METALS AND ENERGY FINANCE

Interrelationship between Technical and Financial Risk in Mineral Projects

Third Edition

Third Edition

METALS AND ENERGY FINANCE

Interrelationship between Technical and Financial Risk in Mineral Projects

Dennis L Buchanan

Imperial College London, UK

With a contribution by Mark H A Davis

World Scientific

NEW JERSEY • LONDON • SINGAPORE • GENEVA • BEIJING • SHANGHAI • TAIPEI • CHENNAI

Published by

World Scientific Publishing Europe Ltd.

57 Shelton Street, Covent Garden, London WC2H 9HE

Head office: 5 Toh Tuck Link, Singapore 596224

USA office: 27 Warren Street, Suite 401-402, Hackensack, NJ 07601

Library of Congress Cataloging-in-Publication Data
Names: Buchanan, D. L., author.
Title: Metals and energy finance : interrelationship between technical and financial risk in mineral projects / Dennis L Buchanan, Imperial College London, UK.
Description: Third edition. | New Jersey : World Scientific, [2025] | Includes bibliographical references and index.
Identifiers: LCCN 2024042372 | ISBN 9781800616523 (hardcover) | ISBN 9781800616622 (paperback) | ISBN 9781800616530 (ebook) | ISBN 9781800616547 (ebook other)
Subjects: LCSH: Financial engineering. | Mines and mineral resources. | Power resources.
Classification: LCC HG176.7 .B83 2025 | DDC 333.79--dc23/eng/20241126
LC record available at https://lccn.loc.gov/2024042372

British Library Cataloguing-in-Publication Data
A catalogue record for this book is available from the British Library.

For any available supplementary material, please visit
https://www.worldscientific.com/worldscibooks/10.1142/Q0487#t=suppl

Desk Editors: Aanand Jayaraman/Gabriel Rawlinson/Shi Ying Koe

Typeset by Stallion Press
Email: enquiries@stallionpress.com

About the Authors

Dennis Buchanan is an Emeritus Professor of Mining Geology, Imperial College London. Professor Buchanan's current research interest lies in addressing the underlying technical principles applied to mineral projects and demonstrating how these influence financial modelling. He has over 40 years of experience in teaching mining geology, mineral exploration and mineral project appraisal and he also created the MSc in Metals and Energy Finance. This was launched in 2006 and he acted as Course Director up until 2021. He continues to contribute to the teaching. This is a joint degree between the Department of Earth Science and Engineering and the Business School at Imperial College. Professor Buchanan has worked as a Mining Geologist in both gold and platinum mines in South Africa and has wide experience as a consultant to industry, as an expert witness and in designing and delivering short courses for industry.

Mark Davis is Senior Research Fellow in the Department of Mathematics at Imperial College, where from 2000 to 2012, he was Professor and Head of the Mathematical Finance Group. Prior to this, he was a Director and Head of Research and Product Development at the London-based investment bank Tokyo-Mitsubishi International, where he worked in a number of areas, including project finance. Mark contributed to the 2nd edition of *Metals and Energy Finance*. He died on 18 March 2020. His Chapter 10 is preserved in this third edition.

Acknowledgements to the First Edition

This book incorporates ideas that first evolved during the delivery of a range of professional development courses in London, Vancouver, Toronto, Stockholm and Johannesburg. The most relevant of the courses is probably "Technical & Financial Evaluation of Mineral Projects" (TechFin) that was launched in 1999 as a joint initiative with the Wits Business School Executive Education programme in Johannesburg and Imperial College Centre for Continuing Professional Development. The original TechFin course included basic concepts of discounted cash flow (DCF) analysis with an introduction to finance and accounting provided by Richard Anderson. Work-shops were based around a set of custom DCF models for a range of different mineral projects. These had limited functionality and utility and were based on pre-funding scenarios.

An early version of IC-MinEval, a Visual Basic-based tool that automated the generation of financial models, developed with Dr Mark Heyhoe at Imperial College, provided the core intellectual property for an Imperial College start-up company. This was launched in 2000 and we called it IC-FinEval Ltd. I was the Chairman, Mark Heyhoe was Technical Director and Roger Haiat was our Commercial Director with Mervyn Jones joining the Board to represent Imperial College. The development of coal and petroleum fiscal modelling tools followed and functionality was undertaken with the support of Professor Tim Shaw and Colin Howard.

Core concepts outlined in this book arose from the collaboration I enjoyed with all these individuals while developing TechFin and IC-FinEval Ltd and I am most grateful to Mark, Roger and Mervyn for the generosity they displayed over the years in sharing their invaluable experience with me which helped to shape my ideas. Tim and Colin remain involved in the programme of joint teaching that we deliver and in the development of the concepts outlined in the book. I continue to value this ongoing professional and academic collaboration.

In 2012, IC-FinEval Ltd was dissolved and the IP transferred to Imperial College but the functionality of IC-MinEval and IC-CoalEval remains available through InfoMine Inc. Simon Houlding, Vice-President of Professional Development for InfoMine and responsible for EduMine, the professional development division, provided outstanding support in this regard. He also supported the delivery of the IC-Mineval-based course "Valuation of Mineral Projects" in Vancouver and Toronto that was launched in 2006.

In 2006 I also launched the MSc Metals and Energy Finance degree as a joint Faculty of Engineering and Business School programme and the structure of this book is based on its teaching modules. Colleagues at Imperial College who have contributed to the delivery of the programme have generously permitted me to use some of their teaching material in preparing this book. Sources are given in figure captions when directly derived from their presentations and these included Professor Jan Cilliers, Professor Olivier Dubrule and Dr Stephen Neethling. Final text on petroleum systems was generated based on extensive discussions with Dr Mike Ala and Dr Peter Fitch during student field excursions along the Jurassic Coast for the MSc students. Dr Fivos Spathopoulos introduced me to the world of unconventional petroleum systems and Professor Mark Sephton reviewed the sections on organic chemistry. My thanks go to all of them for sharing their knowledge with me. I take full responsibility though for the views expressed in this book.

Thanks are due to the companies and organisations that granted me permission to reproduce images either obtained while I was on site at their operations or taken from their own image or photo galleries. These are identified in the figure captions. Many of the insights described in this book arise from professional exchanges with hosts during site visits. I am also obliged to my son James who checked my thermodynamic and spreadsheet calculations and helped with the minerals engineering perspectives.

All the material in the book has been presented to the 2014/2015 cohort of postgraduate MSc Metals and Energy Finance students who proved to be the most discerning and attentive of recipients. I must acknowledge their active feedback which encouraged me to justify all contentions made and re-visit first principles in a way that would not have been possible had I been working in isolation.

Finally though this book could not have been written without the support and patience of my wife Vaughan and to her my grateful thanks. She acted as my own private copy editor. Her queries about confused sentences inevitably identified sections where there was underlying uncertainty in my own mind about the best approach to use in addressing the topic. Revising the sentence clarified the concept, at least in my own mind, but I hope also for the reader.

Dennis Buchanan

Acknowledgements to the Second Edition

I would want to reaffrm all the acknowledgements given in the original book and just add that all the material in the new edition has been presented to the 2017/2018 cohort of postgraduate MSc Metals and Energy Finance students, who have continued the tradition of providing active feedback. My grateful thanks to them for their constructive engagement.

Dennis Buchanan

Acknowledgements to the Third Edition

I would want to reaffirm all the acknowledgements given in the first and second editions of the book, adding only that all the material in this new edition has been presented to the 2023/2024 cohort of postgraduate MSc Metals and Energy Finance students, who have continued the tradition of providing active feedback. My grateful thanks to them for their constructive engagement.

Dennis Buchanan

Contents

List of Abbreviations

AIM	Alternative investment market
AMD	Acid mine drainage
ANFO	Ammonium nitrate and fuel oil
ATBI	After tax before interest
BIF	Banded iron formation
bpd	Barrels per day
BS	Black and Scholes
Capex	Capital costs
CAPM	Capital asset pricing model
CDOs	Collateralised debt obligations
CDS	Credit default swap
CEng	Chartered engineer
CEO	Chief executive officer
CMMI	Council of Mining and Metallurgical Institutes
CRIRSCO	Committee for Mineral Reserves International Reporting Standards
CSG	Coal seam gas
EBITDA	Earnings before interest, taxes, depreciation and amortisation
DCF	Discounted cash flow
dmtu	Dry metric tonne unit
EIA	Environmental impact assessment
EITI	Extractive industries transparency initiative
EPC&M	Engineering, procurement, construction and management
EPT	Excess profit tax

EV	Enterprise value
FCFF	Free cash flow to the firm
FEED	Front end engineering design
FLNG	Floating liquefied natural gas technology
FPSO	Floating production storage and offloading
FTFS	Full technical feasibility study
FVF	Formation volume factor
F–T	Fischer–Tropsch
GDP	Gross domestic product
GRV	Gross rock volume
ICMM	International Council on Mining and Metals
IFC	Issued for construction
IFC	International Finance Corporation
IFRS	International Financial Reporting Standards
IFT	Issued for tender
IMMa	International Mining and Minerals Association
IOGs	International oil groups
IoM3	Institute of Materials, Minerals and Mining
IPO	Initial public offering
IRR	Internal rate of return
ISA	International Seabed Authority
JORC	Joint Ore Reserves Committee
JV	Joint venture
LIBOR	London Inter-Bank Offer Rate
LLR	Loan life ratio
LME	London Metal Exchange
LNG	Liquefied natural gas
LPG	Liquefied petroleum gas
LSE	London Stock Exchange
MC	Monte Carlo
MMbbls	Million barrels
Mtpa	Million tonnes per annum
N/G	Net-to-gross ratio
NAV	Net asset value
NOCs	National oil companies
NPV	Net present value
NSR	Net smelter returns
NYMEX	New York Mercantile Exchange

OpCosts	Operating costs
PAIBT	Profit after interest before tax
PAIT	Profit after interest and tax
PBIT	Profit before interest and tax
Pdf	Probability density function
PEA	Preliminary economic assessment
PERC	Pan European Reserves and Resources Reporting Committee
PFS	Preliminary feasibility study
PGE	Platinum group element
plc	Public limited company
PLR	Project life ratio
ppm	Parts per million
PRMS	Petroleum resource management system
PSC	Production sharing contract
PV	Present value
REE	Rare earth element
ROM	Run of mine
ROV	Real option valuation
SAAS	Software as a service
SAMREC	South African Institute of Mining and Metallurgy
SCF	Specialist commodity funds
SEC	US Securities and Exchange Commission
SFO	Serious Fraud Office
So	Oil saturation
SPE	Society of Petroleum Engineers
STOIIP	Stock tank oil-initially-in-place
tpa	Tonnes per annum
tpd	Tonnes per day
TSX	Toronto Stock Exchange
VE	Venture exchange
VMS	Volcanogenic massive sulphide
WACC	Weighted average cost of capital
WTI	West Texas Intermediate

Chapter 1

Extractive Industry Finance and Mineral Economics

1.1 Introduction

This book is a third edition of the original of the same title published in 2016 by World Scientific Publishing, with the second in 2019. Both covered the field of extractive industry finance, which is a specialist subset of economics. Chapters 2–9 have been revised, with a contribution on *Quantitative Finance* written by Mark Davis added as Chapter 10. A set of four additional case studies has been included in Appendices, bringing the total to seven.

In 2023, information technology stocks represented the largest sector of the benchmark S&P 500 Index, comprising 27.5% of the index's value. The top five are Meta (META) (formerly known as Facebook), Amazon (AMZN), Apple (AAPL), Netflix (NFLX), and Alphabet (GOOG) (formerly known as Google). The top five most valuable tech firms were worth a collective $4.55 trillion at the start of 2023, down an astonishing $2.9 trillion from the previous year. That compares to the combined value of $454 billion for mining's top tier, but there is recognition that metals are essential for most manufacturing processes, with prices linked to exchanges which reflect the fundamental aspects of supply and demand.

The main characteristic of conventional engineering is that it should incorporate a design element. I have argued, after the 2008 financial crisis, that a poorly designed financial model that results in loss for investors (including anyone who pays into a private pension fund) has equivalence with conventionally engineered models and accurate determination of risk, as exemplified by the Titan sub implosion — a consequence of design failure. The 2008 financial crisis was triggered by the failure of the investment banking world to understand the full implications of the Black–Scholes model and real option pricing. In selling sub-prime mortgages, no one fully appreciated that house owners in America were exercising a real option — the right but not the obligation to pay the banks. They simply handed the keys to their homes back to the mortgage companies and moved out. Exposed, in all its gory details, in the excellent film *The Big Short*. Realising that there is no way he will not lose his house, Larry uses the knowledge he gained in his economics class to begin a strategic foreclosure in the film *Larry Crowne*, also worth watching.

Financial engineering as a discipline was accepted by the UK's Engineering Council some 10 years ago when I put forward the above arguments, allowing graduates of the MSc in Metals and Energy Finance programme at Imperial College to apply for Chartered Engineering registration as the course is accredited.

The financial services sectors make little distinction between the mining and petroleum extractive industries, but it should be recognised that mining is just part of the extraction stages that include down-stream processing, while coal is as important a source of energy as petroleum. The choice of *Metals and Energy Finance* for the title of this book therefore allows for a broader treatment of both the technical and financial aspects of the extractive industries.

The concept of "mineral economics" has the connotation of supply and demand although it does incorporate elements of finance. The term "economic geology" is historical in its origin and is concerned mainly with the processes involved in the concentration of metals. The term "mineral deposits studies" is preferred in this book. The term "petroleum economics" tends to cover capital and cost estimates, whereas petroleum fiscal modelling provides the basis for investment decision-making. This book addresses petroleum fiscal modelling.

There are some notable similarities between mineral and petroleum projects. Both are based on depleting resources and therefore companies are under constant pressure to replace reserves. The products are commoditised and globally traded on both spot and futures markets as well as being based on long-term contracts (iron ore, coal and gas supplies). These are products that have low demand elasticity, are capital intensive, require long development lead times and are associated with high technical and commercial risk. There are also environmental compliance and regulatory burdens associated with the development of all natural resource projects.

The book identifies the investment opportunities that are being offered across the whole spectrum of the mining cycle by relating this to the various funding options in the progression from exploration through evaluation, pre-production development, development and, finally, into production. It also addresses the similarities of natural resource projects, whether minerals or petroleum, while identifying their key differences.

1.2 Financial and Conventional Engineering

Fundamental to the approach used in this book is the contention that financial engineering should be considered equal to conventional engineering, as it has a design component. To ensure optimal investment return in natural resource projects, conventional engineering is blended with financial engineering. Timing is critical in optimising return on investment and innovative use of financial engineering can enhance returns to investors. Financial models can identify where sensitivities on investment performance indicators are a function of technical assumptions used in conventional engineering.

In addition to the previous technical and financial material I have developed for this 3rd edition, I have added three new case studies to the three original studies given in the Appendices. These case studies illustrate share performance metrics, including share price, earnings per share, and price–earnings ratios. These, in turn, are linked to cash on the balance sheet and a dividend stream. These new case studies also provide an in-depth treatment of dilution and accretion with respect to rights issues. Thus, they are quite topical.

With many mining operations at the transition from open pit to underground mining where sub-level, panel and block caving methods are able to maintain the rate of production, the role of financial engineering has been enhanced. The tradition in the mining industry is to fund these types of projects from the cash flow generated by an existing operation. The alternative is to ring-fence the project as a discrete investment based on allocation of capital made up of a combination of debt and equity and then to demonstrate the level of return that can be generated. In any geared financial model, the use of debt in funding the capital expenditure permits discounting based on an equivalent to the corporate cost of capital which should further enhance Net Present Value. This results in much greater transparency in decision making which must enhance business development.

There is an important narrative around timing where delay in initiating development of the underground mining will result in a fall-off of ore to the plant which adversely impacts on cash flow. Some develop a shaft system based on cash flow generated from the open pit operation while others make use of debt in funding major programmes of capital expenditure. Where shaft sinking has been funded from equity this should allow treatment of this major cost as sunk capital that provides early access to the ore. As a consequence having vital pre-production infrastructure, such as shafts, in place during construction of the rest of the surface and underground facilities delays in bringing the operation into full production will be short and the ramp-up will be steep.

The book includes a section on the feasibility study. The traditional engineering approach will simply treat this as a study which determines if a project is technically possible. Any investment in a mining project needs, however, to generate a revenue stream that not only covers the cost of extraction but also an Internal Rate of Return (IRR) that exceeds the discount rate selected. In the case of a major mining company, this would be the corporate cost of capital. If the

IRR does not exceed the corporate cost of capital, then it would not be feasible to proceed with the investment in the project as mining is not then a commercially viable option.

If debt is to be used and project finance arranged, then the investment banks and independent engineers will be involved in construction monitoring. Once the project is brought on stream, the independent engineers will again audit actual performance against design expectations. The role of independent engineers, appointed by the investment banks providing project finance, is also to ensure technical robustness through sound design, realistic capital cost estimates, and adherence to construction schedules. Independent audits are also done for mining funds and/or for acquisition, where the focus is slightly different, as the client is often taking on some equity risk and not just debt risk.

A major mining company with existing production capabilities would be in a better position to ensure economic completion tests which will be passed on time. Loans will then go non-recourse on schedule and future risk is then shared with the investment banks. Those elements are included in the book.

Where project finance is used and the lending goes non-recourse, the only remaining security for the investment bank is the ore reserve. The central role of ore resource evaluation in mining finance is also recognised.

The key theme emerging within the mining industry is the role of technical innovation needed to release value through replacing labour intensive mining methods with mechanisation. Before full productivity from the investment in equipment can be achieved, given the level of technical sophistication involved in a modern mechanised mining operation, skilled human resources are needed and these aspects are also covered. Significant technical risk is often associated with the performance of the processing plant and to reduce this the design must take into account the specific mineralogical characteristics of the ore. The book therefore includes an introduction to extractive metallurgy.

All deposits will eventually be mined out so the role of exploration and evaluation must be part of the narrative and the cycle of value creation is a theme that is addressed through detailed treatment of mineral and petroleum geoscience.

1.3 Professional Development

Extractive industry finance recognises that major changes in the international mining and petroleum industries over the last decade have significantly increased the demand for professionals with skills that blend technical and financial engineering with a business perspective. It is now considered perfectly respectable for financial engineering to merit the UK's Engineering Council's Chartered Engineer (CEng) qualification, particularly where finance is combined with the technical aspects of mining, metals and petroleum. A poorly designed financial model can have as big an impact on a business as structural failure in construction. Financial models of case studies covered in this book demonstrate how financial engineering can be used to offset risk associated with operational issues that impact on the original financial performance indicators. An example would be the reduction in net present value as a consequence of unexpected delays in meeting production targets.

The recognition of the importance of these concepts has resulted in a demand for both postgraduate training and professional development courses. The earlier version of the book is used to support the delivery of the MSc in Metals and Energy Finance degree at Imperial College which is a joint Faculty of Engineering and Business School programme. The book also supports a range of courses delivered through the Imperial College Centre for Continuing Professional Development as well as by Vancouver-based Edumine who also provide the platform from which Excel financial models used in the book can be downloaded.

The fundamental basis for the interest in metals and energy is that the assets are tangible and produce commodity-based products that are an integral part of the natural geological environment. The products are traded internationally and generate cash in hard currency in countries in which the resources are located. It follows, however, from this that no matter how smart the financial engineering associated with investment structures, if basic estimates of grade, tonnage and recoveries for metals or the volumetrics and recovery assumptions for hydrocarbons are wrong because of a flawed understanding of mineral or petroleum geosciences, then the whole basis for a valuation and investment decision will also be flawed.

1.4 Hydrocarbons

The emphasis of this book is not only on metals but also on energy, and is not confined to conventional oil and gas associated with petroleum systems. Part of the book is devoted to coal, which in 2016 supplied 28% of world energy needs (see Table 1.1). As will be noted, oil, natural gas and coal, which are collectively described as fossil fuels, provide 85% of energy needs

Career opportunities lie with professionals working in the energy transition business who have the skill sets needed to manage the process of moving from fossil fuels (coal, oil, and gas) to green technology. Energy can be generated not only through combustion but also from electrochemical reactions, and that must be part of the strategy for transitioning to a decarbonised future. This requires recognition that fossil fuels will be needed by society in the present. To keep global warming to no more than 1.5°C — as called for in the Paris Agreement — emissions need to be reduced by 45% by 2030 and reach net

Table 1.1. Consumption by fuel type in 2016.

Commodity	Oil equivalent	
Oil	4,418.2	33%
Natural gas	3,204.1	24%
Coal	3,732.0	28%
Nuclear energy	592.1	5%
Hydro electricity	910.3	7%
Renewables	419.6	3%
	13,276.3	100%

Source: BP Statistical Review of World Energy, 2017. http://www.bp.com.

zero by 2050, which requires the development of green technology. This includes revisiting the role of nuclear energy generation.

Upstream extraction techniques for petroleum and coal are normally different, with the former recovered from wells while the latter is associated with mining, but the Athabasca tar sands operations in Canada are essentially mining operations although classified as petroleum projects.

There is also a convergence between petroleum and coal in the downstream processing stage of Sasol's Secunda plant in South Africa where the Fischer–Tropsch (F–T) process is used to convert coal to petroleum products. This includes the development of conventional petroleum gas resources to enhance the gas-to-liquid capabilities of the F–T process. Theoretically, carbon dioxide generated by the process could be cooled and liquefied and then utilised to recover residual hydrocarbons from mature oil reservoirs.

Pilot projects are being linked to coal mining, carbon sequestration and methane production. Carbon capture and storage, and the utilisation of methane emissions permits operators to attract carbon credits and participate in active carbon trading.

For these reasons, the investment community often makes little distinction between petroleum and coal mining, as both sectors are energy-related and commodity-based. The book covers the detailed financial modelling of coal projects and an in-depth treatment of hydrocarbon fiscal regimes based on both tax and royalty and production sharing contracts. The interplay between gas (and liquefied natural gas (LNG)) prices and oil prices only adds to the mix.

1.5 Energy Transition

There is also a completely fresh thread in this edition of the book on energy transition. This starts with the decarbonisation of natural resource industries and the role played by oil and gas companies in developing renewable energy. This includes the treatment of the circular economy and the role of recycling. Major mining companies are starting to highlight their strategic position in supplying nickel, cobalt, and copper, which are critical metals in the manufacture of

Li-ion batteries, while some junior exploration companies have, as a core part of their business plan, the intention of producing graphite, which is used as the anodes.

Rare earth element (REE) resources are highly topical and are part of the narrative around electric vehicles and the neodymium magnets used in their motors. The reality is, however, that for some deposits, such as those needed to produce commercial levels of REEs, significant volumes of phosphoric acid by-product would be generated. A further example would be the role of hydrogen as an alternative to coking coal in steel production, where the practical strategy has yet to be developed, given that the cost of power required for direct reduction is 100 times greater than that of a conventional processing route. The book would provide an authoritative source of information in this type of commercial narrative.

In the early 1980s, I acted as a specialist advisor to the Lords Select Committee on the European Communities on Strategic Minerals and drafted the report that was published by HMSO in July 1982. Many of the issues surrounding criticality and vulnerability were prescient with respect to the current major initiatives around the energy transition and the role of critical minerals. This would include the U.S. Department of Energy's "Mineral Resources for the Energy Transition" Infrastructure Law and Inflation Reduction Act, the European Commission's list of critical raw materials (CRMs) for the EU, and the UK's Department of Business, Energy and Industrial Strategy policy paper on critical minerals. The book would provide an informed perspective on these issues of the day.

Management and Business

Chapter 2

Cash Flow Modelling and Financial Accounting

2.1 Introduction

This chapter considers the links between the "accounting model" (potentially net profit, earnings per share, price to earnings ratio, even return on investment %) and the "economic model" (the present value of the project's expected future cash flow). It outlines the way in which cash flow information is constructed from basic project details and then represents that information as a set of accounts, as this is widely used for presentation and reporting of financial information. It could be argued, however, that cash flow information is much more useful.

The accounting model includes provision for funding to ensure cash flows never go negative, while the economic model is prefunding. Capital costs and the delay involved during development and before production starts generating revenue mean that the initial net cash flow will be negative. In general, petroleum fiscal models, with the complexity of provision for production sharing contracts, are essentially economic models usually discounted by the corporate cost of capital of the major petroleum company developing the project.

For mineral projects, particular attention has to be paid to the treatment of the key independent variables, such as grade, and dependent variables, such as grade-tonnage relationships, and the way these influence the rate of mining, associated costs, and optimisation of the value of a project. Petroleum projects are based on initial volumetrics, segment production and annual production profiles, revenue, operating costs, and capital costs.

The distinction between technical appraisal and financial factors will also be addressed, and the reason why discounted cash flow (DCF) models need to be integrated correctly into financial accounts will be explained. This will be linked to concepts of shareholder value and the role of gearing to maintain an efficient balance sheet.

The most important part of a DCF model is the revenue row (metal price × grade × plant recovery). The central considerations are:

- the application of the principles of quantitative finance as applied to price volatility, including hedging and real option valuation (ROV)
- the role of geostatistics in resource evaluation
- technical risk associated with plant performance and design and grade yield curves.

All draw on the concepts of probability and stochastic treatment of variables. Revenue assumptions are not deterministic but are associated with uncertainty. These concepts are applicable at the pre-feasibility study (PFS) stage, where net present value (NPV) optimisation can take into account the interrelationship between the time value of money, the cost–capacity relationship, and the impact of economies of scale in any manufacturing process, including mining, as well as the choice of cut-off grade in grade–tonnage curves limited by maintaining mining continuity.

At the full technical feasibility (FTFS) stage, the financial models assume a fixed capacity in terms of throughput in millions of tonnes per annum. The optimisation of NPV is restricted to gearing ratios, and the final choice is used to generate the bank's lending term sheet, which includes the exact repayment schedule and hedging programme. These are all concepts that will be considered in later chapters.

2.2 Principles of DCF Modelling

John Burr Williams (27 November 1900–15 September 1989) was an American economist who developed *The Theory of Investment Value*, based on his 1938 PhD thesis, in which he articulated the theory of DCF-based valuation. As a starting point in building a DCF model for a mineral project, it is often assumed that the projects are at the pre-production and pre-investment stages. The principle of DCF is based on the logic that money received in the future is worth less than that same amount received today, due to the opportunity for earning additional revenue on that sum if it were to be invested elsewhere. Suppose there is a choice of receiving \$1,000 today and investing it or receiving \$2,000 in 10 years' time. Which is the most valuable outcome? The answer clearly depends on the prevailing interest rate. If it happens to be 5%, the money would be worth \$1,629 at the end of 10 years, so it would be better to wait On the other hand, if the current rate happens to be 10%, the sum would be worth \$2,594 in 10 years' time, so it would be preferable to take the money now and invest it. The breakeven interest rate in this scenario is about 7.2%.

Modelling incremental DCF analyses the financial viability of a project by not only testing that generated revenues are substantially greater than costs and debt service requirements but also by measuring the present value of those profits. The underlying philosophy in DCF analysis is that the project is to be compared with investing the same stream of cash flows elsewhere.

One of the essential questions in DCF analysis is how to choose the discount rate. At the pre-funding stage, this is essentially set by the investor or the new business division of the natural resource company. DCF can then be used to determine the NPV of the project, which is essentially a present valuation of the potential of the deposit to generate future profits. NPV is calculated as follows:

$$NPV = C_0 + \frac{C_1}{(1+i)} + \frac{C_2}{(1+i)^2} + \cdots + \frac{C_n}{(1+i)^n},$$

where C is the net cash flow at year n and i is the project discount rate.

Projects with an NPV greater than zero will produce greater revenues than their costs at the minimum acceptable rate of return (the discount or hurdle rate). Mutually exclusive investment opportunities are ranked by magnitude of the NPV.

The internal rate of return (IRR) and payback period of a project can also be calculated from a model of future cash flows. IRR is essentially the discount rate at which the NPV at time zero of all cash flows is equal to zero and is calculated as follows:

$$0 = C_0 + \frac{C_1}{(1+i)} + \frac{C_2}{(1+i)^2} + \cdots + \frac{C_n}{(1+i)^n}.$$

Solving for i gives the project's IRR. A project is profitable if the IRR exceeds the opportunity cost of capital (the project's discount rate), and mutually exclusive scenarios are ranked by magnitude of the IRR.

Payback period is simply the time taken for the initial capital investment to be recovered by the stream of annual positive cash flows and is not generally used alone for making an investment decision, as it takes no account of the time value of money.

Clearly, the choice of discount rate is a fundamental factor in the evaluation of an investment opportunity, whether a mineral or a petroleum project. The impact on the present value factors used to discount a net cash flow for the selected period is demonstrated in Fig. 2.1.

The curves are essentially derived from annuity tables based on end-of-year scenarios, which assume yearly cash flow occurs at end of year. Each year is discounted for a full year, plus previous years. To undertake the calculation based on mid-year scenarios, assume yearly cash flows occur, on average, halfway through the year. For the most realistic scenario, the discount factors are adjusted by subtracting 0.5 from the exponent, and the assumption is that cash flows occur at start of year. Discount factors are then adjusted by subtracting 1.0 from the exponent.

Some key points arise from these curves. For a discount rate much above 6%, the value of net revenue generated after 15 years has a diminishing impact on the present value of the project. It could be argued that for long-life projects of 25 years and greater, the technique will significantly undervalue the opportunity. This effect is amplified as the discount rate is increased to the point that the curves start becoming asymptotic. Applying a discount rate much

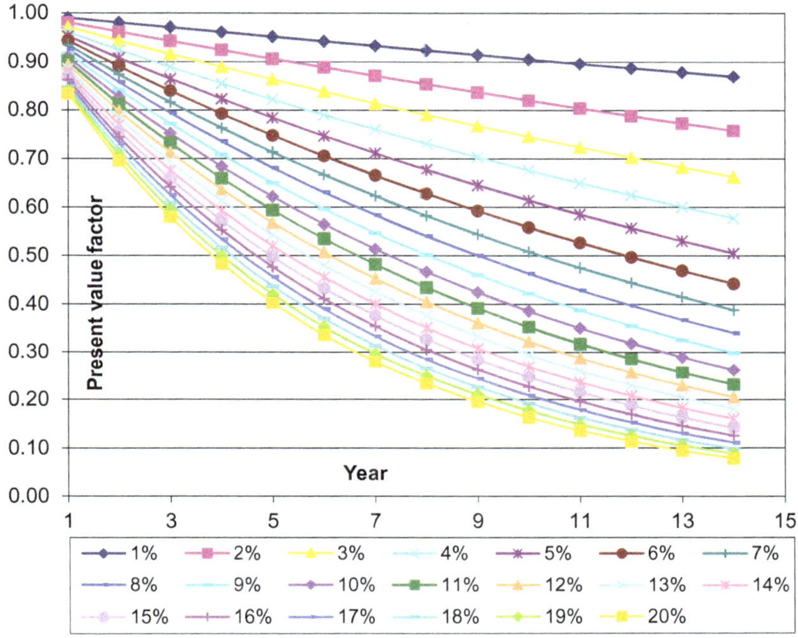

Figure 2.1. Impact of different discount rates over time.

above 15% requires an exceptional project before the NPV justifies making an investment. Successful mining entrepreneurs have made reference to the "tyranny of NPV" in appraising mineral projects and advocate using a 0% discount rate, which gives the true value of long-life projects. It might be said that this is a strategy followed by the Chinese government in its acquisitions, given that the priority is securing control of the supply of industrial minerals.

There is a separate insight that is provided by the curves at the start of the project life when they are steep. Unless the scenario is modelling the refurbishment of an operation already in production with an existing cash flow, there will be a period during development and construction when no revenue is being generated. The delay will have been estimated from the engineering design, and any delay in the original assumptions will have a profound impact on the NPV. Reasons include incorrect assumptions that ore characteristics have on plant design and the distortions that arise when clients start requesting changes after detail work has started. Delays, once expenditure has been committed that defers revenue generation, can compromise the whole financial integrity of a project that has to be reviewed in the context of the original risk factors.

Natural mineral resource projects, with finite reserves and fixed production capacities, which permit accurate prediction of project life, are probably particularly amenable to the application of DCF techniques. For example, product price assumptions can also be predicted reasonably reliably. However, they are less suited to other sectors such as telecoms and pharmaceuticals where products have short shelf lives depending on network systems, tariffs, and patents. A smelter with a fixed capacity but unlimited life is more difficult to value using the DCF technique, as the PV of net cash flow after 20 years is very low for any discount above 5%.

The IRR can have multiple roots. Where a model has a positive NPV, with an IRR that exceeds the discount rate, then as the discount rate increases and approaches the IRR, the NPV will converge to zero. Continuing to increase the discount rate beyond this point will generate a negative NPV, but in some circumstances the NPV can start reversing this trend, and the curve can revert and again approach zero. This might be because the capital cost assumptions used for the initial periods of the project became steeply discounted. The NPV of projects with high closure costs may, counter-intuitively, improve as the discount rate increases, as the impact is reduced once the present value factors 10–15 years into the future have been applied.

In a marginal project, the cumulative cash flows may never become cash positive, so the point of payback is never reached. As a consequence, the model is relatively insensitive to the choice of discount rate. A promoter in these circumstances may elect to use a discount rate of zero, implying that the project remains worthy of investment as it is insensitive to the choice of discount rate, but this approach is somewhat disingenuous. In a good project with an early payback and significant positive cash flows from that point a lower discount rate would significantly enhance the NPV.

Unlike most petroleum projects, a mineral project may have a relatively slow ramp-up period before production gets up to "cruising altitude". Failure to achieve the projected ramp-up after the start of production, resulting in a delay in reaching design capacity, will further compromise the NPV owing to the shape of the present value curves in the early stages of a project. The corollary of this is that by exceeding ramp-up expectations, additional value can be created.

The overall performance of a project is often best assessed from a graphical presentation of the cash flows, as depicted in Fig. 2.2. Initial negative cash flows associated with capital expenditure are replaced by positive cash revenues as production starts. Undiscounted net cash flows depicted in Fig. 2.2 will contribute to cumulative net cash flows, which establish the breakeven point in a project. Both this milestone and the maximum cash exposure have important practical implications for investors.

The model shown is unlikely to have a positive NPV at a 10% discount rate and may never break even. It is important to note that this is an economic model, not an accounting model. In accounting terms,

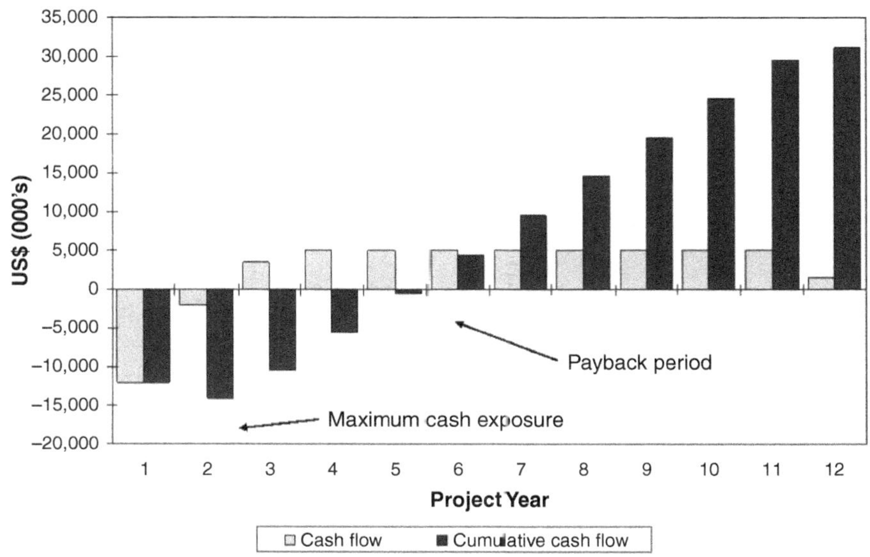

Figure 2.2. Cash flow for a mineral project.

Fig. 2.2 is essentially unable to be implemented. Capital is needed to fund the cost of development. The overall cash flow should never go negative in a financial model designed to make a final investment decision. The NPV is, however, determined from the economic part of the financial model. To determine the NPV from cash flows from the post-funding scenario would generate an infinite IRR as there is no value that would satisfy the condition needed to generate a zero NPV. There are some circumstances in which the financial model of an operation in production where refurbishment is paid for from cash flow never goes cash negative. These can generate an infinite IRR and are good projects to acquire. As a performance indicator, IRR is obviously not particularly useful in such circumstances and could be quite misleading.

Even where no artefacts are generated, such as an infinitely high IRR, DCF performance indicators will not in themselves provide an objective basis for an investment decision. Three hypothetical scenarios are given in Table 2.1.

Project A may be attractive to one of the major international mining companies as the potential NPV would be material but not essential for their business. Project B may be too small for the international mining company, but attractive to a mid-size company with existing operating mines and market capitalisation of, say, $1 billion, as the NPV and reasonable IRR could make a significant difference to their share price. For an exploration company listed on the London Stock Exchange's (LSE) Alternative Investment Market aiming to bring their first mine into production, Project C with its high IRR

Table 2.1. Scenarios illustrating the range of economic performance indicators for three different mining projects.

Project	A	B	C
Capital cost (million)	$500	$250	$25
Mine life (years)	25	15	10
Discount rate	8	10	15
NPV	$1.5 billion	$750 million	$75 million
line IRR (%)	12	15	50

would be attractive. The NPV is, however, too low to be of interest to the mid-sized company and simply a distraction for the international group.

A financial model is clearly no substitute for understanding the business case for investing in a natural resource project. It does, however, provide a good reality check on the level of return that can be expected. For this reason, it should be kept as simple as possible at the early stages of project evaluation.

When generating a DCF financial model, a distinction should be made between the use of "nominal" versus "real" value, "inflation or deflation" in considering costs, and "escalation" when dealing with metal prices. Furthermore, regardless of the location of the project, it is often best to use US Dollar capital costs, operating costs, and obviously metal prices. As a first pass for countries with high rates of inflation (such as South Africa and Russia), use US Dollars for both costs and revenues. It permits the removal of the impact of variable exchange rates between the local currency and the US Dollar.

If "real" value is defined as the nominal figures adjusted for inflation, then the implementation of tax is going to require deflating net cash flows back to nominal before the NPV can be determined. This makes it more difficult to retain an intuitive feel for the model. It is not therefore recommended for the early stages of project evaluation.

In summary, the use of the terms "inflation" or "deflation" applies when considering costs and "escalation" applies when dealing with commodity prices in the financial model. To put this into context, a captive coal mine will often negotiate an escalation clause in long-term supply contracts to an electrical power utility. Future tax liabilities will be determined accordingly. Treatment of inflation is quite a separate matter and adds an additional level of complexity, which is why it is recommended that a model be based on nominal values, assuming real terms after tax cash flow are wanted as the result. Although it is not a requirement to do so, most companies will use nominal cash flows as a basis of their analysis. If using a nominal cash flow, it should be discounted using a nominal weighted average cost of capital (WACC), see Section 2.5. If using a real terms cash flow, discount should use a real terms WACC. In theory, the same result would be obtained since a "present" value NPV is stated for the period in which nominal is the same as real. There is no such thing as a "real NPV" or a "nominal NPV": NPVs are by definition present values, and therefore NPV derived from real cash flows must equal the NPV derived from nominal cash flows at the specified reference date.

When building into the model the role of derivatives, a hedging strategy can be implemented. This becomes relevant where project finance is involved and allows consideration of forward curves for currency and metal prices, which will be either in backwardation (which assumes that the prices will be lower in the future compared to today's spot price) or going into contango. That fixes in the metal prices based on the proportion of metal hedged and the length of the hedge. There might even be a currency hedge. In summary:

- *Real*: nominal adjusted for inflation
- *Inflation and deflation*: applies to costs
- At the pre-feasibility stage, use nominal when generating a preinvestment DCF model
- *Escalation*: applies to metal prices
- At the investment stage may hedge metal.

This approach should not be confused with forward predictions on future supply and demand scenarios that would influence price forecasts. Use the term "inflation or deflation" in considering costs and "escalation" when dealing with commodity prices in the financial model. Most companies will use nominal cash flows as a basis of their analysis.

2.3 Valuation of Mineral Projects Based on Technical and Financial Modelling

2.3.1 *Introduction*

The valuation of mineral projects is best undertaken based on a DCF model. This requires a deposit with an indicated resource as defined by the reporting codes (see Section 3.4.1). Alternative methods include comparable transactions, which normally apply to exploration properties and require identification of market capitalisation of several junior companies with licences covering similar metallogenic characteristics. Finally, there is the appraised value method, which assumes that the value of a property is either enhanced or diminished by an exploration programme. Funds expended that develop the potential of the project will enhance value proportionately. The reality is that in most cases the exploration process will eliminate targets, and that expenditure has to be written off.

Exploration and evaluation costs (development costs) are capitalised if future economic benefits are reasonably assured. This requires the definition and confirmation of "probable reserves" by a competent person. The NPV generated by a DCF model equates to the intrinsic value of the project. This is normally used as a base line for determining the "market value" of the asset, and for a single-project company, that should set the price of the shares if listed. Any market turbulence increases the need to understand the interrelationship between technical and financial risk in order to recognise potential investment opportunities. The key consideration is the intrinsic value of a mineral project. Where current market conditions undervalue the true long-term worth of assets, which are then reflected in low share prices, strategic planning can identify opportunities. There are many ways to value assets, all of which may be justified even if they give different results. An estimated current value is not the same as fair value, or market value in accounting terms. Valuing assets is an art, not a science. Market value may be based on discounted cash flows and share performance metrics, as illustrated in Extended Case Study 4 (copper-mining company) in Appendix D, but imagination and interpretation matter more, for example strategic business agendas.

In a situation where a buyer is negotiating with a vendor and a value is agreed, this acquisition cost needs to be considered in relation to the NPV. If this is the same, then the return on the investment will be the discount rate selected. There may well be resistance from the buyer to paying the full market value. If, however, the buyer is working on a separate strategic agenda, then they may well be prepared to pay more than the NPV.

Valuations of public companies are derived from a range of share performance metrics, which include the following:

- Basic Market Capitalisation = Basic Shares Outstanding × Share Price
- Fully Diluted (FD) Market Capitalisation = Fully Diluted Shares Outstanding × Share Price
- Fully Diluted Shares Outstanding = Basic Shares Outstanding + In-the-Money (ITM) Options
- ITM Options = Number of Options where Strike Price < Share Price
- Enterprise Value (EV) = Market Capitalisation + Debt – Cash & Cash Equivalents – Investments
- Net Asset Value (NAV) = Net Present Value (NPV) – Debt + Cash + Investments
- EBITDA = Earnings Before Interest, Taxes, Depreciation, and Amortisation.

The application of these metrics is illustrated in Extended Case Study 4 (Appendix D). A NAV model assumes that the company does not increase its existing reserves, so when these assets are depleted, there's no value left.

Share performance metrics include share price, earnings per share, and price earnings ratios. These in turn would be linked to cash on the balance sheet and a dividend stream. Financial models are, however, a forward-looking perspective pre-funding and do not reflect actual predicted financial accounting results. A dividend stream is not assigned, so cash will build up on the balance sheet. If this happened to an actual company, it would be a candidate for a takeover. What shareholders want in a mining company in those circumstances is for the cash to be reinvested in new quality projects. This would be reflected in a higher share price and provide the basis for fresh capital through a rights issue. See Extended Case Study 6 (Appendix F).

2.3.2 *Treatment of sunk capital*

The scenario present for an operating mine is somewhat different from a normal mineral project valuation as it is a going concern with sunk capital. The implication of the role of sunk capital is that future production will be put into the slipstream of the existing mine infrastructure. A valuation will need to provide very clear indications on the weight (if any) placed on the sunk capital. In Extended Case Study 4 (Appendix D), the NPV is derived from the estimated future cash flows expected to arise from the continued use of mining infrastructure.

If the valuation is going to be determined simply from the future net cash flows projected from the present, then the arithmetic of the model will ensure it is going to generate a very much higher number than if the original capital cost of establishing the project is offset against the NPV. It needs to be recognised in preparing the valuation, however, that in a takeover or acquisition situation, sunk capital could be added to the valuation by the vendor, as a buyer should be prepared to accept that a mine operating as a going concern has much more value than an undeveloped pristine *in situ* resource. There is no right or wrong outcome, and as a consequence, disputes may arise when a joint venture partner wishes to disinvest, which can end up having to be resolved in a formal legal arbitration process.

Sunk capital should be distinguished from working capital. If the latter is not returned to the financial model at the end of the project's life, it is not compliant with this definition. Junior exploration companies routinely seek fresh equity for operating expenses, which is called working capital; however, should projects evolve into operating mines, that expenditure in accounting terms is treated as sunk capital. That, in turn, should not be a significant portion of the overall capex. Some entrepreneurs ignore that convention. If a shaft system on a project, aimed at undertaking trial mining and securing bulk samples, is funded by fresh equity and subsequently excluded from the financial modelling undertaken as part of securing full funding for the development of the mine, this significantly enhances the valuation of the project.

The need for a valuation of a going concern arises when the company feels that the market has discounted the share price and it needs to reassure shareholders. This becomes critical if the operation has exhausted its working capital and could go into receivership. Closure probably needs to be considered if the company is in this type of financial distress, and the cost associated with placing the mine on care and maintenance would need to be deducted from the valuation. The lower valuation could provide a "book-end" to the exercise.

There is some debate about the use of DCF for valuing very large deposits because it tends to undervalue long-life projects. A valuation should therefore, if possible, be considered in relation to comparable transactions to determine that it is consistent with market perspectives. The valuation would also be considered in relation to the approach used in asset acquisition within the mining industry. It is recognised that for strategic reasons, a company may choose to pay more to acquire a mineral or mining asset than the value generated by a DCF financial model.

In the aftermath of the 2008 financial crisis, projects under construction that had not made sufficient provision for the capital cost found that they were unable to raise additional capital from either the banks that provided the original debt or from existing shareholders. The consequence in some cases was the liquidation of the holding company but of course in others an opportunity for any natural resource company with large cash holdings. Given the combination of a distressed sale and the promise of relatively minor levels of investment to complete the construction of a project, the acquisition cost may be well below the theoretical valuation based on a DCF model.

If the price paid for an asset is subsequently shown to have been based on an inflated valuation, this will need to be reflected as an accounting impairment. This is a reduction in the recoverable amount of a fixed asset or goodwill below its carrying amount. Most accounts recognise and document the values of all assets: fixed assets, current assets, etc. These values are set by the current market. However, the value of most assets changes over time and in some cases dramatically so.

In summary, the valuation of an existing project would assume 100% ownership by the holding company, and the NPV is compared with the current market capitalisation. This should provide the basis for determining if the shares are undervalued or overvalued compared to the underlying models. Debt can be ignored for this part of the exercise. In particular, there would need to be an explanation for the original capital cost of building the operation. It could be treated as sunk, and therefore the NPV is only dependent on future cash flows. Provided there is a reasonable mine life remaining, this should generate an enhanced NPV. The market may not, however, agree with this perspective (which is where the amount of debt becomes relevant), and this would be reflected in a share price lower than a model might predict.

2.4 Analysis of Risk and Uncertainty

The minimum level of information needed to generate a basic DCF model for a small hypothetical underground gold mine is given in Table 2.2. The treatment of depreciation is given in the table and will reduce corporate tax liability but is not considered part of the overall cash flow, although perhaps it should be. Capex of course impacts cumulative cash flow and sets breakeven. There is, however, little merit in being too rigorous in the treatment of depreciation at the pre-feasibility, pre-funding stage, where there is going to be huge uncertainty in any NPV generated.

We need much greater rigour at the funding stage. By integrating cash flow with financial accounts, taxable income can be determined correctly on the current year's profits. This in turn permits the correct treatment in the financial model of profits after tax before interest (ATBI), profit before interest and tax (PBIT), profit after interest before tax (PAIBT), and profit after interest and tax (PAIT). See Section 2.5.1. Also of course, at the funding stage, changing from straight-line depreciation over the life of the mine to loss carry forward will enhance NPV because more cash is retained in the early stages of the project when present value factors are high. If, however, the financial viability of a project is dependent on this type

Table 2.2. Minimum information required for a base case financial model of a gold project.

Variable	Value and units	Comment
Mining method		Underground.
Construction period	2 years	
Resource	3.24 million tonnes	This is the amount of *in situ* mineralised material.
Mining dilution	9%	**9%** which means that for every 9.1 tonnes of ore we extract we will also extract 0.9 tonnes of sub-economic rock. Having some dilution is normal, as it is often caused by mining conditions, but the key is to keep it to a minimum as it is also often caused by poor grade control.
Grade	10 g/t	In the calculations a conversion 31.1 grams per troy ounce is used.
Plant recovery	90%	The *in situ* grade here is **10 g/t** and we have been given a plant recovery of **90%**. Based on these figures, we have 32.4 tonnes of gold *in situ* of which we are able to extract 29.16 tonnes.
Ore mined	1,000 tonnes/day	Assumes ore mined at a rate of 360,000 tonnes per annum and, unrealistically, no ramp-up period.
Mine life		Based on 9% dilution over the entire life of mine we will be extracting 0.29 mt of sub-economic material, or a combined total of 3.53 mt. This gives a mine life of around 10 years.
Capital cost	$55 million	Estimate for the project (mine, mill and processing plant) and we assume this is split **40%:60%** over the 2-year construction period.
Operating cost	$44 per tonne	Estimate for the cost of mining and processing.
Working capital	25%	This is set as a proportion of annual operating costs equivalent to 3 months. It is assigned at the start of production in year three of the project and then returned at the end.

Table 2.2. (*Continued*)

Variable	Value and units	Comment
Metal price	\$300 and \$1,000 per troy ounce	Base case and escalated scenario.
Royalty rate	2%	Determined from net revenue and essentially a resource rent.
Tax rate	35%	This is based on the operating margin.
Depreciation		This is based on straight-line depreciation which allows us to use the Capex to reduce the taxable income by the same amount each year of production.
Discount rate	8%	

of difference in the tax code rather than on technical variables such as grade, plant recovery, operating costs (Opcost), and capital costs (Capex), then it is clear that the most optimistic estimates have already been made and that the project is obviously marginal.

It should be noted that in attempting to undertake an independent evaluation of a project, establishing even this level of information can be a real challenge.

Once the financial model has generated the NPV and IRR, these performance indicators are presented as deterministic outcomes often to an unrealistic level of precision. A much more useful approach is to undertake sensitivity analysis on key variables. The common approach is to generate a sensitivity diagram in which the selected variable is flexed, while the associated variables remain fixed. To ensure that the impact of the selected variable remains comparable to the others in the analysis, the project life must remain the same.

Flexing dilution, the mining rate, ramp-up, and the size of the resource will change the project life. This essentially constrains the use of a sensitivity diagram to grade, plant recovery, Opcost, and Capex. Changing dilution changes mine life, as would mine recovery. You cannot then compare this impact on the NPV simultaneously with plant recovery, grade, Opcost, and Capex, which do not change mine life. You are comparing apples with pears. Obviously, you can flex dilution by itself, and that will impact NPV as high dilution extends mine life, and although all the metal is recovered, receipt of cash towards the end of the mine life is delayed. In a DCF, this must lower the NPV.

It follows that where mining recovery is reduced, the mine life is reduced, and where there is a limited resource, this will reduce NPV. There is also the risk of over-capitalisation if mine life is too short for the installed capacity. For a very long mine life, a DCF generates little value for cash flow beyond 20 years at a discount rate of +10%, so reducing mine recovery has little impact on NPV.

As the key row in the financial model is revenue derived from grade multiplied by plant recovery multiplied by metal price flexing, any one of these variables by the same relative proportion will have the same impact on revenue and therefore on NPV.

The results of the sensitivity analysis on grade, Capex, and Opcost are given in Figs. 2.3 and 2.4.

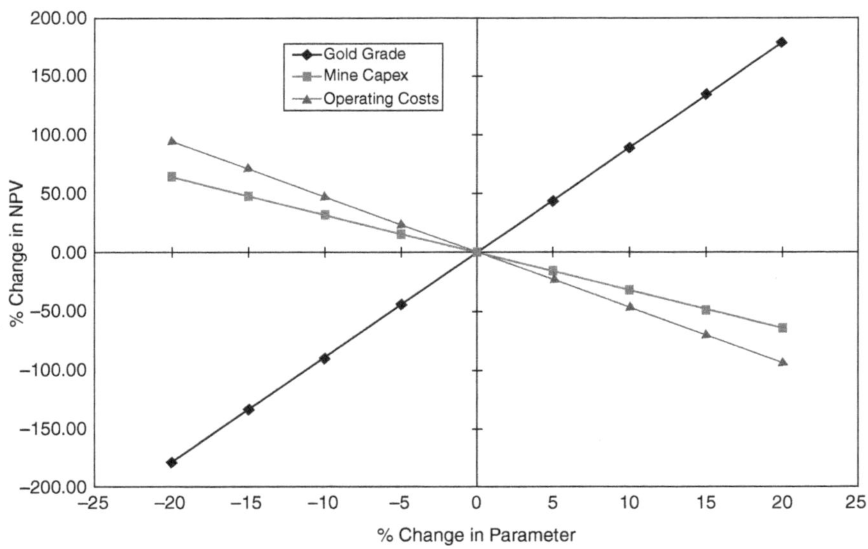

Figure 2.3. Sensitivity diagram for the base case of a hypothetic gold project which at $300 per ounce generates an NPV of $11.61 million and an IRR of 12%.

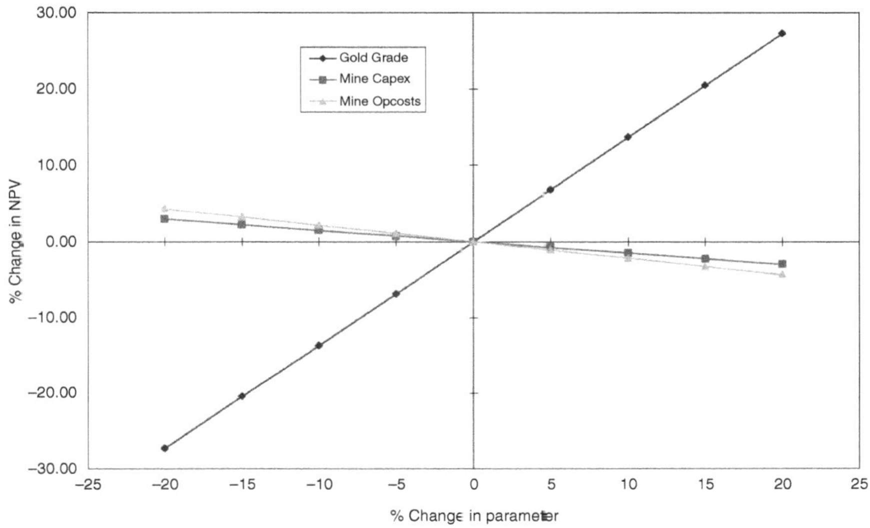

Figure 2.4. Sensitivity diagram for the base case of a hypothetic gold project that when run assuming a gold price of $1,000 per ounce generates an NPV of $263 million and an IRR of 72%.

The base case is clearly marginal. A characteristic of this type of scenario is that a 20% increase in the capital cost of the project will halve an already poor NPV. If grade proves to have been overestimated by 10%, the project will not be viable.

Taking the same base case and using a gold price of $1,000 per ounce generates the sensitivity diagram given in Fig. 2.4. As can be seen, a 20% increase in the capital cost has a trivial impact on NPV. If grade proves to have been overestimated by 10%, the project remains robust. It is these macro factors that should be considered in undertaking an initial evaluation of a mineral project. A marginal project is seldom enhanced to any significant degree by focusing on reducing capital cost estimates. It is more productive to consider the potential of the deposit to host a larger resource of mineralisation present at a higher grade than the scenario being modelled.

The use of a sensitivity diagram does recognise the merits of moving from a deterministic to a probabilistic approach, but being constrained to flexing only one variable at a time is clearly not realistic.

In the real world, grade, plant recovery, Opcost, and Capex will be associated with their own level of uncertainty. Monte Carlo (MC) simulation provides a powerful technique to assess risk and uncertainty by recognising that, as a first approximation, each variable will contribute to a range of NPV outcomes. A good example of the application of the technique is given by Hayes (2014), who explains it as follows:

> *The inputs of a DCF are forward looking estimates, and subject to uncertainty. For example, capital and operating costs are estimated prior to constructing a mining project, but are not known with certainty until they are fully incurred. Monte Carlo Stochastic simulation attempts to account for this uncertainty in DCF inputs by enabling use of probabilistic inputs and producing probabilistic outputs. Important inputs are identified and assigned as random variables with distributions as defined by the modeller. These distributions can be based on historical trends, forward projections, industry standards and professional judgement. To produce results, a set number of iterations of the DCF are calculated. The value of the stochastic input variables changes with each iteration, varying within the bounds of the distributions assigned by the modeller. Consequently, the NPV, and any other output variable produced by each iteration of the DCF is different. The values of the output variable(s) are saved and collected until an adequate number of iterations is completed.*

A commercial product such as Oracle@ Crystal Ball is the leading spreadsheet-based application suite that can be used for predictive probabilistic modelling, forecasting, simulation, and optimisation. A deterministic base case DCF financial model of the type used in the gold project can be uploaded into Crystal Ball, and the variables grade, plant recovery, Opcost, and Capex considered in the sensitivity analysis are then replaced by defined assumptions. These need to be constrained by the practical experience of how real projects might behave.

This might take into consideration that for a gold project, grade would typically be a positively skewed lognormal distribution with a mean of 10 g/t but a standard deviation of 4 g/t, suggesting a small probability of some high grades of up to 18 g/t. These assumptions can be verified through a discussion with the geostatistician responsible for the resource estimation. Plant recovery with an estimated mean of 90% and with a standard deviation of 2% suggests that there is only a small probability of plant recovery exceeding 94%. Such an insight would be derived from pilot plant test work on bulk samples.

Operating and capital costs might mirror a triangular distribution where minimum, maximum, and most likely values are known from similar operations. The probability of cost overruns can be accommodated by defining an asymmetric distribution biased towards a higher but defined value. These distributions are illustrated in Figs. 2.5–2.8.

The output would typically comprise the NPV presented as a defined forecast frequency distribution with associated statistics such as mean, median, and standard deviation. The output can also be plotted as a cumulative frequency plot.

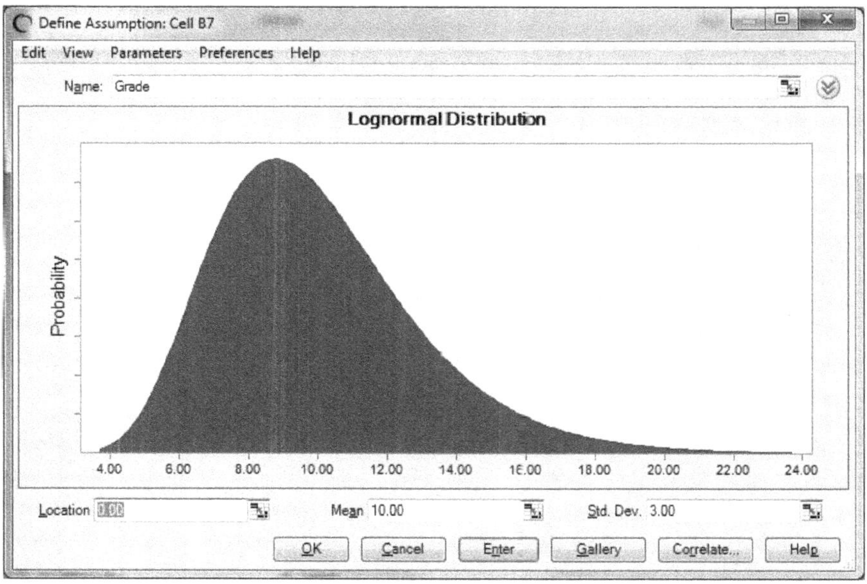

Figure 2.5. Distribution of grade.

Note: This figure was generated by an academic version of Crystal Ball licensed to Imperial College London.

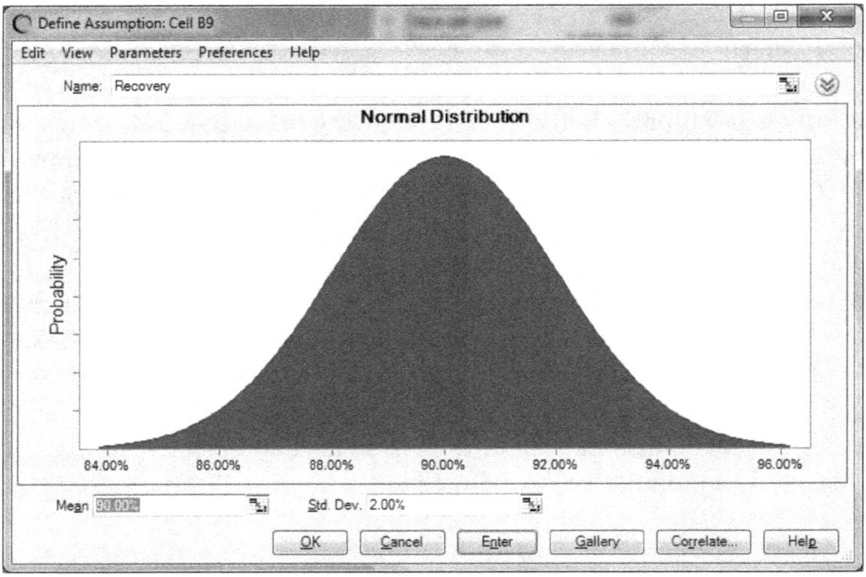

Figure 2.6. Distribution of plant recovery.
Note: This figure was generated by an academic version of Crystal Ball licensed to Imperial College London.

An example of the type of output generated from an MC simulation is given in Fig. 2.9.

This recognises that a range of outcomes is possible based on the uncertainty associated with the estimation of grade, plant recovery, Opcost, and Capex, which are treated as independent variables but this may not be the case. Dependencies include grade and plant recovery and both Capex and Opcost. Correlation coefficients range from −1 to +1. If negative, as one variable increases, the other decreases. If zero, there is no relationship between variables, and if positive, as one variable increases the other also increases.

The mean value of NPV should converge to the base case generated in the deterministic model but recognises that low grade may coincide with low plant recovery. In the real world, there may be a correlation between plant recovery and its associated operating and capital costs. The method permits modelling these as dependent

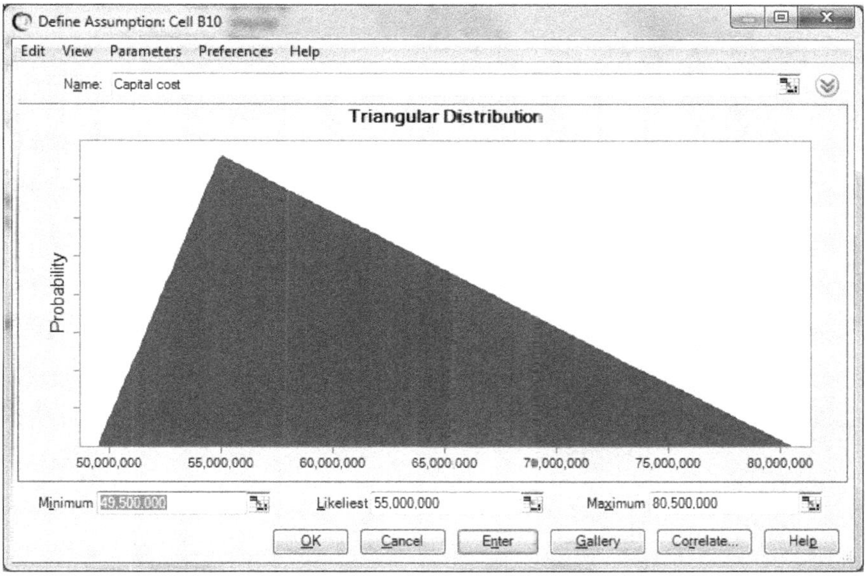

Figure 2.7. Distribution of Capex.

Note: This figure was generated by an academic version of Crystal Ball licensed to Imperial College London.

variables. The software is able to apply correlation coefficients, and while this should not make a significant difference to the mean, it will reduce very low or very high outliers.

This technique comes with a health warning — not all investors welcome having the uncertainty associated with a natural resource project being demonstrated in this way, particularly if one of the outcomes is a finite probability of a negative NPV. On the other hand, it can also demonstrate the robustness of a project and the probability of a high NPV. The techniques of MS simulation are best applied to projects at the prefeasibility and pre-funding stages.

There is seldom any merit in using sensitivity analysis or MC simulation to flex metal prices as the outcomes are simply self-fulfilling. The appropriate application of MC simulation to metal prices is to set up a real option valuation, as outlined in Sections 4.8 and 11.3.

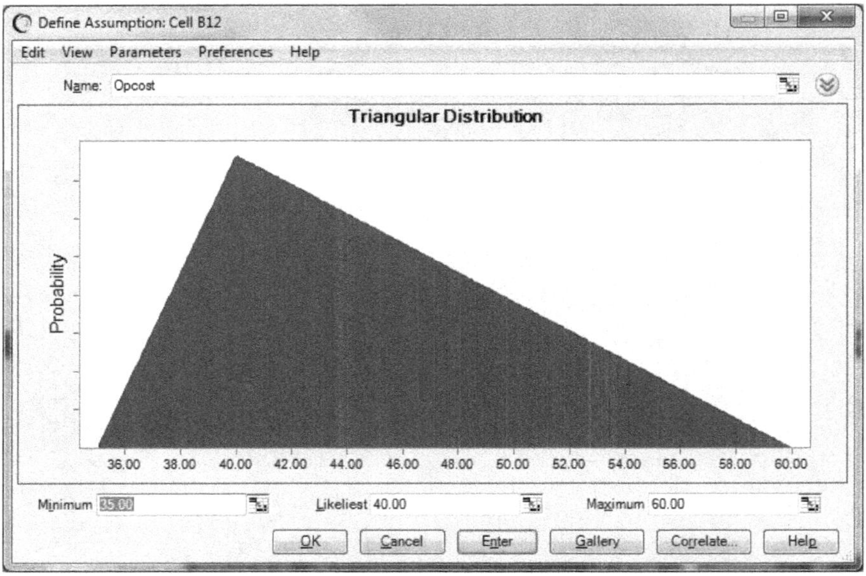

Figure 2.8. Distribution of Opcost.

Note: This figure was generated by an academic version of Crystal Ball licensed to Imperial College London.

2.5 Project Finance and the Cost of Equity

2.5.1 *Introduction*

Project finance is the funding (or financing) of long-term infrastructure, industrial projects, and public services using a non-recourse or limited-recourse financial structure. The debt and equity used to finance the project are paid back from the cash flow generated by the project.

Project financing is a loan structure that relies primarily on the project's cash flow for repayment, with the project's assets, rights, and interests held as secondary collateral. Project finance is especially attractive to the private sector because companies can fund major projects off-balance sheet and has particular relevance to mining projects where the product can be traded on open markets.

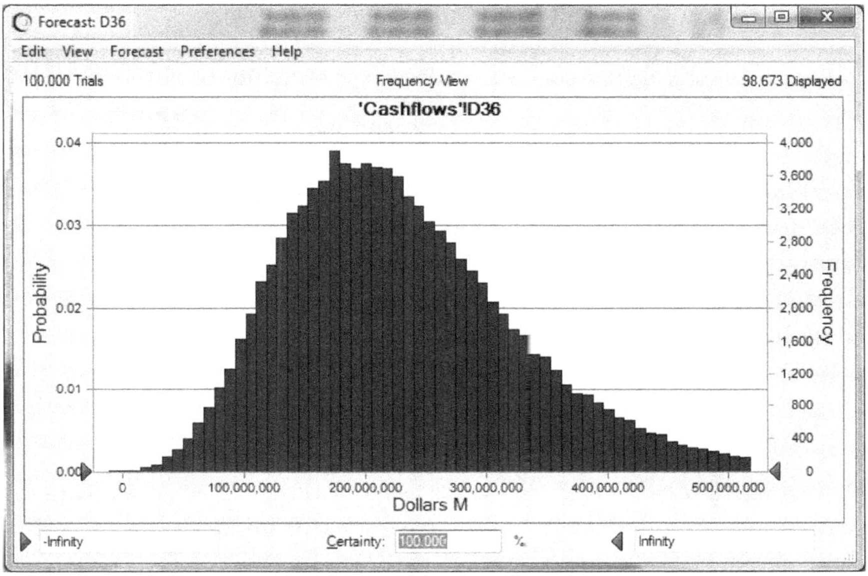

Figure 2.9. Frequency distribution of NPV based on an MC simulation of a gold project in which grade, plant recovery, operating costs, and capital costs are treated as independent variables.

Note: This figure was generated by an academic version of Crystal Ball licensed to Imperial College London.

These in turn offer the opportunity to apply the principles of derivative trading and hedging strategies.

Structured finance is a financial instrument available to large financial institutions or companies with complicated financing needs who are unsatisfied with conventional financial products. Since the mid-1980s, structured finance has become popular in the finance industry. Collateralised debt obligations (CDOs), synthetic financial instruments, collateralised bond obligations (CBOs), and syndicated loans are examples of structured finance instruments.

2.5.2 *Discount rate and cost of capital*

There are two methods of discounting that can be used to calculate the NPV in a financial model. The pre-determined discount rate can be used or the WACC. This is calculated as follows:

$$(\text{tax-adjusted cost of debt} \times \text{percentage debt})$$
$$\pm (\text{cost of equity} \times \text{percentage equity}).$$

For tax purposes in important jurisdictions (including the United Kingdom), interest on debt is treated as a business expense. It is, in other words, tax deductible, but dividends are not. As the NPV is calculated on the cash flows before funding but after tax, an allowance is made for the tax relief of interest payments on debt. The cost of debt is therefore calculated as follows:

$$\text{Tax-adjusted cost of debt} = \text{interest rate} \times (1 - \text{tax rate}).$$

Determination of WACC requires assumptions on the tax rate. A tweak in gearing, though, would have a greater impact than an equivalent percentage change in the tax rate. In the US, the Federal corporate tax is 21% with no special provision for mining companies, and most state taxes are around 5%. So, a straight 26% rate can be used for the base case tax assumption. The WACC thus varies according to the debt-to-equity ratio of the project's funding structure. The cost of equity is generally higher than the cost of debt, reflecting the higher rate of return required by the equity holders in comparison to the "cheaper" interest rate on debt. Thus, the greater the percentage of total capital funded by debt, the lower the WACC and thus the more favourable the calculated NPV. This is an essential principle behind the consideration of the use of project finance.

Treatment of tax requires the integration of an economic model with an accounting model. At the investment stage, the cash flows should not go negative and where debt is used in combination with equity, the cash flows must be integrated with financial accounts. In Table 2.3, simple links from the cash flows through to the profit & loss account and the balance sheet are shown. The model includes project funding showing the cash flow impact of raising equity and debt to fund the development of the project and their presentation in the balance sheet. The model also includes the effect of depreciation and tax on profitability together with the treatment of working capital,

Table 2.3. Integrated economic and accounting model for a simple gold project demonstrating the interrelationship between DCFs and the financial accounts.

Year	0	1	2	3	4	5
Annual mined ore (t)	0	50,000	100,000	150,000	150,000	150,000
Annual depletion	0	3.7%	7.4%	11.1%	11.1%	11.1%
Total mined, including waste (t)	0	75,000	150,000	225,000	225,000	225,000
Recoverable gold (000's g)	0	248	496	744	744	744
Cash flow (000's US$)						
Capital expenditure	−18,300	−550	0	0	0	0
Cash from sale of gold		1,744	4,419	7,210	8,257	8,373
Operating expenses paid:						
per tonne mined		−503	−1,028	−1,553	−1,575	−1,575
per tonne treated		−611	−1,248	−1,886	−1,913	−1,913
Fixed overhead		−250	−250	−250	−250	250
Tax paid		0	0	0	−64	−402
Cash flow before funding 1	**−18,300**	**170**	**1,893**	**3,521**	**4,455**	**4,233**
Debt funding	14,999	0	0	0	0	−5,000
Interest charge	−1,200	−1,200	−1,200	−1,200	−1,200	−1,200
Cash Flow before equity 1	**−4,500**	**−1,370**	**693**	**2,321**	**3,255**	**−1,967**
Equity funding	6,001	0	0	0	0	0
Annual cash flow	**1,500**	**−1,370**	**693**	**2,321**	**3,255**	**−1,967**
Accumulated cash	1,500	131	823	3,144	6,399	4,433
NPV factors @ 8.00%	**1.0000**	**0.9259**	**0.8573**	**0.7938**	**0.7350**	**0.6806**
Annual PV's	**−4,500**	**−1,268**	**594**	**1,843**	**2,392**	**−1,338**
Accum NPV	**−4,500**	**−5,769**	**−5,175**	**−3,332**	**−940**	**−2,278**

(*Continued*)

Table 2.3. (*Continued*)

Year	0	1	2	3	4	5
Profit & loss account						
Sales revenue	0	2,093	4,884	7,675	8,373	8,373
Less cost of goods sold	0	−1,059	−2,284	−3,447	−3,738	−3,738
Less depreciation (not a Cash flow!)	0	−698	−1,396	−2,094	−2,094	−2,094
Less interest (is in the Discount rate!)	−1,200	−1,200	−1,200	−1,200	−1,200	−1,200
Prof it before tax	**−1,200**	**−864**	**4**	**934**	**1,341**	**1,341**
Assessed loss cfw	**−1,200**	**−2,064**	**−2,061**	**−1,127**	**214**	**1,341**
Taxable income	**0**	**0**	**0**	**0**	**214**	**1,341**
Tax payable	**0**	**0**	**0**	**0**	**−64**	**−402**
Less prov for tax	0	0	0	0	−64	−402
Profit after tax	**−1,200**	**−864**	**4**	**934**	**1,277**	**939**
Balance sheet						
Assets:						
Cash balance	1,500	131	823	3,144	6,399	4,433
Debtors	0	349	814	1,279	1,396	1,396
Inventory	0	353	644	934	934	934
Fixed assets (net)	18,300	18,152	16,756	14,661	12,567	10,472
Total assets	**19,800**	**18,984**	**19,037**	**20,019**	**21,296**	**17,235**
Liabilities:						
Creditors	0	48	97	145	145	145
Debt	14,999	14,999	14,999	14,999	14,999	10,000
Equity	6,001	6,001	6,001	6,001	6,001	6,001
Accumulated P&L	−1,200	−2,064	−2,061	−1,127	150	1,089
Total claims on assets	**19,800**	**18,984**	**19,037**	**20,019**	**21,296**	**17,235**
Diff (if any!)	0	0	0	0	0	0

Source: Reproduced with permission from Richard Anderson.

inventory build-up (equivalent to an ore stockpile), creditors (also called payables), and debtors (also called receivables).

By integrating cash flow with financial accounts, taxable income can be determined correctly on the current year's profits. This in turn permits the correct treatment in the financial model of profits ATBI, PBIT, PAIBT, and PAIT. Where debt is used for funding and the cash flows are discounted by WACC, it is clearly important that this be based on ATBI in order to determine NPV. Using WACC to DCFs that have already derived benefit from tax relief on interest would generate an artificially enhanced (and incorrect) NPV.

A financial model which integrates cash flow with financial accounts also permits a more realistic treatment of depreciation from straight line over the life of the project to loss carried forward where the taxable income is equal to the current year's profits (PBIT or PAIBT as appropriate) plus the previous year's losses (with losses carried forward indefinitely). This will generate an enhanced NPV, as the tax benefit is obtained earlier in the life of the project when present value factors give greater weighting to profits ATBI.

Under International Financial Reporting Standards (IFRS), profit & loss account and the balance sheet are designated "income statement" and "statement of financial position", respectively. UK-based companies are still using the old terms in their financial statements, and the familiar terms are retained in this narrative.

2.5.3 *Optimisation of gearing*

As the gearing changes, so does the NPV. The obvious reason why initially the NPV increases with increased levels of debt is because of the greater relief on tax and because the cash flows are being discounted by the cost of debt, not equity. The lower cost of debt allows for a WACC lower than the cost of equity when the latter is determined from the standard capital asset pricing models (CAPM), which then significantly enhances the NPV.

The measure of the riskiness of a share is illustrated in Fig. 2.10. The beta (that is, the gradient of the plotted line) is a measure of a stock's volatility relative to the volatility of the market and is the

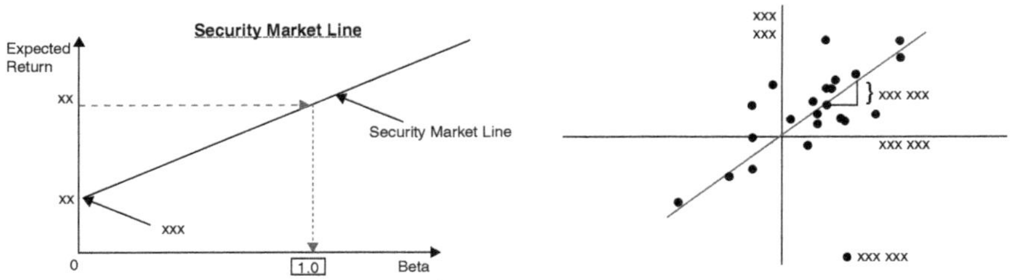

$$[r_f + \beta(r_m - r_f)]$$

where ...

r_f = the risk-free rate (e.g. US treasury bills)	3.0%
r_m = the equity market return	15.0%
(rm − rf) =	12.0%
β = the volatility/risk of the security/project	1.00
Cost of Equity therefore . . .	15.0%

Figure 2.10. Capital asset pricing model: Beta is essentially a correlation coefficient between the share price and the market average. This is a positive slope. A beta of 1.00 means a perfect match and a low cost of equity.

covariance of the securities return against the return of the market index, divided by the variance of the market index as follows:

$$\beta = (\text{Covariance of the stock with market average})/$$
$$(\text{Variance of the market average}).$$

A share that has a beta of 1.00 has the same return as the market. If a beta is below 1.00, it is less volatile than the market, and if above, it is more volatile. The variables are then used to determine the cost of equity, as indicated in Fig. 2.10. Beta factors can be determined by statistical analysis of share prices over time, or from dedicated market information services that can provide beta factors for a range of companies.

Assuming the cost of equity is based on a gearing of 30% debt, then at a tax rate of 30% and an interest rate of 8%, the WACC is 12.18, as shown in Fig. 2.11.

Any attempt to model gearing does obviously require that the cash flow model be integrated into the financial accounts, primarily

Interest %	Tax %
8%	30%

	DEBT	EQUITY	WEIGHTED AVERAGE
1. After-Tax Cost of Debt	5.6%		
2. Estimated Cost of Equity		15.0%	
3. Debt/Equity Gearing	30.0%	70.0%	
4. Cost of Capital	1.7%	10.5%	12.18%

Figure 2.11. Determination of WACC.

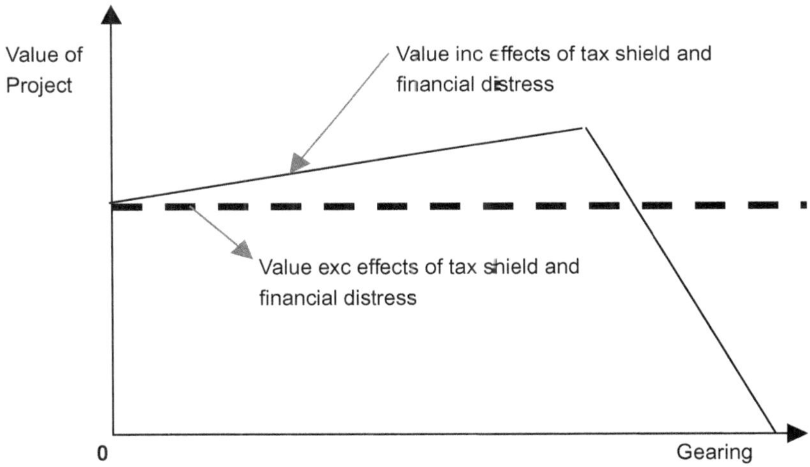

Figure 2.12. Gearing optimisation.

so that the effect of tax can be correctly determined. Changing the gearing changes the risk and therefore the cost of equity and the cost of debt. The effect is shown in Fig. 2.12.

The limiting factor is that as the level of debt increases, so does the risk of default on meeting repayments on principal and interest. The CAPM recognises this, and so the cost of equity increases. This will start offsetting the advantage of discounting by the WACC, and NPV will, after reaching a maximum, start decreasing. For large natural resource companies, the Treasury Department will usually calculate the company WACC.

Pit optimisation algorithms have to assume a discount rate fixed by the parent company, so the operation cannot use a gearing optimisation approach where the subsidiary cannot act as an independent company and raise fresh equity and secure debt from an independent investment bank. They must use the parent's corporate cost of capital. This must impact stripping ratios and may even sterilise some ore — a source of some frustration to planning departments on mines.

2.6 Petroleum Fiscal Regimes

A basic DCF model for a petroleum project will have many of the same elements as one set up for a mineral project. The project life will be derived from the production segments defined by annual production. The major difference is that, after a period of production in which volumetrics will be determined by the well infrastructure, there will normally be an exponential decline in production.

The volumetric used in setting up the model is based on a single value for the recoverable reserves. The production rate is then modelled over time using three segments — ramp-up, plateau, and decline, each with their own input parameters. Bear in mind that there are an infinite number of combinations that can produce the same total field life volume. This needs to be linked to the decline rate in the final segment, so that the total volume produced matches the total reserves. The same result can be achieved by adjusting the plateau rate, plateau duration, ramp duration, or the maximum of production periods in the model. The correct choice should be governed by reservoir performance, and it is not valid to simply squeeze or extend the production profile into the time available.

There is then the separate issue of the economic life of the project. This is termed the "economic limit" and is determined by the balance of revenues and costs over time. An example of a petroleum financial model is given in Fig. 2.13 based on a linear decline curve, demonstrating the relationship between the economic limit and total operating costs.

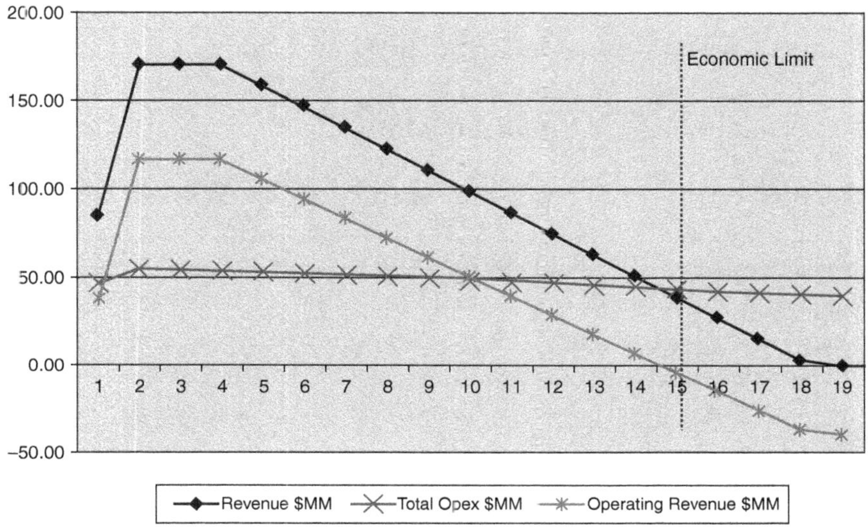

Figure 2.13. Cash flow for a petroleum project showing unconstrained and economic limit before tax cash flows.

There are three main types of hydrocarbon fiscal regimes. These are:

- tax and royalty (concessionary) regimes
- production sharing contracts (PSC) or agreements
- risk service contracts.

Of these, the PSCs are the most complex. They are normally bespoke agreements specific to a field of jurisdiction, and unintended consequences can arise once development and production commence (see Section 11.8). They are essentially complex tax structures, which means that the relatively straightforward link falls between tax-adjusted cost of debt used in mineral projects funded using debt. The choice of discount rate therefore tends to revert to the overall corporate cost of capital of the international petroleum company undertaking the development.

PSCs are modelled using revenue, cost recovery and profit split, and partner carry. The end result is an after-tax cash flow, which forms the fundamental basis for further analysis involving financing and gearing scenarios. Concessionary fiscal regimes are modelled using depreciation and hydrocarbon taxes, corporation tax, and royalties. These are covered in further detail in Sections 4.5 and 11.7.

2.7 Generation of Financial Models

The application of IC-MinEval software was developed at Imperial College, London. It is an Excel^{TM}-based spreadsheet Visual Basic program automating all stages required to produce models for a wide range of mineral projects. IC-MinEval produces a balance sheet and profit and loss account from the cash flows, with tax provisions linked to the profit and loss account. The cost of debt is calculated, as is the WACC and the cost of equity. Output modules include the base case DCFs, as well as key financial ratios and performance indicators such as NPV, IRR payback, and maximum cash exposure. Sensitivity analysis can be undertaken on key variables.

IC-MinEval was transferred to an Imperial College start-up company called IC-FinEval Ltd. and a coal version of IC-MinEval — IC-CoalEval — was developed and essentially incorporated the same functionality as IC-MinEval. This was followed by IC-Petroval, which modelled the cash flow models of oil and gas, projects based on volumetrics, segment production and annual production, revenue, Opcost, Capex, unconstrained and economic before tax cash flows, depreciation and tax and royalty, after tax cash flow and tax royalty, and production-sharing contracts (revenue allocation, carry, and cash flows). IC-Petroval remained as a beta version in the development stage, and the application was never made available for general use.

The functionality of both IC-MinEval and IC-CoalEval was delivered over the internet through the software as a service (SAAS) system with InfoMine Inc. This functionality is now delivered through Imperial College's Software Hub and is available to students and continuing professional development delegates.

Chapter 3

Strategic Management

3.1 Introduction

This chapter considers the investment and value creation opportunities that are offered across the whole spectrum of the mining life cycle. The interrelationship between the life cycle and the drivers is illustrated in Fig. 3.1.

A key driver in the minerals business is that natural resources have finite limits and therefore value creation is derived from an expansion of resources or reserves. An understanding of the life cycle of a project from exploration through to production helps identify those areas where value can be, and is, created.

The life cycle of an asset can be characterised by a number of stages. Each stage increases the level of certainty over the size of the potential resource base, the quality of the ore, and the likely costs and methods of extraction and benefaction.

As producing and development assets are often valued using a discounted cash flow methodology, reducing risk naturally increases the value. Earlier stage assets can be valued on a probabilistic method (expected present value) considering a range of likely payoffs, the capital expenditure required to gain those payoffs and the risk that expenditure will be incurred without success. Again, progression from exploration through evaluation to pre-production, utilising pre-feasibility and feasibility studies, decreases risk and enhances value through elimination of uncertainty over scale or quality of ore bodies and/or costs and timing of exploitation.

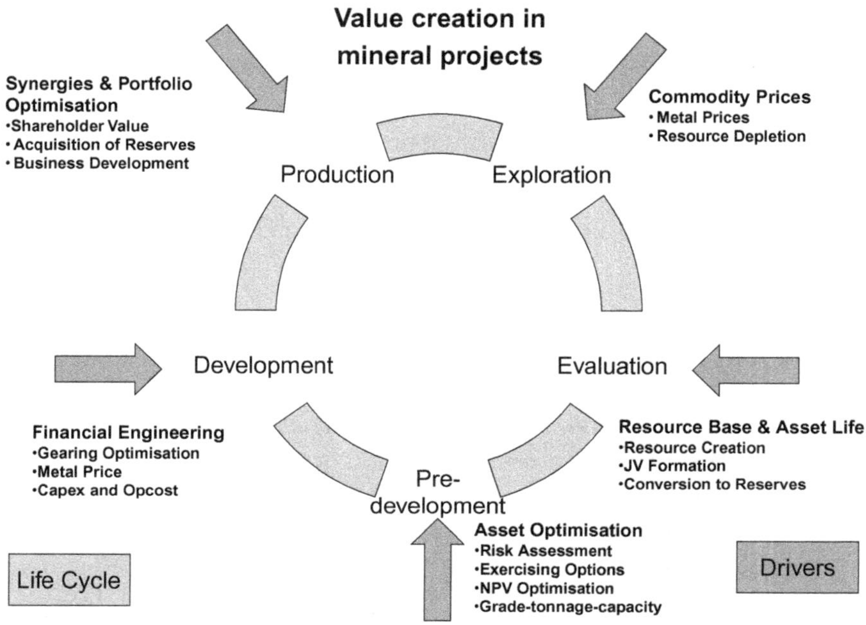

Figure 3.1. The cycle of value creation in mineral projects.

3.2 Exploration Stage

The proportion of targets identified at the exploration stage that will eventually emerge as operating mines is very small. The exploration and early evaluation stage is dominated by junior mining companies who generate value by screening areas and evaluating prospects. Given the relatively low success rate, the risk attached to such activities is high but junior mining companies make this exploration activity a core competence.

This is illustrated diagrammatically in Fig. 3.2. The high rate at which targets are eliminated at the generative and exploration stages demonstrates the importance of maintaining a pipeline of targets.

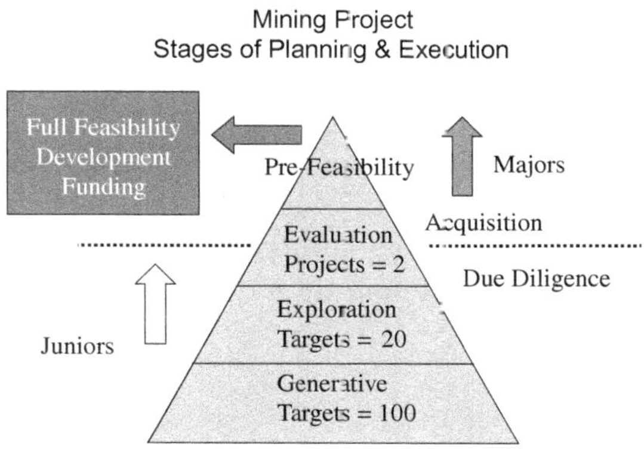

Figure 3.2. The pyramid reflecting the evolution of a gold mineral exploration and evaluation programme based on data from an exploration licence in Central Asia.

Once the pre-feasibility stage is reached, the costs of commissioning an asset can exceed the funding available to the junior miner, which will need greater resources to exploit the asset. Larger mining groups are attracted to the fresh asset in order to enhance their reserve base, and they are able to bring greater financial and technical capabilities to bear. Hence, the evolution of an exploration target into a mine will also often be accompanied by a series of mergers and acquisitions as the junior exploration company aligns with a larger mining group. This is a mutually beneficial arrangement allowing the mining groups essentially to undertake exploration by proxy, while from the exploration company's perspective entering into a joint venture with an established producer enhances their ability to raise equity funding. The need to create value by adding metal reserves to their underlying asset base is an important driver in encouraging major companies to invest in the exploration sector dominated by the junior companies. The higher risk associated with investment in early stage exploration is offset by the lower cost of securing a significant stake in the venture compared to the cost of a farm-in into more advanced projects.

3.3 Drivers

3.3.1 *Introduction*

Under either the expected present value or the DCF approach, there are a number of drivers that can be seen to impact strongly on value, regardless of volatility in commodity prices. As well as the obvious financial, geological and operating drivers, other aspects, such as entry to a new market, diversification of currency or commodity risk may also add value.

Use of broader metrics such as enterprise value (EV) — the economic measure that reflects the market value of a whole business as a ratio of earnings before interest, taxes, depreciation and amortisation (EBITDA) — or EV/production or EV/reserves need careful consideration as two projects with similar current earnings, production rates and/or reserves may not be equal. Differences may arise either in potential scale of the project (a pure production metric may ignore future growth plans), sunk costs (later stage projects may already have invested significant capital in removing overburden or on procurement of assets) or mine life (one asset may be closer to decline or require higher future costs to maintain production). These broader metrics are however much more useful in the valuation of corporate entities which may contain many projects in a range of stages of the life cycle.

3.3.2 *Commodity prices*

Whilst end commodity prices are an obvious driver of value, they are outside the control of the mining entity, except where hedging is undertaken. Volatility in product price curves over the potentially long life of a mine, however, makes the revenue projections difficult. Operationally, this volatility impacts on the economics of the mine, decisions on optimising the design of the pit (as revenue estimates may change views on economic cut-off grades) and even the scale of development. For example, it may be worth scaling up quickly to gain access to higher short-term prices.

Additionally, volatility and recent high commodity prices have resulted in many major mining companies having low gearing and cash-rich balance sheets. These companies need to invest cash surpluses in extending reserves in existing operations, locate extensions to known mineralisation or acquire existing operations and known undeveloped deposits. Capital expenditure in the global mining industry has fluctuated over the last decade and has to be balanced against the need to generate profits. Boards know that they must either use their cash intelligently by developing new mines or they must return it to shareholders.

High metals prices of course also impact at an operational level. Locking in pay levels while commodity prices are high will, however, result in higher operating costs, leaving profits more vulnerable to any future falls in the price of the metals produced.

Companies and analysts often plan based on forecasts showing commodity prices falling (or rising) to historic averages. Even if historic averages represent the appropriate longer-term base level of prices, future spikes may increase returns in due course. Longer-term prices when demand and supply reach equilibrium are driven by costs of production. It is likely that the downside of below average prices is far exceeded by the potential scale of any spikes. There is a risk of conservatism in asset assessments and the inherent optionality in longer-term assets being forgotten.

3.4 Resource Base and Asset Life

3.4.1 *Mineral resources*

Successful exploration leads to evaluation involving complex geostatistical concepts of sampling practice and geological continuity, principles of uncertainty, spatial control on sampling, ore body modelling, grade–tonnage relationships and selection of cut-off grades. These are covered in Chapter 7.

Following the 1997/1998 Serious Fraud Office (SFO) prosecution of individuals involved in the Butte Mining flotation and the

1997 Toronto Stock Exchange (TSX)-listed Bre-X Minerals fraud, described by Jennifer Wells in her book of this title (see also Section 7.3), the professional bodies in the United Kingdom, Australia, South Africa and Canada undertook a major revision of the codes for reporting mineral resources. These are identified by their acronyms (for example, JORC[1] — Australian Institute of Mining and Metallurgy — and SAMREC[2] — South African Institute of Mining and Metallurgy) and in plain English such as the Standards and Guidelines for Resources and Reserves — Canadian Institute of Mining, Metallurgy and Petroleum (CIM).

These professional organisations, together with the Geological Society of South Africa and the London-based Institute of Materials, Minerals and Mining (IoM3) jointly revised all their reporting codes in early 2000 and continually revise them. The IoM3's efforts evolved into the International Mining and Minerals Association (IMMa) and the Pan European Reserves and Resources Reporting Committee (PERC) Code. The mineral classification system is summarised in Fig. 3.3. There is also the Committee for Mineral Reserves International Reporting Standards (CRIRSCO). This was formed in 1994 under the auspices of the Council of Mining and Metallurgical Institutes (CMMI), a grouping of representatives of organisations that are responsible for developing mineral reporting codes and guidelines in Australasia (JORC), Canada (CIM), Chile (National Committee), Europe (National Committee PERC), The Mongolian Professional Institute of Geosciences and Mining (MPIGM), Russian National Association for Subsoil Use Auditing (NAEN), South Africa (SAMREC) and the USA (SME). Finally, there is the United Nations Framework Classification (UNFC) for Resource Management who regularly deliberate on the issues as a bureaucratic exercise. UNFC is not used by the mining industry for reporting purposes, and it is not a mandatory reporting framework.

---

[1] Joint Ore Reserves Committee.

[2] SA Code for the Reporting of Exploration Results, Mineral Resources and Mineral Reserves.

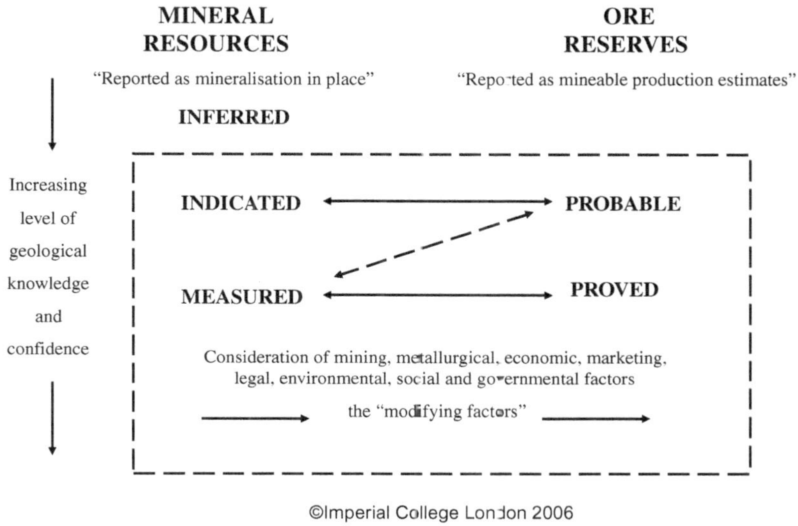

Figure 3.3. General relationship between exploration results, mineral resources and ore reserves. Reserves = Proven + Probable. Resources = Measured + Indicated + Inferred (Inclusive of Reserves).

Promoters of mineral projects attempting to secure funding from investors through an unlisted company will sometimes ignore the various codes for reporting mineral resources and reserves in their promotional material. Small low grade placer deposits (both gold and diamonds) are often selected as the core asset for this type of promotion. There will often be a general heading of "Gold Reserves" and there may even be the use of the term "Proven" or "Proved". Revenue for unit volume of alluvium mined and processed in these types of deposits would normally be insufficient to cover the operating costs, let alone the capital needed to establish a mining operation. Such projects would certainly not generate any return on investment and therefore to use the term reserve (rather than resource) in promotional material is inaccurate and misleading. The term reserve should only be used where technical and financial evaluation has demonstrated that the deposit is able to support a viable commercial operation.

In the United Kingdom, a company promoting a mineral project as having a reserve can draw the attention of the Department of Business, Energy and Industrial Strategy who can carry out an investigation. If considered expedient in the public interest, they can seek to have the company wound up on the grounds of lack of commercial probity and misrepresenting to members of the public the features of the assets. If this is challenged by the Directors of the company, the matter can be taken to the Companies Court.

The codes are essentially qualitative descriptions of uncertainty that are based on quantitative techniques. For minerals, a resource category will be allocated by a geostatistician based on complex mathematical algorithms that combine concepts of statistical uncertainty with the spatial relationships between samples. Probabilistic concepts are simplified into deterministic estimates but it is up to the geostatistician to allocate the resource in mineral projects to the inferred, indicated or measured resource categories. Financial modelling also provides an objective basis for distinguishing between resources and reserves. Unless you can demonstrate that mineralisation allocated to an indicated or measured resource category can also provide the basis for a positive NPV and an IRR that exceeds the discount rate in a DCF it cannot be described as a reserve.

Clearly as a project moves through the life cycle the ore body will move from resource to reserve and through inferred, indicated to measured. This progression is matched by value creation, as more certainty is gained over the quality and scale of the ore body and projects become financeable. The issue of conversion from resource to reserve is something the technical director must take direct responsibility for by making sure that resource blocks are not confused with mining blocks, dilution, and mine recovery is correctly determined and then other key variables such as plant recovery are incorporated into the pre-funding financial model.

While these codes were prepared for the equity markets and development projects, they are now also being routinely applied to mature active mining operations. In these circumstances, revisions to the definitions are normally introduced by the mine planning group as the level of sampling undertaken in an operating mine will always exceed that available for a development project (see Chapter 7).

There is a risk, however, that investors will assume that the level of sampling undertaken on pre-production projects needs to be comparable with those in operating mines exploiting similar styles of mineralisation, rather than that defined in the international reserve and resource codes.

Where inferred and indicated resources are very large, giving rise to potentially long mine lives, an NPV derived from a DCF model where cash flows are discounted at standard rates would not provide adequate weighting to revenues generated beyond 10–15 years. Indeed, given the impact of discounting, doubling the mine life may only add 10–20% to the value. This tends to undervalue large projects even where a large probable reserve is demonstrated. Alternative strategies for assessing the valuations of these types of projects need to be considered. The application of real option analysis, that takes into account such variables as product price volatility, can result in valuations with a premium over the determined NPV.

In a climate of shortage of supplies, there is every incentive to increase production capacity of long-life projects. Notwithstanding the need for additional expenditure on evaluation drilling and capital investment in the operation, the financial models may indicate enhanced NPVs for the same original resource based on the incremental production. Clearly it is not feasible to accelerate production in all cases, but scaling operations may add significant value.

Recent opinion is that more importance should be given to inferred resources even if they are not being given more weighting in valuations. Promoters are now being encouraged to generate "what if" DCF scenarios even though the codes restrict the application of economic modelling to indicated resources. This is based on the premise that the potential for a positive NPV must be demonstrated if the cost of closer spaced drilling needed to take the resource from the inferred into the indicated category, is to be justified (see Chapter 7).

3.4.2 *Petroleum resources*

The corresponding reserve classification for petroleum reserves is given in Fig. 3.4.

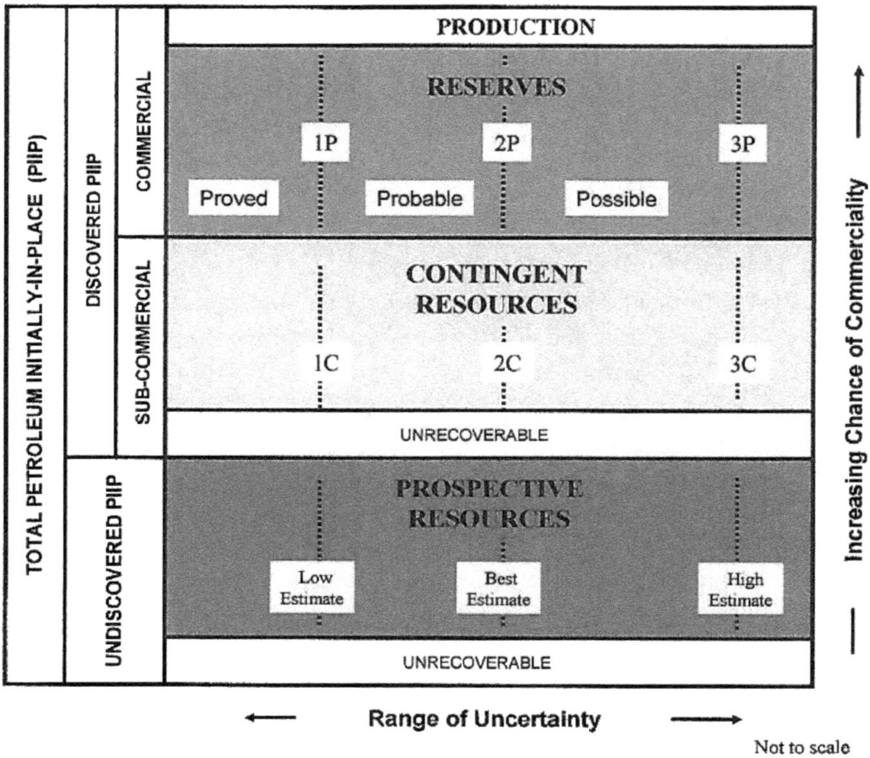

Figure 3.4. Society of Petroleum Engineers reserve classification: petroleum resources management system.

Probabilistic reservoir estimation techniques and simulation technology are used to determine the underlying key relationship between "total petroleum-initially-in-place" and "estimated ultimate recovery". Most oil and gas analysts understand that the 1P reserves (proven only), which the US Securities and Exchange Commission (SEC) require, are no basis for valuing the future earnings potential of a company. They will look at risk-weighted 2P (proved + probable) reserves (see Section 4.6). Companies are mostly interested in ensuring they have a rigorous, auditable system to support their estimate of the reserves submitted to the SEC. Directors won't get sued for taking a calculated geological risk, but they will get sued for not having a system to back up their numbers.

While there are obvious similarities in the resource and reserve nomenclature in petroleum and minerals, direct comparisons are probably not possible. The approach to extraction is of course also fundamentally different.

Energy projects such as coal, uranium and oil sands are essentially mining projects and can be accommodated within the Minerals Reserve Code.

The NPVs of all oil and gas projects were historically based on a simple DCF using a standard discount rate of 10% (designated PV10) for SEC-reporting purposes. Companies are probably happy to report normalised NPV10 numbers to SEC. This convention is, however, rarely the basis of share price valuations. Predictions of the price of petroleum company shares should be derived using the same gearing considerations as used in the minerals industry. In reality, due to the complexity of petroleum fiscal models, DCF models are often based on the corporate cost of capital.

3.5 Funding Options and Sources of Capital for Advanced Projects

Sources of capital to develop a mineral project include the following:

- Debt markets (includes corporate bonds)
- Capital markets (includes the stock market and equity)
- Sovereign wealth funds (such as the Mubadala Investment Company managed by the Emirate of Abu Dhabi)
- Private equity (such as La Mancha Resource Capital)
- Governments
- Institutions and agencies (such as the African Development Bank and the United Kingdom's Foreign, Commonwealth and Development Office).

A listing on the main LSE is not possible for companies involved only in exploration — the company must have at least one project associated with a probable reserve. It is an option that is restricted to companies undertaking or proposing to undertake extraction on a commercial scale.

For projects evolving into the development phase, project finance becomes an option. Banks exposed to the level of risk associated with a mining project will naturally take a conservative view. The development phase of a project would normally involve a joint venture (JV) with experienced operators.

Once projects have advanced to the stage of a full technical feasibility study, valuations determined from financial models based on a simple discount rate and a probable reserve will tend to approach the full potential NPV of the project. For a single project company, this would also tend to be the same as its market capitalisation.

Clearly volatile commodity prices increase tensions between miner and financier. Nevertheless, in the absence of a JV with a larger miner (with access to traditional corporate finance based on lending capacity across its portfolio), a junior miner will have to risk losing upside in order to secure the finance needed to progress the project.

3.6 Synergies and Portfolio Optimisation

To expand beyond its current reserve base, the major mining group will normally either have to buy an existing deposit or discover a new one. As many major mining houses have delegated exploration to the juniors, new reserves will generally be built via acquisition. If the type of deposit sought has to be large and high grade, then it is probably blind (there is no surface exposure) and will be very difficult to delineate or very expensive to acquire if already developed. Nevertheless, there is a drive by the majors to acquire companies with existing reserves.

Past major acquisitions have shown that value can be created by mega-mergers even at the top of the commodity cycle. Some corporate acquisitions involved multiples of NPV being paid. But how can value be created if acquisition cost exceeds that determined using a conventional DCF-based valuation? Portfolios of projects may, however, be value creative beyond plain vanilla DCF, from a corporate perspective, through elimination or diversification of currency, country or commodity risks.

Additionally in the corporate context, significant cost savings may be achieved, longer-term credit ratings improved (giving access to cheaper bank financing) and new competencies or enhanced reserve bases acquired. In this respect, valuing a miner based on the sum of the parts of the NPVs of its stand-alone projects may be erroneous. The NPV of the combined corporate holdings could easily exceed that of the underlying assets owing to the inclusion of future growth in blue-sky projects. The corporate holding in this context provides investors with a vehicle to invest in both the underlying commodities but also a management team with proven abilities in growing the business. In this context, the use of EV/EBITDA multiples becomes more useful. It is not just the current earnings and reserves that are important, a premium may be warranted for either organic or acquisitive growth. It is this momentum and the desire to maintain it that may partially explain the seemingly high prices that were paid for mineral projects prior to 2008. Another explanation for a multiple of NPVs arising is recognition of the conservatism that often pervades mineral and project assessments. If original technical, geological and commodity price assumptions are all set at conservative levels and then a low or normal discount rate applied, prices paid for assets will appear as a multiple of NPV as more optimistic scenarios are modelled.

3.7 Value Creation in Mineral Projects

Recent volatility in metal prices and its impact on the mining sector has increased the need to understand the interrelationship between technical and financial risk. The key consideration is the intrinsic value of a mineral project. Where current market conditions undervalue the true long-term worth of assets, which is then reflected in low share prices, strategic planning can identify opportunities. The following sections review strategic approaches for evaluating projects at the pre-feasibility stage and identify the underlying financial and technical principles which apply to mineral projects. Particular attention will be paid to the treatment of the key independent variables, such as grade and dependent variables, like grade–tonnage relationships and the way these influence the rate of mining, associated costs and optimisation of the net present value of a project.

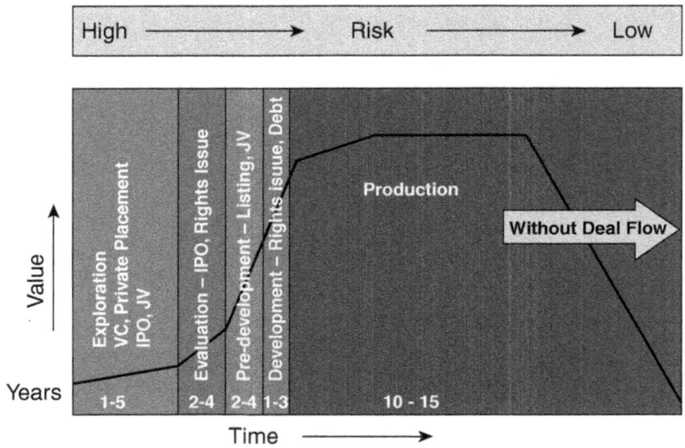

Figure 3.5. Single project mining company stages of development and funding options.

Professionals in the investment community appreciate that the higher the risk the greater the opportunity for significant returns on an investment in the sector and the leveraged position gained in the underlying commodity via an investment in a natural resource business, whether minerals or petroleum. This is illustrated in Fig. 3.5.

Key boundaries on the value-added line are the inflection points when exploration transitions into evaluation and evaluation into predevelopment. The experienced investor might reason that once production starts that is the time to sell down a holding as the reality of mining becomes evident. Figure 3.5 is of course simply a generic view in terms of funding. A major mining company could fund all the stages from internal resources.

3.8 Funding Options for Mineral Projects

3.8.1 *Introduction*

Sources of capital funding for mining projects include the following:

Equity markets. Liquidity is dependent on being listed on an exchange. This strategy is especially suitable for early-stage exploration and evaluation, but founders could lose control of the holding company. Once listed, the platform provides the basis for a rights issue, which normally supplements debt at the development stage. See Case Studies.

Traditional bank debt (loans). This is a form of credit that the borrower is required to pay back with interest. Secured against the borrower's assets, it has the highest seniority. This includes project finance, as described in Section 2.5. Debt finance poses a particular risk for weaker companies because, given a default, the banks can and do foreclose.

Corporate bonds. These are investment products that yield interest. They are riskier for investors and therefore command higher interest rates than loans. Most companies that have sold high-yield bonds have producing mines. They have the advantage of being able to lock in long-term interest rates and can be used to pay back shorter-term bank debt as part of prudent balance sheet management. Furthermore, they do not have the same restrictions as loans, such as covenants. When interest rates are high, there would be less incentive for a mining company to raise capital through a corporate bond.

Convertible bonds. This is a type of debt that can be swapped for equity if a company's share price rises to a specific price. It allows the company to borrow at a cheaper rate than that of a traditional bond. This avoids immediate dilution which comes with selling new shares. See Extended Case Study 6 (Appendix F).

3.8.2 *Pre-initial public offering*

For the junior mining company with largely exploration assets, raising equity on a stock exchange (also referred to as a "listing"), funding options are often limited to private placements (PPs), with valuations very difficult to establish and often highly subjective. This does, however, allow the investor to link the higher risk associated with investment in early-stage exploration with the lower cost of securing a significant stake in the venture compared to more advanced projects.

For a pure exploration project, the best option is to establish an unlisted company with backing from a limited number of private investors who have a major stake (shareholding). These are either venture capital funds or PPs. There is no liquidity for the shares they hold. This is the first step for any entrepreneur. See also Section 8.2.

Private equity typically undertakes investments of $100 million and above in mineral projects at the advanced evaluation, development, and early production stages. They would often have a controlling interest in the mineral project and usually raise their funds from institutional investors.

Venture capital is a form of private equity but targets start-up companies with early-stage exploration projects and usually raises its funds from high-net-worth individuals.

A company holding an exploration licence with some advanced properties may seek to raise capital to, say, undertake a programme of evaluation drilling through a PP rather than an initial public offering (IPO). Funds raised via an IPO where the shares are publicly traded on an exchange are subject to more regulatory scrutiny than those for a PP. PP offerings are normally sold to professional investors.

3.8.3 *Listing*

The prospectus for a listing must have a technical report, prepared by an independent consultant (Competent Person's Report), which in turn may include all the elements of a pre-feasibility study. It may not be necessary to have a full technical feasibility study completed (see Chapter 8) if funds are to be used for, say, additional drilling or trial mining.

A listing on one of the main exchanges such as the LSE is not possible for companies involved only in exploration — the company must have at least one project associated with a probable reserve. Once the target generation/exploration stage has been completed under a reconnaissance permit and the company has confirmed the presence of significant mineralisation, a public listing might be possible on one of the specialist exchanges such as the LSE's Alternative Investment Market (AIM) or the TSX's Venture Exchange (VE). The majority of Canadian public mineral exploration and mining companies are listed on either the Toronto Stock Exchange ("TSX") or TSX Venture Exchange ("TSX-V"). The TSX is the senior exchange and has more stringent listing requirements. TSX-V is subject to simpler continuous disclosure requirements and has two categories of listing requirements for mining issuers as reflected below. The minimum quantitative and distribution requirements highlighted below need to be met for TSX-V issuers. You cannot generate a DCF or undertake a preliminary feasibility study (PFS, see Section 8.3) without an indicated resource according to JORC, SAMREC, CIM, etc. codes. Once you have achieved that, you could expect to generate an NPV of $200–$500 million.

Once you have decided that this is the opportune time to go public and list on a public market, you prepare a prospectus based on AIM, the Australian Stock Exchange (ASX), TSX, etc., guidelines which includes the Competent Persons/Qualified Persons Report. Clearly this is a pointless exercise if it is not linked to attracting investors. Investors are not going to come to you, you have to approach them with a compelling reason why they should invest in your company.

If you conclude that you need $30 million for the next stage of evaluation drilling, then that is what you must raise. You create say, 160,000,000 shares at 25 cents per share; 120,000,000 will be issued.

No fund manager is going to take up all the shares on offer but for reputable specialist commodity funds (SCF) it is hardly worthwhile investing less than $6 million which would give them 20% of the company. They may object and say that for $6 million they want 30% of the company. You will then need either to lower the price of the share or issue more shares to the fund. You then move on to the next fund manager saying that a well-known fund is taking 20% and of course you are pushing against an open door. The word may then get out onto the street and private investors have the opportunity to apply, but this would be only a small proportion of funds flowing to a new natural resource IPO. An IPO is underwritten by an investment bank.

You then list and on the first day of trading your share price goes up to 30 cents. Everyone is happy and your market capitalisation is $36 million. You got your pricing about right. See Extended Case

Study (Appendix F). There is no merit in overpricing the shares as this will result in poor after-flotation performance. That is the value of your company. You then start spending the money on your drilling, achieve the milestone outlined, generate an NPV of, say, \$200 million following a PFS based in part on metallurgical tests and preliminary engineering — the market believes this and so your Market Capex reflects this number. Your SCF sells out, say, half of its 20% stake for \$20 million having now made \$14 million for its shareholders.

Shares outstanding refers to all shares currently owned by stockholders, company officials, and investors in the public domain, but does not include shares repurchased by a company. A share option is a contract that gives the holder the right, but not the obligation, to buy or sell outstanding shares at a specific price and at a specific date and is used by the organisation managing the listing. A share warrant is similar to a share option issued by the company itself.

$$\begin{aligned}&\text{Basic Market Capitalisation}\\&\quad = \text{Basic Shares Outstanding} \times \text{Share Price}.\end{aligned}$$

Number of shares created will obviously be related to the price of an individual share and the amount raised. The aim for a junior is to have a share that is priced around one dollar as this tends to be the benchmark regardless of the market capitalisation. When trading in the range of cents, small changes in the price can be announced as significant in percentage terms. Also, shares are traded in multiples of pence or cents, not fractions of them.

As the price increases to the level of hundreds, then a share split might be considered to encourage trading, originally introduced partly as a way of making purchasing round lots of 100 shares more affordable. This will not change the value of the stakeholding. Nevertheless when the price of a single share approaches \$1,000 and a share split is made, the overall equity valuations do tend to increase. This tends to lift the overall market capitalisation. A company can exploit this artifact. Instead of simply cutting the price and increasing the number of shares, it issues a new class of shares with no voting rights. Typically, founders and executives hold shares with voting rights, which allows greater control.

3.8.4 *Share buyback and mergers*

A share repurchase is a programme by which a company buys back its own shares from the marketplace, usually because management thinks the shares are undervalued, thereby reducing the number of outstanding shares. The impact is the opposite of dilution and should help the share price by adding to demand. The company is essentially returning capital to shareholders.

An additional driver in the mining industry, following a recovery in commodity prices and the build-up of cash, is handing money back to shareholders through dividends and share buybacks, which signals aversion by directors to buying up assets that may never deliver returns, as happened prior to the 2008 financial crisis. The emphasis is on maximising shareholder returns over deal-making and investment. See Extended Case Study 6 (Appendix F).

In implementing a share buyback and retiring stock, the company ensures that future income is divided among a smaller number of stakeholders. It will help improve profitability on an earnings-per-share basis by reducing the number of shares in circulation. With a share buyback for the same share price and greater earnings, the P/E ratio falls; therefore, with good technical fundamentals, the share price should rise but is more likely to flag in the absence of investment opportunities, essentially returning cash to shareholders rather than investing in new projects — a poor substitute for strategic vision. Stakeholders retaining their shares should see a rise in the share price and therefore an increase in the value of their holding.

Higher borrowing costs will act as a disincentive for a company to buy back its shares. It could also be argued that a company should return capital via dividends, but buybacks are more flexible as they can be scaled back when conditions change. Cutting a dividend, however, often leads to a drop in the share price.

The corollary of share buyback occurs when fresh equity is raised to develop a new project. See Extended Case Study 5 (Appendix E). The market should recognise that the future benefits of development and share price increased, and overall stakeholding was accretive.

In a friendly company merger, synergies are sought, permitting the whole to be greater than the sum of the parts. Share offerings or issuances of new ordinary shares are made in exchange for assets. In the Sibanye-Stillwater/DRDGOLD transaction, West Rand tailings provided additional resources, and 265 million shares were issued by DRD to Sibanye, equating to a 38.05% stake. The value created per share must be sufficient to offset the dilution of existing DRD shareholders. If the value created exceeds this, then the transaction is accretive.

Typically, dual-class shares are created when founders and executives hold shares with greater central (and voting) rights, while the general public holds shares with lesser or no voting rights.

3.8.5 *Share structure case history*

You have set up a company, have created 200 million shares and obtained an exploration permit to undertake a modest programme of diamond drilling on a platinum prospect in South Africa. You have raised $13.5 million through a PP in which you have issued 50 million shares at a price of 25 cents each based on a deal structure with a Venture Capital fund holding 55%, the Founders holding 25% and a Strategic Partner holding 20%. In addition, 10 million shares have been allocated as options and have been taken up at a price of 10 cents in the proportion in which the Venture Capital fund hold 40%, the Founders hold 50% and a Strategic Partner holds 10%.

After completing a successful programme of exploration, you have concluded that you need $60 M for the next stage which would be to undertake evaluation drilling as part of an IPO on the Toronto Stock Exchange. You issue 120,000,000 shares at 50 cents per share and secure the commitment of Fund Managers to take up 65% of the offering at this price. The Venture Capital fund decide not to acquire any more shares (they are not seeking a long-term commitment), the Founders commit to acquiring 5% of the new issue and the Strategic Partner takes up the remaining shares (30%). All options are exercised at 25 cents per share.

Determine the shareholding of the Venture Capital fund, the Founders, the Strategic Partner and the Mining Funds post the IPO and the overall cost to each of the stake holders (including the cost of exercising options). Under requirements of Black Economic Empowerment guidelines in South Africa, the Strategic Partner should eventually have a 26% stake holding. Has this been achieved post the IPO? The answers are given in Table 3.1.

The share price when trading opens settles at 65 cents per share. What would the value of the project be worth to each of the stake holders? What would the capital gain be to each of the stake holders at a price of 65 cents per share? What is the total amount raised post IPO?

What valuation approach would the underwriters of the IPO have used to recommend a price of 50 cents per share given that an indicated resource has yet to be established and therefore the technique of discount cash flow cannot be used? Indicate whether or not this was the appropriate price giving reasons. Outline the possible scenarios on the movement of share price as the evaluation drilling is undertaken and the results become available to the market.

As the share price goes up to 65 cents on the first day of trading, the valuation was correct. The investors have seen a reasonable gain while the promoters have not lost an opportunity to secure much more than the \$62.5 M raised. The predicted market capitalisation would be \$117 M. See Extended Case Study 6 (Appendix F).

As evaluation drilling is undertaken and the news flow confirms the potential of the project and an indicated resource is defined, then a DCF valuation can be undertaken based on a PFS that would include metallurgical tests and preliminary engineering. The NPV should be greater than the Market Cap on listing which should then be reflected in the share price. Cash balance in the treasury will have fallen as the evaluation drilling programme was completed. Fresh equity funding raised through a rights issue would probably be needed if the project is going to be developed into a mine. This would be used to cover the cost of a full technical feasibility study and perhaps trial mining (see Chapters 8 and 9). The final stage of building the mine would involve a combination of debt and equity, the latter raised through a further rights issue, resulting in further dilution. The expected significant enhancement in the overall value of the

Table 3.1. Deal structure and share price.

	Number of shares created	Number of shares issued	Shares optioned	Option stike price	Share price	Capital raised	Structure			
							Venture capital fund	Founders	Strategic partner	Mining funds
Private placement	200,000,000	50,000,000			$0.25	$12,500,000	55%	25%	20%	0%
Shares							27,500,000	12,500,000	10,000,000	
Cost							$6,875,000	$3,125,000	$2,500,000	$0
Share options			10,000,000	$0.10		$1,000,000	40%	50%	10%	
Shares optioned							4,000,000	5,000,000	1,000,000	
Cost							$400,000	$500,000	$100,000	$0
Total		50,000,000				$13,500,000				
IPO (New issues and pre-exercise of options)		120,000,000			$0.50	$60,000,000	0%	5%	30%	65%
Cost							$0	$3,000,000	$18,000,000	$39,000,000
Shares already held							27,500,000	12,500,000	10,000,000	
Options exercised		10,000,000			$0.25	$2,500,000	4,000,000	5,000,000	1,000,000	
Cost of exercising options							$1,000,000	$1,250,000	$250,000	
Total shares issued		180,000,000					0	6,000,000	36,000,000	78,000,000
Total shares held							31,500,000	23,500,000	47,000,000	78,000,000
shareholding after IPO (post-exercise of options) total cost to stakeholder/total amount raised post IPO						$76,000,000	18% $8,275,000	13% $7,875,000	26% $20,850,000	43% $39,000,000
Price post IPO					$0.65					
Value of shareholding to each stakeholder capital gain to each stakeholder (value)							$20,475,000 $12,200,000	$15,275,000 $7,400,000	$30,550,000 $9,700,000	$50,700,000 $11,700,000
Capital gain to each stakeholder (percentage)							147%	94%	47%	30%
Total amount raised by IPO						$62,500,000				
Predicted market capitalisation						$117,000,000				

project as illustrated in Fig. 3.5 should more than offset any reduction in the value of an individual share. See Extended Case Study 5 (Appendix E). To work properly when putting in additional funds to offset dilution, shareholders expect a significant enhancement in the overall value of the project so that this would more than offset any reduction in the original value of an individual shareholding.

The valuation of mineral projects is best undertaken based on a DCF model. This does, however, require a deposit with an indicated resource as defined by the reporting codes. Alternative methods when this does not apply include:

- Comparable transactions which normally apply to exploration properties and require identification of market capitalisation of several junior companies with licences covering similar metallogenic characteristics.
- The appraised value method which assumes that the value of a property is either enhanced or diminished by an exploration programme. Funds expended that develop the potential of the project will enhance value proportionately. The reality is that in most cases the exploration process will eliminate targets and that expenditure has to be written off.

For a listed company that has operating mines, accounting-based metrics can be used which include:

- Net Asset Value (NAV) – Net Present Value (NPV) – Debt + Cash + Investments
- NAV/Share
- Enterprise Value (EV) = Net Present Value – Debt – Cash & Cash Equivalents – Investments.

3.8.6 *Joint venture agreement*

Having identified a deposit potentially able to support a commercially viable operation, the Directors will then need to consider how it is going to get into production. This is when reality sets in — pyro- and hydrometallurgical technical issues around downstream production of, for example, platinum group metals (PGEs) from an initial concentrate are highly complex.

The development phase of a project would normally involve a Joint venture (JV) with experienced operators. Putting together a JV requires a valuation of the assets of the junior as a basis for the determination of the vend-in conditions for the major, and a clear set of targets to identify when trigger points are reached. Usually this is linked to the delivery by the major of a pre-feasibility and a full technical feasibility study. These need to be defined with rigour if disputes are to be avoided. In the event that the major decides not to proceed, a claw-back clause is often included in the terms of the original JV agreement. Announcing the JV will of course be good for your share price.

The vend-in conditions will be dependent on the valuation you have managed to achieve and this has to be linked to market capitalisation if the company is listed. The gold standard for a valuation is to be able to generate a DCF analysis. This requires, however, that the project be associated with an indicated resource. Even for advanced-staged exploration this milestone may not yet be present. Comparable transactions require identification of market capitalisation of several junior companies with licences covering similar metallogenic characteristics. The appraised value method assumes that a property's value is either enhanced or diminished by an exploration programme and that funds expended will produce value which will be proportionate to the expenditure. Of course, if drilling sterilises a potential target then the accrued costs need to be written off, so additional expenditure on a prospect can end up reducing the valuation. Intangible assets can be added to valuation determined using the above methods. These include local infrastructure, deferred expenditure and compliance with minimum expenditure requirements.

The basic structure of a typical JV agreement is given in Fig. 3.6. As major miners often explore by proxy via JVs with junior miners, the alternative strategic approach to acquiring mature developed assets is to vend into a large project post-discovery but

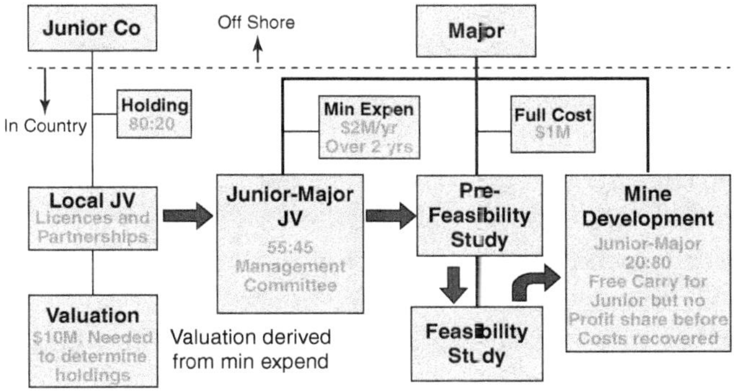

Figure 3.6. Components of a JV.

predevelopment. At this point, there is still some project uncertainty but the major has the ability to utilise experienced project development staff to accelerate the project and reduce project risk. This gives the ability to create value within the project itself as well as through the addition of reserves to complement the major's existing operations.

A major international mining company seeking to enter into a JV with a junior company holding a prospecting right where a base metal exploration project has entered the evaluation drilling stage needs to take into account the following:

- The profile of the junior
- The merits of the property and project
- The structure of the likely business relationship
- The legal framework of the JV agreement
- The relationship between the vend-in expenditure, the valuation of the project and the target shareholding to be acquired.

The earlier the major can vend in, the less they pay for a significant shareholding. At the same time, the more the junior concedes as a shareholding the greater the dilution for the junior's founders. This effect may be offset by the enhanced share price arising from a successful JV. The assumption is that the major will use their funds to supplement the junior's cash to convert a larg(ish) inferred resource into an indicated resource to allow a pre-feasibility and then possibly a full technical feasibility to be prepared.

Figure 3.6 should also be considered in relation to Fig. 11.6 showing a tax-efficient company structure. In a perfect world, the junior company would have a corporate structure such that expensive re-structuring is not needed if an exploration programme is successful and a significant discovery made. In the real world, legacy agreements with local strategic partners and sources of funding mean that restructuring is often needed.

3.8.7 *Project finance*

For projects evolving into the development phase, project finance becomes an option. Banks exposed to the level of risk associated with a mining project will take a conservative view. They generate an information memorandum which incorporates a full technical feasibility study. The factors involved include the following:

- Metal price assumptions and hedging
- Capital, opcost, contingency and reserve tail assumptions
- Sensitivity analysis and role of tax
- Gearing performance indicators
- Gearing optimisation
- Multi-partner modelling.

This is discussed in more detail in Section 8.6.

3.9 Multi-partner Modelling

Having tapped most of the world's mineral resources that are easy to mine, major mining companies are now being forced to take on complex projects in countries like Mongolia where foreign ownership and exploitation of natural resources are highly sensitive issues. As a consequence, the award of any mining licence in that country is predicated on the Mongolian Government having a 34% stake holding. The Government is essentially the strategic partner. The financial models that are needed to accommodate this type of investment constraint were first developed for the South African circumstances where Black Economic Empowerment (BEE) compliance required a target 26% stake holding in projects for the "historical disadvantaged" and was a condition of awarding mining licences. The intention was that this would eventually provide a controlling interest for what would also be strategic stake holders.

IC-MinEval generates a simple multi-partner scenario of three stakeholders which can mimic the free carry element (which assumes this is the strategic partner), the promotor and the fund managers, providing equity from the various markets. If the legislation requires a strategic stake holding (whether it be 26% or 34%), there have to be some concessions. The key one is that if the strategic partner's contribution to the cost of developing the project through mechanisms such as equity and shareholder loans, the entities providing the facility must be able to recover their initial investment. Usually this is in nominal terms but ideally it should be in real terms and before dividend streams are distributed according to shareholding that is compliant with minimum stake holder requirements.

Unless this strategy is accepted, there is a high risk that the investment simply does not go ahead. Essentially once the project starts generating annual profits, the strategic partner would need to agree to use its share of earnings to repay the money it has borrowed. Once those debts are paid off, the strategic partner can start to receive dividends. This carried interest arrangement recognises that the strategic partner has not had to put up a single cent to fund its share of the development costs. The downside is that it will not receive any dividends until the debt has been paid off.

This approach is simply asking for trouble and it would be sensible to make provision for at least a token dividend stream to the free carry strategic partner while the cost of the investment is being recovered by the mining company and fund managers. IC-MinEval's multi-partner functionality can model this scenario. If the strategic partner is the Government, then arguing that the state is receiving royalties and tax revenues is unlikely to convince an electorate.

Back-engineering a "deal" struck by an entrepreneur with the Minister of Mines into an actual financial model is a non-trivial task.

If, as was the case in South Africa, BEE was an attempt at social engineering then unintended consequences can arise. Wealthy black entrepreneurs legitimately representing the "historical disadvantaged" element were both able and willing to pay for their stakeholding up to the required 26%. This allowed them to obtain full and immediate benefit from projected valuations in new mineral projects, but potentially not all the expectations of rural communities where the deposits were located were met.

3.10 Discussion

Estimates of the grade and tonnage in the full technical feasibility study may be no different from those used for pre-feasibility, but may well include the results of trial mining, bulk sampling and pilot treatment. This level of technical information would not usually fall within the scope of a pre-feasibility study. Permitting and environmental impact assessment (EIA) (see Section 4.1.1) also need to be in place. A full technical feasibility study will also provide the verifiable cost and performance predictions. These are needed for the economic completion tests when operations funded from debt progress from the recourse to non-recourse stage. These issues are discussed in Chapter 8.

Major international mining companies act virtually as their own investment banks in setting cost of capital. Projects evolving into the development phase therefore provide a favourable investment environment for a rights issue, exchange-listed convertible bonds, high yield notes and structured corporate loans.

High commodity prices also provide a platform from which debt can be quickly repaid. Strong cash flow enables acquisitions to be debt-funded and gearing reduced as the acquisition is digested. Reasonably rapidly, the acquirer is able to un-gear its balance sheet or that of the target, leaving capacity for further acquisitions or green-field investment. When there is an appetite for mining stocks, this gives the major the option of raising new equity, or even funding from cash flow.

3.11 Transitioning to Business Leadership Roles

While the major mining companies have the expertise to assess the key technical issues that affect the sector which when incorporated into financial models is used to rank the investment opportunities, there will always be an inherent uncertainty associated with such quantitative performance indicators. The techniques of quantitative finance can assist the softer skills needed to make good commercial and business decisions. To arrive consistently at sound business decisions also requires consideration of the role of leadership, in particular judgement, intuition and experience. The Director who gets it consistently correct is obviously worth a great deal to a company. There is no substitute for experience and natural ability.

Bridging technical volatility and interpersonal influence and persuasion is central to achieving decision quality and leadership in the sector. Leadership in the industry involves navigating personal, technical and financial risks to create value. Technical and financial appraisals of mineral projects remain only theoretical models of what projects may develop into. A feasibility study cannot give completely reliable results. Performance indicators (NPV, IRR, payback, loan life ratio, etc.) may all indicate a project is viable. Implementation needs to be considered within the context of technical, financial and legal risk while taking into account the importance of getting to understand personal and organisational decision biases and blind spots. This involves raising awareness of one's approach to decision-making and recognising that it is qualitative, intuitive and probably subjective. Developing the professional skills that enable a Director to consistently arrive at appropriate business decisions is obviously worth a great deal to a company. To achieve this requires an environment where all factors can be reviewed in an open and objective manner. Decision-makers need to be approachable. Seniority and position should not be used to dictate strategic decisions, or poor projects will advance into development and good projects will be rejected.

Needless to say Business Schools have long recognised the importance of formalising these factors and they are part of the academic discipline of Organisational Behaviour Management (OBM). This is a form of analysis which applies psychological principles derived from experimental observations and is used to improve individual and group performance and worker safety. It covers the following topics:

- Leadership models and transitions from personal performance to management and leadership
- Leadership derailment
- Delivery of Myers-Briggs Type Indicators (MBTI), Fundamental Interpersonal Relations Orientation (FIRO) and feedback
- Psychology of team dynamics
- Effective meetings
- Managing successful negotiations
- Thomas Kilmann Conflict Mode Instrument
- Watson Glaser Critical Thinking Appraisal.

Executive Education of this type really needs to be delivered by suitably qualified faculty and would normally be included as part of an MBA programme. The reader is encouraged to read around the topics. Anyone who has observed the disastrous consequences of strongly opinionated individuals insisting they are right when in fact their judgement was flawed will appreciate the risks involved in not taking into account the impact of personal bias and should be aware of this when being asked to be part of a collective decision-making process.

Chapter 4

Management of Projects, Markets and Supplies

4.1 Constraints on Mineral Resource Development

4.1.1 *Environmental impact assessment*

There is a disconnect in society between the necessary requirement to minimise the environmental impact of mining during production, including the obligation under a mining licence to fully rehabilitate the site once mining has ceased, and the nostalgia for historical mining districts. An excellent example of the transition from industrial dereliction to historic heritage is the 19th century pump house of Cornwall built during the peak of the tin and copper mining period, forming the backdrop to the BBC *Poldark* television series. Mining also has an archaeological context. The Las Medulas gold mine in Spain was developed by the Romans with description given by Pliny the Elder, Gaius Plinius Secundus (AD 23–August 25, AD 79) in Book XXXIII of his *Naturalis Historia*. The massive excavation was created through the extensive use of hydraulics with viaducts extending up to 100 km from the site. The alluvial gravels were then washed into gorse-lined sluices and gold recovered after the gorse was dried and burnt. This is now a World Heritage site.

Prior to mining, an Environmental Impact Assessment (EIA) must normally be undertaken. This would include consideration of surface water, groundwater, air quality, soils, land use, socio-economic issues, human amenity (noise, vibration and traffic), archaeology, landscape and visual impact. Each of these aspects would in turn need baseline conditions and potential impacts to be determined and a strategy to mitigate impact put forward. This would involve provision for environmental management and monitoring. The scale of the task and the need for an interdisciplinary approach means that the work is best undertaken by specialist environmental services companies who employ biologists, engineers, social scientists, archaeologists, hydrologists and many other specialists. They in turn will need to co-ordinate their work with consultants undertaking the detailed engineering design stages (see Section 8.5.3) who may need to accommodate constraints required for the mining licence to be awarded. The siting and design of tailings dams is often a particularly contentious issue (see Section 9.5.1).

4.1.2 *Sustainable development and the moral case for mining*

Given the global reach of natural resource projects, there are international guidelines on their development. The perception that mining is harmful to the environment has resulted in governments taking greater control of their countries' mineral resources. The policy has been described as "Resource Nationalism". Examples of this would be the voiding of the concession that First Quantum Minerals had to operate the copper-gold Cobre mine in Panama and the Government of Serbia revoking Rio Tinto's permits to develop the Jadar lithium-borate project. This exemplifies that, without a social licence, approvals for a mining licence will not be issued. This is in the context of the narrative around critical minerals and the importance to Europe of a local source of lithium for EV batteries. It is always a revelation as to the number of agencies involved in reconciling extraction with environmental impact within the context of the entire life cycle of the project, which includes the closure plan. This is why the permitting process is best undertaken by specialist environmental service companies, as outlined above.

The argument put forward by the mining industry to justify the development of a project, namely that it offers employment, enhances the GDP for the host country, and generates tax revenue, can be considered patronising. Local communities can (and do) take the view that they own mineralisation associated with a deposit and any exploitation must be undertaken with their engagement. This, in turn, involves very significant commitments of time by senior executives of the mining company. Even when a deposit is being mined, this engagement must be maintained. The destruction at Juukan Gorge during the extraction of iron ore in Australia highlighted the importance of building relationships with the traditional owners of the land being exploited as well as getting indigenous people into leadership roles in the company. As an example of how getting this right can expedite the mining process, Ni laterite mining in Indonesia is expanding because local communities are stakeholders in its success, and the government has a direct equity interest.

The Equator Principles provide a risk management framework adopted by financial institutions for determining, assessing and managing environmental and social risk in projects and are primarily intended to provide a minimum standard for due diligence to support responsible risk decision-making.

The World Bank also provides guidelines for the development of base metal iron ore and coal mining as well as copper smelting and steel manufacturing.

The International Council on Mining and Metals (ICMM) was established in 2001 to act as a catalyst for performance improvement in the mining and metals industry. They state, "It is self-evident that no matter where we are in the world, metals and minerals are a part of our everyday life. Simply put, the 'green' version of almost anything means the use of more metals. But ICMM doesn't see this as a license for industry to mine them at all costs. Quite the contrary, we see the imperative to mine with principles".

The Extractive Industries Transparency Initiative (EITI) is a global standard to promote open and accountable management of natural resources. Stakeholders include all the international mining and oil companies. It seeks to strengthen government and company systems, inform public debate and enhance trust. In each implementing country, the initiative is supported by a coalition of government, companies and civil society working together.

The question that has to be asked is to what extent does an international mining company, when operating in a developing country, have an obligation to ensure that the revenues accruing to the host government are spent in a way which brings about broad, sustainable economic development and not wasted through mismanagement and corruption? What are the obligations of a mining company to influence the behaviour of government in a host country to ensure an equitable distribution of benefit flowing from the development of a large projects? Should they demand economic and political reforms as a condition of their investment, or adopt a "non-interference" strategy (as Chinese mining companies have tended to do)?

Given the decision by Rio Tinto to temporarily halt development of the Oyu Tolgoi project in Mongolia, what are the risks of undertaking mining extraction of natural resource projects which represent a significant proportion of a host country's GDP? Is there a case for applying the approach used by the petroleum industry based on a PSC rather than a tax and royalty regime which is likely to reduce political sensitivities (see Section 2.4)? Governments know perfectly well that with a well designed Production Sharing Contract the income to the treasury could be exactly the same as a tax and royalty regime.

Where major infrastructure projects are needed to release value from bulk commodity deposits such as iron ore or coal projects, the role of the International Finance Corporation (IFC) part of the World Bank Group becomes important as a moderating influence. The European Bank for Reconstruction and Development can have a role in addressing corporate governance issues.

An ideal legislative framework should be consistent, transparent, fair to all, and open. It should encourage responsible investment, with reasonable economic rent being paid to the country and local community for the right to explore and then extract minerals.

As far as practicable, it should discourage speculative license applications and asset sitting while encouraging exploration activities and mining operations.

Permits/licences should be issued for standard lengths of time (and be extendable, if necessary, according to set and known rules) and should apply the principle of "use it — or lose it".

Exploration permits/licences should be made available/issued at a nominal base fee in a fair and transparent manner and in such a way that, if there is more than one interested party, a fair and transparent competition for the permit is undertaken.

Modest royalties and taxes should be paid for the benefit of the country and local community and based on the recovered value extracted.

Jobs should be given to the local community and nationals where possible, and where skill sets are lacking, training programmes to enable localisation should be deployed to create long-term capacity within the local population.

The system must be efficient in that there should not be any undue delays in the issues of licences and permits upon the correct receipt of documentation, so that investors and projects are not unduly burdened with the cost of waiting time.

Landowner rights and rights of access should be protected, but eminent domain and expropriations should be deployed in the case of significant national interest.

All reasonable efforts should be used to protect the environment as far as practicable, with mitigation built in to construction and operation plans to prevent and contain pollution, and reparations on mine closures should be properly funded.

All geological, cadastral, and other relevant information should be reported to the agency for natural resources in a timely manner, and when permits are available, they should be freely available to interested parties.

Employees, contractors, sub-contractors, communities, and every stakeholder should work in conditions of safety and not be harmed.

If such a regime were to exist, then this would encourage juniors to initiate a programme of mapping followed by diamond drilling; however, this needs convincing endorsement by the government on the clarity and stability of licences. There has to be a clear pathway from exploration success to obtaining mining permits.

The obvious focus would be on known deposits based on any heritage of geological mapping, trial mining, and infrastructure development. The aim would be to generate a resource of sufficient size that can support a well-founded, modern mining and mineral processing operation.

4.1.3 *Occupational health and safety*

Given the key role that good management has in a mining operation, any objective assessment will need a site visit. The first expectation is that there should be evidence of good housekeeping. If the site is a mess, then that is visible evidence that it is poorly managed. An untidy workplace is also inherently unsafe. Operators will have to deliver what the manager demonstrates through action is really wanted, not what is said is needed. This impacts on safety: a manager can talk about safety but will be ignored if on inspection he or she passes unsafe situations without comment. On a visit, one should be able to tell whether all staff respect the manager. If they do, then the person is clearly doing things right. The operation will only really give priority to safety when the manager refuses to pass an unsafe situation until it is fixed. There are no unsafe mines, only ones with unsafe management (personal communication, Professor C.T. Shaw).

The same is true about other aspects of a mining operation. This is one of the reasons why so many waste tonnes end up in the plant — most managers really want to get their daily tonnage come what may. It is very rare to have a manager who worries more about how many ounces of gold arrived at the plant rather than how many tonnes of ore.

In the final analysis, if the management really wants a clean, tidy, safe operation they will get it. It will also almost certainly be a highly efficient one as a result. Needless to say, the situation with a poorly managed operation will not be improved by abstract analysis and investing further funding could simply reward complacency.

4.2 Cost of Environmental Compliance and Closure Provision

The cost of meeting the requirements for compliance with environmental constraints might start with comparing the NPV of two identical projects — one with permitting in place and the other, say, 2 years away from this stage. A DCF model of the former would generate a significantly higher NPV as the revenue stream would be brought forward. While it might imply that the difference between the NPVs of the two projects is the cost of complying with environmental constraints, this would be wrong. It is simply an artefact of DCF modelling. For this reason, it is recommended that financial models should assume that permitting is in place.

Environmental compliance can also generate an artefact in a DCF model when there is a significant cost of rehabilitation at the end of the mine life where, counter-intuitively, increasing the discount rate can improve NPV.

A DCF model generates results that reflect the true financial impact of compliance with permitting requirements for reducing environmental impact during production and undertaking site rehabilitation after closure once a mining permit has been awarded. These are from costs that include the following:

- *Bullet payment at the end of the mine life.* This is a fixed amount which is payable at the end of the mine life for the environmental rehabilitation of the mine site, retrenchment costs, etc. As this is discounted in a financial model, it is usually not material but there have been examples of projects which have such huge cleanup liabilities that the NPV improves as the discount rate increases. This counter-intuitive outcome arises because the liability is being reduced in the model.
- *Environmental sink fund at beginning of production.* This is usually an alternative to the above and is a fixed amount which is payable before the start of production and acts as an environmental bond to cover the cost of the environmental rehabilitation of the mine site. This applies to a country such as the Republic of Ireland which has a legacy of environmental dereliction which the state has had

to deal with. This cost is undiscounted so will reduce NPV by the equivalent amount.

- *Annual environmental costs during production.* A well-designed mineral operation should have provision for rehabilitation built in as an integral part of the cycle of extraction and disposal of waste rock and tailings. For example, on the mining side, double handling should be avoided. On the processing side, waste rock should not be mixed with sulphide-bearing low-grade ore and chemically unstable sulphide in tailings should be kept in a reducing environment (see Section 9.6.2). Under these circumstances, environmental compliance should not add significantly to base case operating costs.
- *Annual rehabilitation costs after mining.* This is the annual cost of rehabilitating the mine site and is not included in either the sink or bullet payments that have been made. A modern project is unlikely to gain a mining licence unless there is a clear plan for closure and site rehabilitation. It will therefore have been designed with this in mind so the cost should not be disproportionate to the cost of development.
- *Number of years for environmental cleanup.* Essentially the length of time after the completion of mining that the annual rehabilitation costs have to be paid. For the reasons given above, this should not exceed 2 years. This is different from the requirement in many countries that there should be site monitoring after closure and rehabilitation. In the European Union, this period is essentially in perpetuity. The Bullet Payment at the end of the mine life may incorporate some type of annuity to fund the process of long-term site monitoring.

Financial modelling can, perversely, be used to demonstrate that the best way of preserving value for future generations is to leave natural resources in the ground where they will remain safe. Net Future Value always exceeds Net Present Value. The trick is to find a mechanism, such as used by the Norwegian Petroleum Fund, which allows sustainable wealth from the current exploitation of a natural resource to be preserved through fiscal modelling.

4.3 Site Visits and Due Diligence

The formal due diligence provides the basis for significant investment decisions. The guidelines are as follows:

- *Objective.* Ensure that all material technical, financial and legal issues are disclosed (the responsibility of the promoter) and reviewed (the responsibility of the evaluator).
- *Obligations of the promoter.* Set up a Data Room. Provide administrative and professional support. Select a set of relevant reports. Provide a digital (Access) database listing of all reports. Arrange site visit. It is counterproductive to overload evaluators with superfluous information. Promoters are not obliged to identify risk elements where these can be deduced from the disclosures.
- *Obligations of the evaluator.* Form an inter-disciplinary team. Assign a suitable amount of time for a site visit (normally around one week). Keep a record of material examined and copied. Formulate questions.
- *Preparation by the evaluator.* Be sure of the reason for the visit and collect all currently available information on the site. Study the available information and question any unclear items — ensure the current status is clear. Prepare a list of items that need to be seen on the site visit, particularly items critical within the constraints of the purpose of the visit. Inform site personnel of items you wish to see that may otherwise be missed on the visit.
- *At site.* Make the purpose of the visit clear from the start. Look for tidiness — a tidy site is almost always an efficient site. Check safety records — there is nothing as unproductive as an accident! Look at the control mechanisms — are they fit for purpose and properly maintained? Make sure to see all the items on the checklist prepared for the visit.

The evaluator on an assignment has to formulate the right questions. Get this wrong and you will simply demonstrate a basic ignorance in understanding that the promoter will take full advantage of. Of course, it works the other way around too.

If you are promoting a project to an evaluator, you want to be able to assess their competence. Post Bre-X (see Section 3.4.1), the integrity of the sampling information should be absolute. Check if in doubt. Gold and diamond projects are particularly vulnerable to salting. Retaining the integrity of technical results in a corrupted programme is, however, very difficult for anyone perpetrating a fraud; a process mineralogist after all reported alluvial gold in Bre-X samples which, for a purported epithermal deposit, was a clear red flag (see Section 7.3).

4.4 Petroleum Fiscal Models

The approach to financial modelling needed to undertake valuations of petroleum assets is given in Section 2.4 and developed further in this chapter. The approach uses the same principles as the valuation for minerals projects in that you start with basic technical assumptions (which of course will be different for a petroleum project). The fiscal factors for a petroleum project can be a lot more complex than for a mineral project. They comprise the following:

- *Tax and royalty (concessionary) regimes.* These are similar to those in mineral fiscal regimes. The title to the resources is owned by the license holder and stakeholders bear costs, receive revenues, and pay royalties and taxes in proportion to their equity. This is illustrated in Fig. 4.1.
- *Production sharing contracts and agreements.* Title to reserves always held by state or its proxy, and the "Contractor" and state enter into contract to explore for and develop reserves. The contractor bears all costs (and therefore risks), and is paid for services out of the project revenues. The contractor is paid via two key mechanisms: Cost Recovery and Profit Sharing as illustrated in Fig. 4.2.
- Service Contracts do not give an ownership right to oil in the ground and the company is simply paid a fee for its services in extracting the government's oil.

		Company share	Government share
Gross revenue (oil price)	$60.00		
Royalty	12.5%	$52.50	$7.50
Assumed cost	$5.65	$46.85	
Special petroleum tax	25%	$35.14	$11.71
Income tax	35%	$22.84	$12.30
Division of cash flow		$28.49	$31.51
Take		42%	58%
Lifting entitlement		87.5%	12.5%

Figure 4.1. Tax and Royalty System flow diagram showing distribution of revenue from one barrel of oil. Taken from a presentation by Paul Wheeler.

			Company share	Government share
Gross revenue (oil price)	$60.00			
Royalty	10.0%		$54.00	$6.00
Assumed cost	$5.65		$48.35	
Special petroleum tax	25%		$35.14	$11.71
Income tax	30%		$19.34	$29.01
Profit oil split contractor	40%		$13.54	$5.80
Profit oil split government	60%			
Division of cash flow			$19.19	$40.81
Take			25%	75%
Lifting entitlement			42%	58%

Figure 4.2. PSC flow diagram showing distribution of revenue from one barrel of oil. Taken from a presentation by Paul Wheeler.

The typical production profile of a petroleum project is illustrated in Fig. 4.3. As production declines, so revenue declines. The point in time at which the revenue has declined to equal the operating costs is known as the economic limit of the field and is illustrated in Fig. 2.13 and discussed in Sections 2.6 and 11.7.

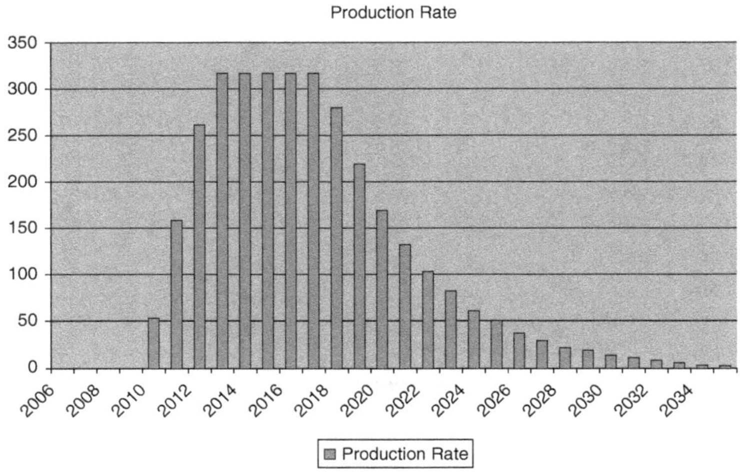

Figure 4.3. Petroleum projects are characterised by decline curves.

4.5 Petroleum Resource Management System

An oil reservoir requires a rock to be both permeable and porous. Permeability measures the ability of fluids to flow through rock (or other porous media). Typical values of permeability for petroleum reservoir rocks range from 10,000 to 100 millidarcies (mD). Porosity is a measure of the volume of voids which cannot exceed 45% (see Section 6.2).

Natural production occurs when the reservoir pressure exceeds the well pressure. This is due to a combination of hydrostatic pressure at the base of a column of water exceeding that for an equivalent column of oil owing to the density difference. This effect reinforces lithostatic pressure which means, owing to the density of sedimentary rocks ($2.6\,g/cm^3$) which is much higher than hydrostatic pressure, that once breached by a well, oil will flow up to the surface with considerable force. Drilling technology must take this into account and blow-out protection is an integral part of the design. The Deepwater Horizon oil spill and the Macondo blowout are testament to the environmental implications of a failure of systems in the petroleum industry.

A floating production storage and offloading (FPSO) unit is a floating vessel used by the offshore oil and gas industry for the production and processing of hydrocarbons and for the storage of oil. Usually based on a (converted) oil tanker hull, it is equipped with hydrocarbon processing equipment for separation and treatment of crude oil, water and gases arriving on board from sub-sea oil wells via flexible pipelines.

Once pressure in the reservoir equals well pressure, flow will cease, which occurs after as little as 10% of the Stock Tank Oil-Initially-in-Place (STOIIP) has been recovered. Secondary production is maintained by injecting gas or water but typically as little as 35% of STOIIP may be recovered.

Decline profiles in production from petroleum reservoirs were modelled via a series of empirical equations proposed by Arps (1945) who developed exponential, hyperbolic and harmonic models for decline curves, constructing a mathematical relationship between the production rate and the decline percentage in each case.

The Arps equations are defined by three key variables:

- the initial rate of production (qi)
- the hyperbolic constant (b) which defines the curvature of the decline
- the decline rate (D).

Fundamental to these equations are the assumptions that production is stable and that production rates are proportional to reservoir pressure. The hyperbolic curve models a decline rate that is proportional to a power rate, which is best applied to gas reservoirs, shale gas, highly fractured reservoirs or those under gravity drainage (Blunt, 2017). Under exponential decline, a constant percentage decline in the production is assumed over time. Such modelling assumptions typically work best in reservoirs above the bubble point without a strong aquifer drive.

The harmonic description is best used for water drive mechanisms and high viscosity oil reservoirs.

Ramp-up, plateau and decline periods are modelled by applying the Arps equation which is defined as follows:

$$q(y) = qi/(1 + (x - 6) \times b \times Di)x - 6b.$$

The inputs for this equation are:

- y, the number of years after the plateau period
- $q\ (y)$, which is the production rate in barrels, y years after the end of the plateau period
- qi corresponds to the plateau value of the production rate
- Di is the initial decline rate
- b is the degree of curvature of the line.

IC-Petroval incorporates a series of forms that provide basic input variables needed to calculate volumetrics as illustrated in Fig. 4.4.

IC-Petroval will model the production rate over time using three segments — ramp up, plateau and decline, each with their own input parameters. Bear in mind that there are an infinite number of combinations that can produce the same total field-life volume.

The simplest approach for calculating recoverable reserves and their associated uncertainty is Monte Carlo Simulation. STOIIP is the amount of oil that is estimated to be present in the reservoir. STOIIP may be multiplied by an estimate of the recovery factor in order to estimate recoverable reserves. This is derived from the following:

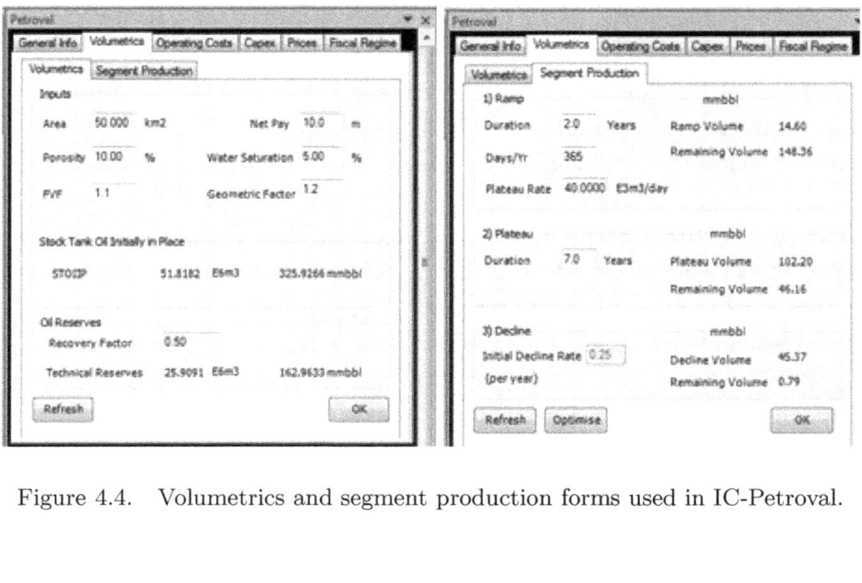

Figure 4.4. Volumetrics and segment production forms used in IC-Petroval.

- Gross Rock Volume (GRV)
- Net-to-Gross ratio (N/G) which is the ratio between the volume of productive (Net) reservoir rock and the total (Gross) reservoir volume
- Porosity (Φ)
- Oil Saturation (So)
- Formation Volume Factor (FVF) relates the volume of oil at stock-tank conditions to the volume of oil at elevated pressure and temperature in the reservoir. Values typically range from approximately 1.0 bbl/STB for crude oil systems containing little or no solution gas to nearly 3.0 bbl/STB for highly volatile oil.

$$\text{STOIIP} = \text{GRV} \times \text{N/G} \times \Phi \times \text{So} \times \text{FVF}.$$

$$\text{STOIIP} = (\text{GRV} \times \text{NG}/\Phi \times \text{So} \times \text{FVF}) \times \text{Recovery Factor}.$$

Recovery Factor is the amount of petroleum in comparison with the total amount which can be recovered and can range from 30–80%.

A Monte Carlo simulation can be generated from the assumed probability density function (pdf) of these five variables in order to generate the histogram given in Fig. 4.5 (in this Crystal Ball

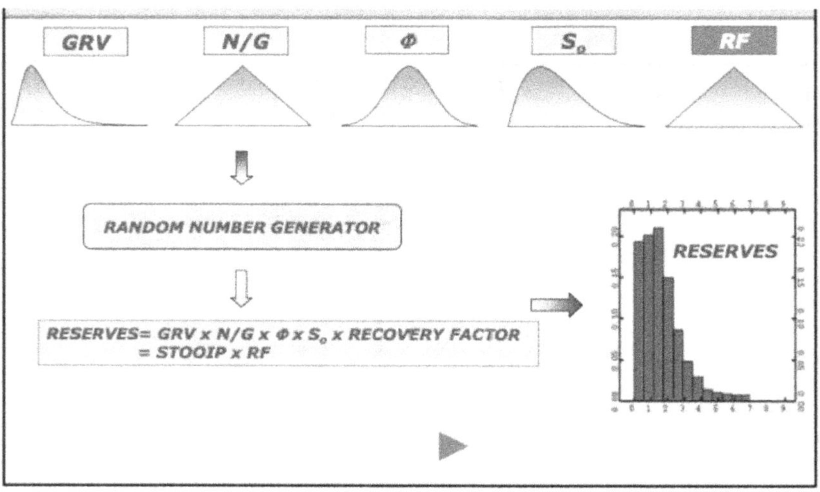

Figure 4.5. Reserves uncertainty quantification by Monte Carlo simulation. Reproduced with permission from Prof. Olivier Dubrule from his teaching slides.

simulation, 100,000 samples of each parameter were generated probabilistically).

Crystal Ball simply calculates the P90 (resp. P10) as the value above which nine-tenths (resp. one-tenth) or 90,000 of the samples (resp. 90,000) are found. P90 and P10 in Fig. 4.6 are 0.13 Mm3 and 0.51 Mm3 respectively. Since the histogram above is clearly lognormal, P90 and P10 could also be calculated from the theoretical quantiles of the lognormal pdf.

Confusion often arises because the nomenclature of P10 and P90 is switched around as compared to the quantile nomenclature of statisticians. What is a q10 (10% quantile) for statisticians is a P90 for petroleum engineers. It means the value at which there is 90% probability that the volume is greater than this value. The same applies to q90 versus P10 on the other side of the curve.

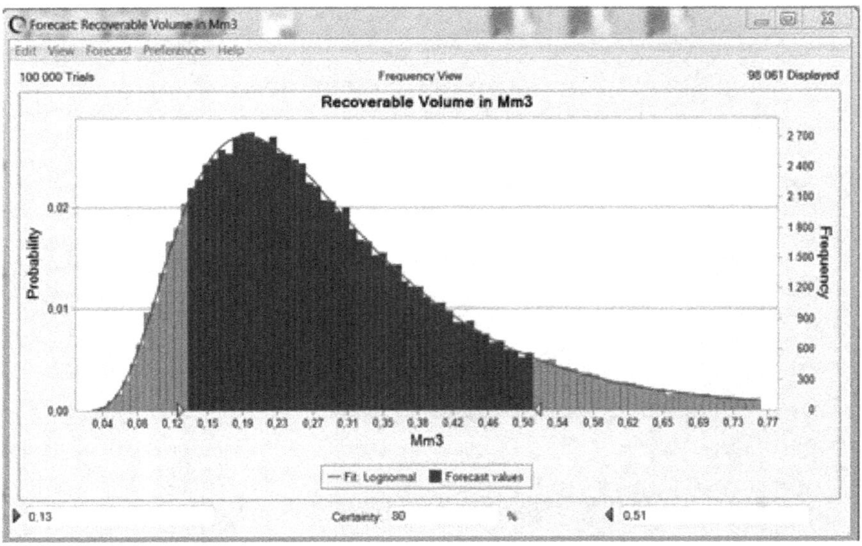

Figure 4.6. Positioning P90 and P10 on the output histogram generated from a Monte Carlo simulation using Crystal Ball from Gross Rock Volume, Net-to-Gross ratio, Porosity, Oil Saturation and Formation Volume Factor (Reproduced with permission from Prof. Olivier Dubrule from his teaching slides).

Note: This figure was generated by an academic version of Crystal Ball licensed to Imperial College London.

This needs to be reconciled with the definitions of the Society of Petroleum Engineers (SPE) Petroleum Resource Management System designations of 1P (Proved), 2P (Proved plus Probable) and 3P (Proved plus Probable plus Possible) Reserves. These are illustrated graphically in Fig. 3.4 with qualitative descriptions of Proved Reserve given as having reasonable certainty.

The two-axis PRMS is illustrated in Fig. 3.4. This a qualitative system based on descriptions but is derived from a quantitative probabilistic approach outlined above. Based on SPE nomenclature given in Fig. 4.7, 1P is therefore 0.13 Mm3, 2P is 0.26 Mm3 and 3P is 0.51 Mm3.

This should be compared with the reporting of mineral resources outlined in Section 3.4.1 and the alternative classification given in Fig. 4.7.

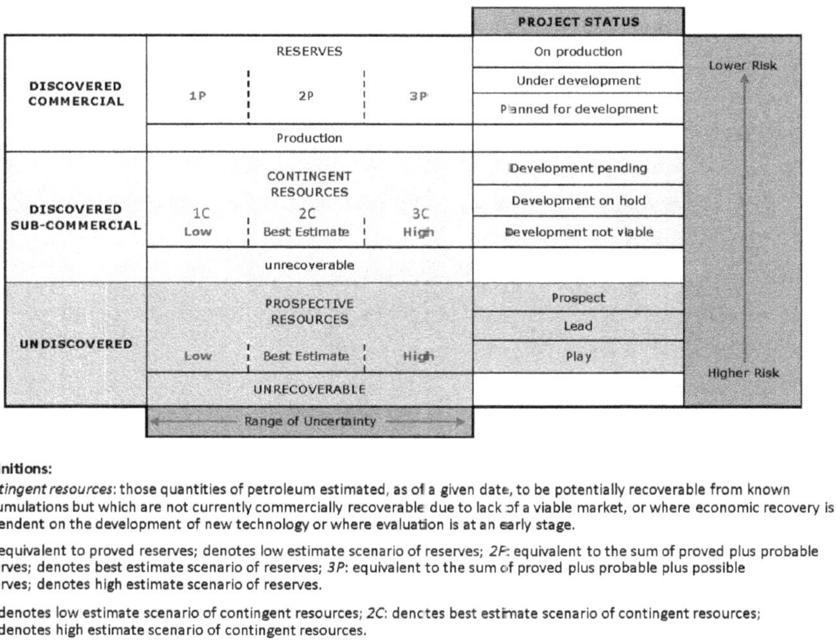

Figure 4.7. SPE Resource Classification Scheme.

4.6 Valuing Oil Companies

While there are obvious similarities in the resource and reserve nomenclature in petroleum and minerals, direct comparisons are probably not possible. The approach to extraction is of course also fundamentally different. Energy projects such as coal, uranium and oil sands are essentially mining operations although classified as petroleum projects. Here conventional mining techniques are used to produce oil indicating that differences are becoming blurred. The investment community in any event often makes little distinction between mining and petroleum — both sectors are commodity-based and are associated with products that have over the last decade been associated with unprecedented levels of volatility. The impact this has on revenue assumptions and determination of economic viability needs to be linked to concepts of probabilistic reservoir estimation techniques and simulation technology used to determine the underlying key relationship between "total petroleum-initially-in-place" and "estimated ultimate recovery".

Most oil and gas analysts understand that the 1P reserves (proven only), which the SEC require, are no basis for valuing the future earnings potential of a company. They will look at risk-weighted 2P (proved + probable) reserves. Furthermore, the NPV of all oil and gas projects is based on a simple DCF using a standard discount rate of 10% (designated PV10) for Securities and Exchange Commission (SEC) reporting purposes. Companies are probably happy to report normalised NPV10 numbers to SEC. This convention is, however, rarely the basis of share price valuations.

Valuation of petroleum projects tends to be a niche skill that has been in demand by both the IOGs and the natural resource teams of investment banks. The current volatility with oil price is therefore likely to increase the career opportunities for professionals in the business development divisions of the natural resource groups as well as the financial services offering advice on restructuring. The boundary condition between resources and reserves as given in Fig. 3.4 can only be addressed when models are integrated into the quantitative fiscal modelling. This integrates volumetrics and decline analysis with oil and gas fiscal systems, concessionary regimes and production sharing contracts. The key concepts around economic limits (see Fig. 2.13) and the stochastic treatment of decline curves within the context of the corporate cost of capital all need to be included in the design of the financial model.

4.7 Gaseous Hydrocarbons

4.7.1 *LPG versus LNG and CSG to LNG*

The organic chemistry and formation of hydrocarbons is given in Chapter 6. Liquefied Petroleum Gas (LPG) includes mixes that are mostly propane (C_3H_8), mostly butane (C_4H_{10}) or, most commonly, mixes including both propane and butane. LPG is derived from petroleum or "wet" natural gas, and is almost entirely from fossil fuel sources, being manufactured during the refining of crude oil, or extracted from petroleum or natural gas streams as they emerge from the ground.

Liquefied Natural Gas (LNG) is natural gas (predominantly methane, CH_4) with some mixture of ethane C_2H_6 that has been converted to liquid form for ease and safety of non-pressurised storage or transport. It takes up about 1/600th the volume of natural gas in the gaseous state (at standard conditions for temperature and pressure). The gas is first extracted and transported to a processing plant where it is purified by removing any condensates such as water, oil and mud, as well as other gases such as CO_2 and H_2S. An LNG process train will also typically be designed to remove trace amounts of mercury from the gas stream to prevent mercury amalgamating with aluminium in the cryogenic heat exchangers. The gas is then cooled down in stages to approximately −162°C (−260°F) until it is liquefied at close to atmospheric pressure; maximum transport pressure is set at around 25 kPa (4 psi).

The process of extracting gas and converting coal seam gas (CSG) to LNG is commonly broken down into industry classifications comprising upstream (the process of surveying, drilling and extracting) and downstream (processing and compressing CSG) which differs both from conventional upstream and combined conventional gas-field–LNG plant projects. The upstream CSG part operates under a different fiscal and ownership regime to an LNG operation. If the LNG plant is already built, the investment sunk study focuses on future value. Production depends on numbers of wells drilled and their average performance.

Engineering challenges related to the subset of geological heterogeneities will need to be considered within the context of their financial implications.

Coalbed Methane/CSG comprises methane which is trapped by adsorption in micropores in coal formation, and is released when a pressure differential develops between the coal matrix and fractures. Water is usually contained in the fractures, and dewatering is required before any gas can be produced.

Floating liquefied natural gas (FLNG) technology makes the production, liquefaction and storage of natural gas possible at sea.

LNG is transferred directly from the floating facility to specific carriers for convenient shipping to countries around in the world. Aboard an FLNG facility, natural gas produced from underwater fields is processed with the advanced design of facilities on board. LNG plant design packs a typical land-based LNG plant into a fraction of its normal size.

A FPSO vessel is designed to receive hydrocarbons produced by itself or from nearby platforms, process them, and store oil until it can be offloaded onto a tanker or, less frequently, transported through a pipeline. FPSOs are preferred in frontier offshore regions as they are easy to install, and do not require a local pipeline infrastructure to export oil.

Once the gas collected from the field enters the plant, the first step of the process is to pass through knock out drums. The condensate will be separated from the gas and thus not be processed. The condensate is then stabilised and put to storage. The gas flow then undergoes a chemical absorption of the acid gas, mainly carbon dioxide, thanks to an amine process. The next step is to dehydrate the gas by molecular sieve before removing the mercury from the natural gas. The removal of mercury is highly desirable as it prevents the damage mercury can do to the aluminium heat exchanger. Using the Joule–Thomson effect, a refrigerant gas at −161°C is used to separate the propane, butane and remaining condensate content from the LNG. At this temperature, all the components are liquid and the separation is possible by using a fractionation column. The separated propane, ethane and methane are then usually compressed, cooled and condensed to be used as refrigerant gas. As it was heated up during the distillation, the LNG is pre-cooled by propane refrigeration. Finally, the LNG is cooled again and liquefied in the Main Cryogenic Heat Exchanger. Once the LNG is cooled, it is transferred to the LNG carrier to be sent all over the world.

In financial modelling, there will be a mismatch in capacity between the mtpa produced by the field and the mtpa produced by the LNG plant. This is due to the "shrinkage" in volumes because the LNG plant burns gas to fuel the plant operation. LNG plant shrinkage is often 10–15%, which could easily explain the difference.

There is a need to account for shrinkage in the financial model since the revenue is only from LNG sold, not produced gas at the wellhead.

4.7.2 *Natural gas and oil pricing*

Historically, natural gas was not priced globally because it could not be easily transported, although the growing LNG business is changing this. A DCF model based on the historical gas price will generate a large positive NPV and attempts have been made to consider the relationship between oil price and gas price to determine more realistic choice of gas price. In order to incorporate oil price volatility the Brownian motion model can be used to predict the future evolution of oil, LNG and LPG prices.

Platts Japan Korea Marker (JKM™) is the LNG benchmark price assessment for spot physical cargoes delivered ex-ship into Japan and South Korea. As these two countries take the largest share of LNG imports in the world, Platts JKM™ is thus a key reference in marking product value/market price from supply source to the destination market.

Pricing of LNG in 20-year long-term contracts has always been linked to an energy index or group of indices, based on the geographic location of the LNG buyer. As the index price changes, LNG price changes correspondingly. US LNG liquefaction projects are offering Henry Hub-linked LNG pricing which is a relatively new pricing index for buyers. The LNG price of contracts then follows an "S-curve evolution" according to the following formula:

$$P = C + \beta X + S,$$

where:

- P is the LNG price (\$/MMBtu)
- C is the base price (\$/MMBtu)
- β is the price slope
- X is the oil price index (JCC in Japan)
- S is the shipment charges.

Butane is derived from a manufacturing process using natural gas as the feed and in liquid form is transported and traded globally when produced to an international specification. The hub of trade is Mt. Belvieu, Texas, just outside Houston. This location serves as the swing for the global market, taking surplus into inventory (salt caverns) and exporting when needed to fill a deficit.

The petrochemical cracker operators are able to swing their feed from propane to "naphtha" (light oilC_{5+} molecules, see Section 6.1) very quickly, and therefore they are extremely price sensitive. Hence, there is a well-known relationship between the Mt. Belvieu reference price for propane and the price of light, sweet crude oil on the New York Mercantile Exchange (NYMEX), the commodity futures exchange and West Texas Intermediate (WTI) that naphtha is referenced to. Cushing, Oklahoma is a major trading hub for crude oil and is the price settlement point for WTI which is also known as Texas light sweet and is used as a benchmark for oil pricing alongside the price of Brent crude from the North Sea.

Although there are short-term deviations from the relationship of Mt. Belvieu reference price at WTI that can last for weeks or even a month or two, over the long term the volume/heat content relationship has remained consistent.

4.8 Real Option Valuation

During periods of low commodity prices, more projects will be marginal but there may be the intuitive view that a project has intrinsic value. This can be determined quantitatively through the application of the technique of Real Option Valuation (ROV). This is based on the Black–Scholes (BS) equation in which any deferred value for a marginal project can be estimated. The volatility variable used in the BS equation is derived from the distribution of the Present Value of Free Cash Flows during the operational period based on a MC simulation of the relevant commodity price volatility. The time to expiry of the option would be linked to practical considerations such as the duration of an exploration licence. This in turn must be linked to the integrity of the award of licences and the principles of security of tenure once exploration results in a discovery and evaluation is completed. Conversion to a mining licence must be subject to compliance with environmental permitting.

This is the appropriate framework for the treatment of commodity prices and is discussed in more detail in Section 11.3 and in the first Extended Case Study given in Appendix A.

If the application of ROV generates a value in the future which is significantly greater than the current value, then it will be worth while retaining the asset. At the time of the expiry or at any stage up to its expiry (so this is an analogue of an American option not a European option which can only be exercised at the expiry date), you have retained the right but not the obligation to continue with the program of evaluation or development. If the price of the commodity (gold, copper, oil, uranium, coal, etc.) has increased then you proceed with further evaluation drilling or to a Full Technical Feasibility Study (FTFS), see Section 8.5. If not, you let the licence lapse and abandon the project.

All of the above follows on from the NPV optimisation process that is undertaken at the Preliminary Feasibility Study (PFS) stage discussed in Section 8.3 and takes into account time-value of money, cut-off grades and cost–capacity relationships. This approach allows the promoter to identify the sweet spot for the project but the NPV expressed as a deterministic outcome must then be considered from a probabilistic perspective. This then loops back to the role of MC simulation outlined above on the selected base case.

4.9 Metals Streaming

The metals streaming business was created in 2004. In this model, a metals streaming company such as Wheaton or Sandstorm Gold makes an upfront payment to a mining company. In return, the metals streaming company obtains the right to buy a fixed quantity of metal. Usually, this is a by-product precious metal (gold or silver) which is often present in base metal deposits and generally represents a relatively small proportion of the overall revenue. The upfront fee will be at a discount to the prevailing spot price to offset the significant risk to the metals streaming company that the metal price will have fallen when the metal is delivered to them by the mining company. This is not the same as a hedge which is designed to remove any risk of price volatility that arises from a physical transaction and requires physical delivery of the metal. The metals streaming company will also be fully exposed to the technical and financial risks that are inherent in an active mining operation. For the year ended December 31, 2022, Wheaton generated revenue of \$6,298 million (43% gold, 54% silver, and 2% palladium) for an upfront payment of \$7,772 million.

Metal streaming would be an attractive option where a company has not made sufficient provision for contingency in Capex estimates after construction has started, but the project is not yet in production. Market conditions might mean that they cannot raise more money through a rights issue from existing shareholders and the banks will not lend further. In those circumstances, a fund could negotiate an even greater discount on the current spot price of the metal compared to a project that is adequately funded.

The metals streaming option may become important for marginal projects in production where low metal prices and high operating costs are creating cash flow problems. It is a quick source of cash but it is obviously capping up-side if metal prices increase. This links into a related narrative which is ceding a proportion of your precious metals under a hedging programme imposed by banks to ensure that future operating costs, debt and interest payments are met.

Where a project is still in development and has entered into a streaming agreement ahead of production and is unable to extract ore then the original shareholders would lose everything. The metals streaming companies are not operators, so they are unable to recover their investment by taking delivery of metal and they are taking on risk.

It follows from the above that while the mine agreeing to provide precious metal to a streaming company will need to accept the discount to the prevailing spot price this is a rational business decision as operational risk is passed on to the metals streaming company. Those companies involved in metals streaming, such as Wheaton, have the expertise to assess such technical risk so it is a niche business that applies only to natural resource operations.

A theoretical study on an analogue pure precious metal project partly financed through metals streaming and royalty financing of by-product metals was undertaken in 2013 as part of a dissertation submitted in partial fulfillment of the requirements of the MSc in Metals and Energy Finance at Imperial College. This involved an analysis of the project's NPVs under different financing scenarios including metals streaming based on the standard terms imposed by the investors on a mining company. These can significantly reduce the project's NPV relative to conventional debt and equity finance. Furthermore, with metals streaming the project will not benefit from increased metal prices as up-side is capped. On the other hand, metals streaming and royalty finance represent attractive solutions when allowing the shareholders of a mining company to avoid massive dilution or avoid dramatic construction delays. A comparison with conventional sources of funding based on debt and equity is given in Table 4.1.

The scale of recent transactions has been noted by analysts who have expressed concern that mining companies are exchanging cash for future value but it is clearly now a mainstream activity in the international mining industry. The mining companies are, however,

Table 4.1. Comparison between different sources of funding for the development of a mining project.

	Debt	Equity	Metals streaming	Royalty financing
Mechanism	The common type in mining is project finance where the principal and interest are repaid from the cash flows once the operation is in production.	Investors secure a shareholding in the company through an initial public offering or subsequent rights issues.	Investor purchases, in exchange for an upfront payment, the by-product production (usually silver or gold) of a mine that it does not own or operate. The cost of future production of the metal is included in the agreement.	Investor makes an upfront financing payment and in exchange gets returns through fixed royalty payments, commonly taken as a percentage of revenues.
Source	Investment banks.	Equity funds and major mining companies.	Royalty and streaming companies.	
Maturity	Linked to mine life.	Not applicable.	Normally bound to the life of the mine but can be flexible.	Normally bound to the life of the mine but can be inflexible.
Constraints	That proportion of metal that generates the revenue needed to cover repayments to bank and operating costs needs to be hedged.	Shares offered in exchange for the initial investment. Recovery of investment	Requires physical delivery of the metal.	Usually cash settled through payments based on revenue.

	Hedging designed to remove any risk of price volatility that arises from a physical transaction and requires physical delivery of the metal.	dependent on the liquidity of shares.		
Advantages	Non-dilutive for equity stakeholders. Tax relief on interest lowers the cost of debt and gearing can be used to optimise the weighted average cost of capital thereby enhancing net present value.	Full exposure to the upside if metal prices increase and for this reason banks will not hedge more than 40% of the metal produced.	Provides early stage capital and is non-dilutive for equity stakeholders. Able to take completion and commodity price risks. Metals streaming and royalty financing will be expensive for the reasons outlined below.	
Disadvantages	The bank will take a conservative view and will want to undertake an independent view on the technical feasibility study which will delay implementation and then maintain tight control on development.	Dilution of founders' stake holding and possible loss of control.	Dedication of the production for the life of the mine. No benefit from any increase in the price of the by-product metal.	Burdens future revenue and detracts from the full benefit of increases in metal prices.

using this cash to expand and develop their operations so there is clearly mutual benefit. Streaming companies can sell their contracts, which could be seen as a type of call option on rising precious metal prices. They can also enter into agreements with producers, allowing them to take only a minor proportion of overall future production, where the precious metal is the major source of revenue. This provides an immediate source of cash without detracting from the chance of raising further equity.

Mineral and Petroleum Geosciences

Chapter 5

Mineral Deposits

5.1 Introduction

The terminology that has developed around mineral deposits is a blend of historical use and more recent attempts to clarify nomenclature used in reporting mineral resources and ore reserves. The traditional connotation of an ore mineral was a museum-quality sulfide or oxide that was often geologically exotic in order to have been collected in the first place. Such specimens are seldom encountered in an active mining operation. The term "mineralisation", when used to describe a mineral deposit, has the connotation of a concentration of minerals able to support a commercially viable operation, but this use also needs to be treated with caution. The term grade is used to report concentration of the metal or mineral and it is the discovery of mineralisation that combines high grade in association with a large mass of host rock that is the ultimate aim of an exploration programme. At that point, a mineral deposit has been identified.

It is important to relate any description of a mineral deposit to the associated mineral or metal type and this provides the basis for classification systems. Type deposits are described in great detail and analogues which have been assigned are identified. Inevitably overlap occurs, some deposits do appear to be unusual and in a class of their own and all deposits will have their own unique geochemical signature and geological setting.

The field of mineral deposit studies is in turn inextricably tied to the discipline of earth science and the study of rocks. These comprise the three well known groups. Igneous rocks fall into two broad compositional types: the high-magnesium and high-iron varieties (ultramafic and mafic rocks respectively) and high-silica and high-alumina varieties (salic rocks). These in turn will be classified according to their mode of emplacement — intrusive or extrusive. Sedimentary rocks are essentially the accumulation of eroded and re-deposited detritus of pre-existing rocks, of chemical precipitation or life processes. Metamorphic rocks are formed when igneous or sedimentary rocks have been subject to high pressure and temperature. These processes in turn are driven by the dynamic mechanism of plate tectonics. Mineral deposits can be located in any three of the rock groups while petroleum is restricted to sedimentary host rocks.

The geochemically abundant elements in the crust comprise Silicon (27.2%), Oxygen (45.2%), Aluminum (8.0%), Iron (5.8%), Calcium (5.1%), Magnesium (2.8%), Sodium (2.3%), Potassium (1.7%) and Titanium (0.9%). The remaining elements comprise just 1% of the crust. These are the geochemically scarce elements. Unlike the petroleum sector, which is able to focus on hydrocarbons, the geochemically scarce elements include the metals that have practical industrial uses, which represents a significant portion of the periodic table. There is, therefore, a significant divide between geological models needed to understand the formation of mineral deposits and the minerals engineering needed to exploit them and the petroleum geological and engineering skills needed to extract hydrocarbons. All are natural resources so the approach to investment funding is very similar.

Coal is a carbonaceous material confined to sedimentary rocks and is covered in Chapter 6.

Each mineral deposit type will have its own unique geological characteristics and earth scientists and exploration geologists will usually specialise in a particular sub-set of a mineral deposit type. It is often prudent to bring in the relevant authority to provide an independent perspective on a deposit after discovery and before embarking on a detailed programme of evaluation and development of a project. It is all too easy to over-simplify the inherently complex physical and chemical processes involved in the formation of a mineral deposit. No matter how proficient the conventional engineering, or innovative the financial engineering, an operator cannot create a single additional ounce of precious metal or kilogram of base metal that nature did not provide. This is why a basic understanding of mineral deposits is needed for anyone involved in the natural resource sector.

5.2 Lithogeochemistry

Chalcophile elements, according to the Goldschmidt classification, will partition strongly with the Sulphur (S) and Arsenic (As) anions and many of the transition elements that have important industrial uses fall into this category. These include Nickel (Ni), Copper (Cu), Zinc (Zn) and Lead (Pb). The Platinum Group Elements (PGEs) act both as siderphile and chalcophile metals and comprise Platinum (Pt), Palladium (Pd), Rhodium (Rh), Iridium (Ir), Ruthenium (Ru) and Osmium (Os). Pt will combine with S and As but is also found as ferroplatinum in alluvial deposits. Gold of course is often present as native metal.

There is no shortage of the geochemically abundant industrial metals of Fe and Al or indeed the industrial minerals such as halite or limestone. To have the combination of high grade ore quality, metals or minerals respectively need to be associated with high tonnages. While this is geologically rare, they will always be low value commodities which means that production will need to be associated with large capacity and the availability of infrastructure. For the geochemically scarce elements, when associated with a sulphide, oxide or present as an alloy or native metal, liberation must be achieved from the host rock matrix (also known as gangue). This permits separation into a concentrate and immediately raises the value of the product by weight (see Chapter 9).

A sulphide not only acts as a powerful collector of metals, but once liberated from the matrix of gangue rock the technique of froth flotation ensures a highly efficient mechanism for its collection and concentration (see Section 9.6.2). Release of the metals from the primary mineral association also takes place as an exothermic reaction in the subsequent downstream pyrometallurgical process. Where metals partition into a silicate phase, release from the mineral phase involves an endothermic reaction. This effectively represents an energy barrier that must be considered in any evaluation of a project.

The simple expression of the relationship between grade and metal price is illustrated in Fig. 5.1.

Outlined below are descriptions of some of the major mineral deposit types. There are notable omissions such as the iron oxide-Cu-Au(-U-REE) deposits "IOCG" types as well as the palaeoplacer deposits of the Witwatersrand in South Africa. A more comprehensive treatment of mineral deposits is given in the book *Introduction to Ore-Forming Processes* by Laurence Robb.

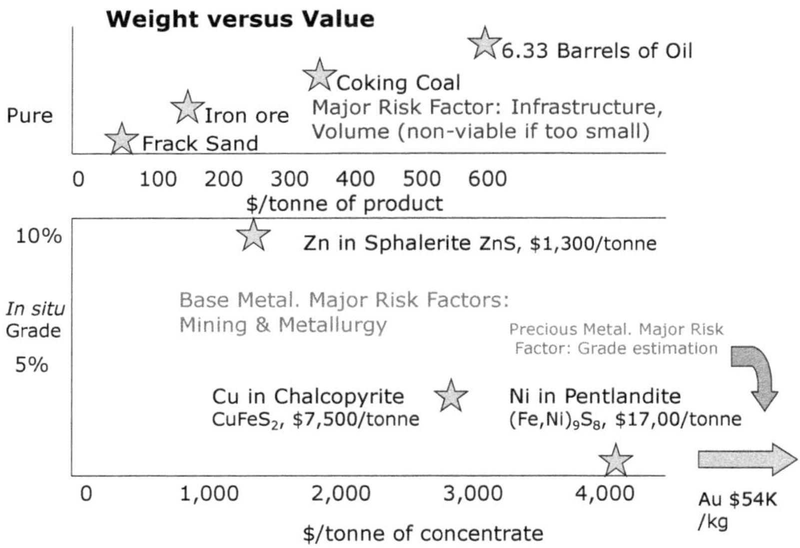

Figure 5.1. Relationship between value and tonnage. Top — geochemically abundant material. Bottom — geochemically scarce elements.

5.3 Diversity of Mineral Deposits

5.3.1 *Rare earth elements*

A good example of the complexity that arises in assessing the economic potential of a mineral deposit hosting geochemically scarce elements is that of the Rare Earth Elements (REEs). The most commercially important are the elements Neodymium (Nd) and Dysprosium (Dy) which in turn are just two of the 14 REEs within the periodic table. Nd is used in the manufacture of powerful magnets. Dy is present in control rods in nuclear reactors where it acts as a neutron absorber in nuclear fission reactions. It is also used in the manufacture of compact discs. Neither Nd nor Dy occur in nature as free elements but are found in the radioactive mineral monazite. This has the formula (Ce, La, Nd, Th)PO_4 containing up to 14% Nd. Dy is not a major constituent of monazite although it may be present in concentrations of up to 0.7% together with the other REEs.

Differential separation of the REEs from monazite into the pure form of each element requires sophisticated chemical processes.

Monazite is present as a mineral in a wide range of primary igneous rocks but given its relatively high hardness (5 on the Mohs scale) and density (5.15 g/cm^3) it will, when liberated by natural processes of weathering and erosion, concentrate in fluvial river, marine coastal and dune systems. As a consequence, it is commonly associated with placer-type heavy mineral deposits which are accumulations of alluvium (gravels, sands and dunes). These in turn provide the feed for heavy mineral alluvial mining operations which produce, as a primary product, the titanium-bearing minerals ilmenite and rutile and the zirconium mineral zircon.

In some placer-type heavy mineral deposits where monazite is present it may be produced as a by-product in the mineral separation process. To exploit a monazite resource, this has to be associated with ilmenite, rutile and zirconium in concentrations and volumes sufficient to justify the investment in a heavy mineral alluvial mining operation. The economics of such an operation normally require a rate of production of about 10 million tonnes of feed per annum and an investment in mining equipment (earth moving and dredging) and processing equipment (gravity and electrostatic) of at least $50 million. The nature of the mining itself involves a major impact on the environment, creating significant obstacles in securing permits. The main areas of the world where monazite is produced are in the US, Brazil, India, Sri Lanka and Australia.

Challenge lies in linking REEs with prices as the separate metals are not traded on an exchange and in understanding both the technical factors and the pricing mechanisms of the products. This is dealt with by linking the pricing mechanism of the REE oxide with the precursor concentrate. The favoured approach is to establish a project specific "basket" price (expressed in US$/kg) which is defined as the value ($) of one unit mass (1 kg) of separated rare earth oxides (SREOs), in which those SREOs are in the same proportion/distribution as the deposit (see Table 5.1). In other words, the total rare earth oxide value applied within a financial modelling is the sum of the REO mineral distribution (%) within the concentrate product multiplied by the associated FOB China REO price.

Table 5.1. REE basket price. Industry practice is for price decks to attribute zero $ values for the lowermost five HREEs (Ho, Er, Tm, Yb and Lu).

Element	EEO concentration split (%)	July 2016 China FOB price (US$/kg)
Lanthanum	12.00	3.75
Cerium	37.80	1.49
Praseodymium	8.00	48.00
Neodymium	26.60	38.90
Samarium	4.00	1.93
Europium	0.90	63.00
Gadolinium	2.20	456.70
Terbium	0.30	410.00
Dysprosium	1.20	185.00
Yttrium	5.80	3.65
Basket price		29.56

5.3.2 *Lithium*

Lithium is a soft metal belonging to the alkali metal group of the periodic table. It is the lightest metal and the least dense solid element. The metal is of particular importance as an anode material, making it a valuable component of high-energy-density rechargeable lithium-ion batteries. These batteries are currently effective and affordable and have few substitutes. Lithium is extracted from both hard rock and brine deposits. The mining and mineral processing of a primary hard-rock deposit of lithium minerals is the precursor to the hydrometallurgical treatment of a mineral concentrate, which produces lithium hydroxide or lithium carbonate. From September 2023, the London Metal Exchange started trading lithium hydroxide. There is, however, a step change in the refining of what is essentially still a raw product to the level of purity required by battery manufacturers. Within this process, there is a range of different grades depending on end use, from disposable e-cigarettes to electrical vehicles requiring a long life. This market is opaque, and end-users will have off-take agreements with refiners that will be commercially confidential.

The recent growth of the lithium demand is mainly due to increase in battery component demand. Lithium has a wide range of other applications, however, and its historical use is not related to batteries but to the ceramics and glass industry.

Hard-rock sources of lithium include the following minerals:

- Spodumene, $LiAl(SiO_3)_2$, contains 3.7% of Li or 8.02% of LiO_2 and traded as a concentrate at \$500/tonne
- Petalite, LiAlSi4O10, contains 4.5% of lithium
- Lepidolite, $K(Li, Al)_3(Al, Si, Rb)_4O_{10}(F, OH)_2$, contains 2.55% of Li or 5.49% of Li_2O.

Lacustrine brines such as Minera Salar Blanco Maricunga in Chile have Li concentrations of 1,163 ppm.

Lithium content is generally reported in terms of lithium oxide (Li_2O), or lithium metal. Lithium Carbonate (Li_2CO_3) and Lithium Hydroxide (LiOH) are the two major forms of lithium products.

5.3.3 *Coltan*

"Coltan" consists of an intergrowth of minerals within the columbite-tantalite group $(Fe, Mn)(Nb, Ta)_2O_6$ for which a nearly complete solid-solution series exists. The super charge-ion batteries rely on proprietary titanium niobium oxide (TNO) ceramic nanoporous anodes to provide transformative performance compared to existing lithium-ion batteries, which rely on graphite-based anodes. The new batteries are expected to provide over double the lithium storage capacity by volume, translating into a threefold improvement to electric vehicle range, up to 320 km, from a 6-minute charge.

5.4 Volcanic-hosted (Volcanogenic Massive Sulphide) Deposits

The idea of massive sulphide formation by volcanic exhalative processes was proposed in the late 1950s for the sulphide ores associated with sedimentary lithologies of the Scandinavian Caledonides. Since then stratabound massive sulphides have been described throughout the world, ranging from the Archaean deposits of Canada to the currently active hydrothermal exhalations observed on the ocean floor ridge-rift systems (see Section 5.9). The term "Volcanogenic Massive Sulphide" (VMS) is used to describe a whole range of deposits which, although they share some common features, may be highly variable in their age, mineralogy and associations. They are normally polymetallic and are associated with Cu, Zn, Pb, Au and Ag. They typically comprise one or more lenses of massive pyrite and chalcopyrite hosted by mafic volcanics and underlain by a well-developed pipe-shaped stockwork zone.

The Iberian Pyrite Belt has been regarded as the type area for VMS mineralisation. This description is based on Carol Halsall's PhD dissertation (1989) that considered the lithogeochemistry of the Rio Tinto area. Although many of the mines have ceased production over the years, the discovery of the Las Cruces deposit (Fig. 5.2) below

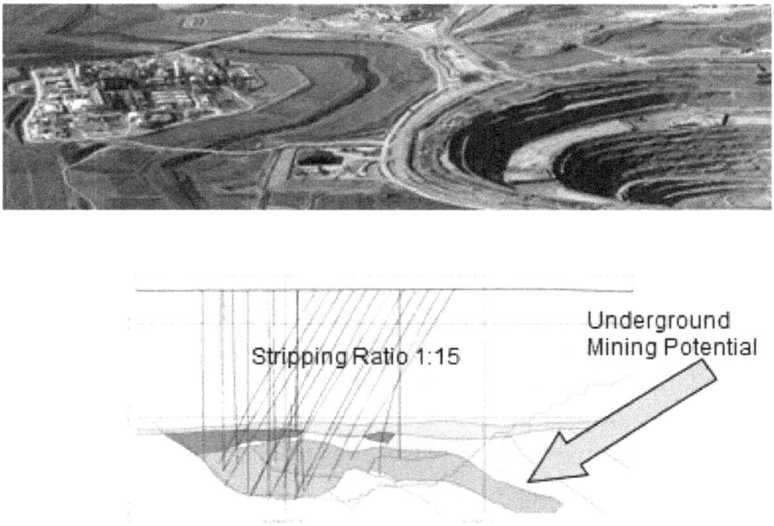

Figure 5.2. Las Cruces VMS deposit comprising 69,000 tonnes Cu (2013 production, operated by First Quantum Minerals). Reserves: 14.1Mt @5.4% Cu.

younger cover outside Seville has demonstrated that fresh discoveries remain to be made. Hydrothermal alteration of the footwall rocks is a characteristic feature of VMS deposits and a good understanding of the genetic process involved provides the foundation to successful exploration.

Conventional models for the genesis of VMS deposits by volcanic exhalation involve interaction between the host rock and large quantities of heated seawater, resulting in the leaching of metals from the footwall rocks and their subsequent deposition as sulphides on the sea floor. Although much of the metal transport and deposition in these systems undoubtedly takes place as a result of the convective leaching process, there is some controversy over the role of intrusive magmatism in the generation of large massive sulphide deposits such as the Kuroko deposits of Japan.

5.5 Mafic and Ultramafic Magmatic Sulphide-hosted (Metal Group: Ni and Cu; Platinum Group Elements (PGEs) — Pt, Pd, Rh, Ir, Ru, Os) Deposits

5.5.1 *Introduction*

Primary nickel sulphide deposits are hosted in ultramaficigneous rocks in Archaean greenstone terrains. Nickel grades are typically 1–5% and tonnages are moderate to high. Copper may be present as an economic by-product. Examples would be Mt Keith in Western Australia and Voisey Bay in Canada.

Orthomagmatic sulphide deposits formed in large, stratiform, layered igneous complexes in Proterozoic cratonic settings. Their origin is intimately associated with the high temperature processes of magma formation and crystallisation. Differences in the stage of geochemical evolution of the source magma results in the economic

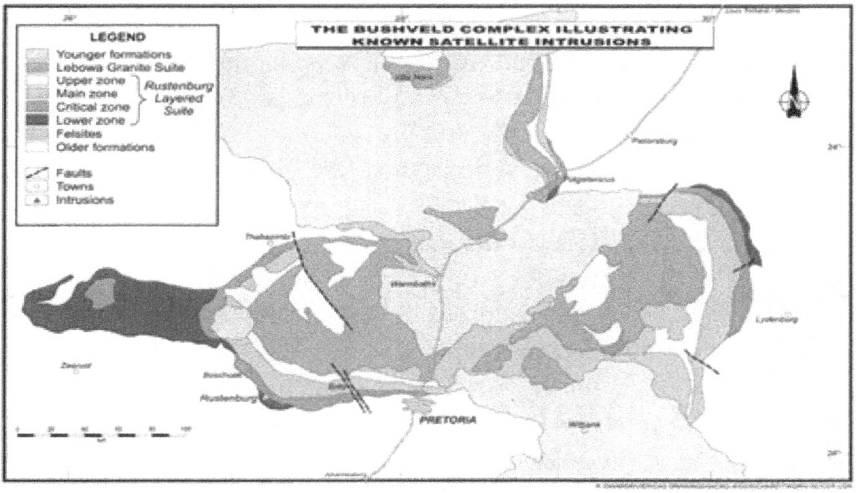

Figure 5.3. Geological map of the Bushveld Complex in South Africa taken from presentation by ARM Platinum. The complex comprises five major subdivisions ("Zones") with a thickness of up to 7 km. Hosts 13 major chromite layers in the Critical Zone, major economic concentrations of PGEs in the Merensky Reef, UG-2 Reef and Platreef. The Nkomati satellite deposit is indicated by the triangle.

concentration of nickel and copper within certain layers, in addition to accessory platinum group elements. The Bushveld Igneous Complex of South Africa is a prime example, hosting the Merensky and UG-2 reefs. These were formed in closed chemical systems unlike the other major horizon, the Platreef (Fig. 5.3).

5.5.2 *Fractionation*

When a large body of mafic magma is emplaced in the Earth's crust, slow cooling takes place. Silicate, oxide and sulphide phases crystallise and sink through the magma chamber to form texturally distinctive layers. The removal of the more refractory minerals in this way depletes or enriches the residual melt in various elements through a process of fractional crystallisation. Enhanced levels of the elements nickel, chromium and vanadium are normally associated with the mafic rocks and enrichment during fractional crystallisation can be sufficient to form mineralised horizons at predictable levels within the intrusion.

Changes in melt composition during fractional crystallisation are illustrated in Fig. 5.4. As can be seen, the Fe (Fe + Mg) ratio of the residual melt increases with fractionation. This is in response to crystallisation of magnesium-rich silicate phases such as olivine (Mg_2SiO_4) and pyroxene ($MgSiO_3$), which deplete the magma in magnesia.

Oxides are represented by ilmenite (FeO · TiO2) and the spinels.

The latter represent a solid-solution series comprising the following end-members: spinel ($MgO \cdot Al_2O_3$) — magnetite ($FeO \cdot Fe_2O_3$) — Magnesio-chromite ($MgO \cdot Cr_2O_3$) — chromite ($FeO \cdot Cr_2O_3$). See Section 5.9.1 for further detail.

Chromium levels in the melt decline in response to the early crystallisation of chromite. The proportion of chromium in the chromite declines with fractionation, while Fe ratios in the chromite are used as a broad index of fractionation. These are normally calculated from the mineral analyses given in weight per cent FeO, Fe_2O_3 and Cr_2O_3 by establishing the weight per cent metal from the molecular weight of the oxide. Cr/Fe ratios can also be calculated from stoichiometric atomic proportions. These apparently arcane concepts are central to

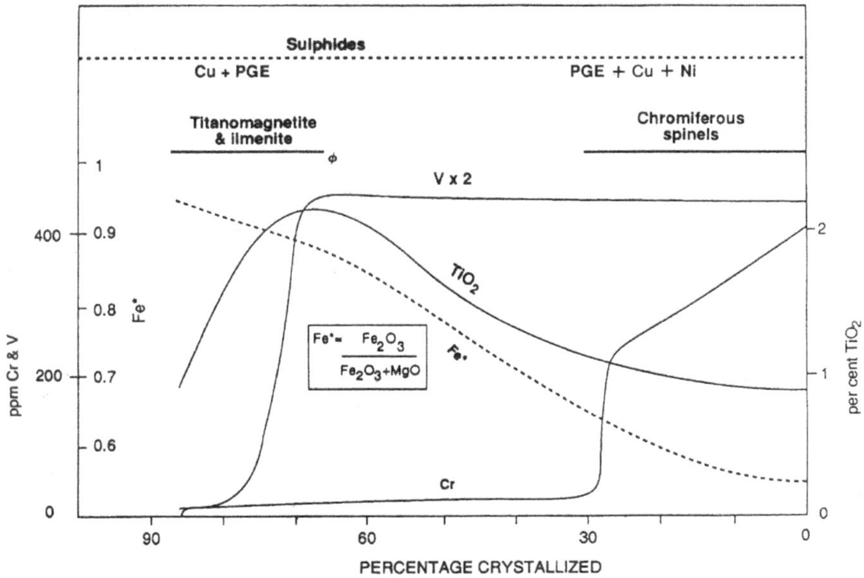

Figure 5.4. Model of fractional crystallisation for Karoo dolerites. Fe_2O_3 represents combined ferrous and ferric values.

any evaluation of a chromitite (a rock made up entirely of the mineral chromite) which is exploited for the production of ferrochromium. As the smelter is paid only on chromium units, the high-quality iron units are essentially being given away free to the stainless-steel producers.

Outokumpu is a major stainless-steel producer, and 70% of the ferrochromium produced at Kemi goes to the parent company, allowing it to reap the benefits from this pricing mechanism. Key chemical variables are that the Cr_2O_3 content of Kemi chromite (the mineral) is 48%. The chromium (Cr^o) content of the ferrochromium produced is 53%. The processing plant produces 1.2 Mtpa of chromite concentrate, which results in 530,000 tpa of ferrochromium. This figure is consistent with the mass balance, whereby 2.26 tonnes of chromite concentrate is needed to produce one tonne of ferrochromium. The benchmark price of ferrochromium is \$1.50/lb, equivalent to \$3.30/kg per chromium unit, or \$3.30*0.48 = \$1.58/kg, or 1,580/tonne. Of the

530,000 tpa of ferrochromium produced, 170,000 tonnes is sold externally to generate a revenue of \$269 million.

Vanadium and titanium levels in the melt display a sharp drop in the later stages of the crystallisation history. Titanium depletion is due to the crystallisation of ilmenite. Vanadium partitions strongly into coexisting magnetite where V^{3+} substitutes for Fe^{3+} because of its similar charge and ionic radius.

5.5.3 *Sulphur solubility*

Studies undertaken on fresh submarine basalts, in which degassing has been inhibited by pressure of sea water, indicate that they contain significantly more sulphur than subaerially erupted basalts. The sulphur in the submarine basalt occurs as a dissolved constituent in the basaltic glass and as small immiscible sulphide droplets. These features can be reproduced in the laboratory; Fig. 5.5 illustrates synthetically produced sulphide droplets consisting of an iron sulphide-oxide phase coexisting in equilibrium with a silicate melt containing 0.15% sulphur.

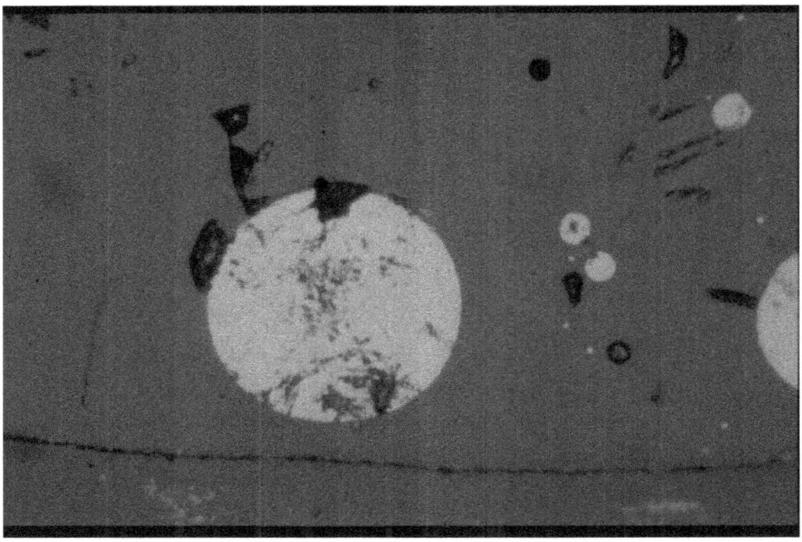

Figure 5.5. Reflected light micrograph of an experimental charge showing immiscible sulphide droplets in a silicate glass. Horizontal field of view = 40 microns. This sulphide–silicate immiscibility is equivalent to the metallurgical matte–slag system.

Once formed, sulphide droplets in mafic and ultramafic magmas will act as collectors for copper, nickel, cobalt and PGEs. The subsequent concentration of the metal droplets, normally through gravity settling, could lead to the formation of ore bodies. The tenor of the ore body will, however, be a function of the partitioning characteristics of the metals between silicate and sulphide melts, as well as the relative proportions of the melts. Early formed sulphide melts will be rich in nickel and on cooling will crystallise pyrrhotite ($Fe_{(1-x)}S$) and pentlandite $(Fe, Ni)_9S_8$.

Sulphides in most intrusive mafic rocks are evenly distributed as a finely disseminated phase. This suggests that the sulphide phase nucleated only at a late stage in the crystallisation history of the magma, allowing insufficient time for settling. The coexisting residual melt will also have been depleted in many of the economically important metals because of their preferential partitioning into earlier crystallising silicate and oxide phases. In the absence of a sulphide phase, nickel will partition into olivine while the silicate melt will become enriched in copper and PGEs. The ratio of Cu/Ni increases, therefore, with fractionation. Subsequent precipitation of a sulphide phase will result in the crystallisation of pyrrhotite, pyrite and chalcopyrite ($CuFeS_2$).

For a mafic magmatic sulphide ore deposit to develop, it is clearly important that the sulphide phase should form very early in the crystallisation history. This would probably require an open system in which external factors can influence the timing of sulphide immiscibility. The characteristics of these factors (based on studying magmatic ore deposits in natural rocks) is limited by the difficulty of obtaining reliable data for their intensive parameters such as temperature and density at the time of formation. By examining experimental systems at magmatic temperatures under controlled conditions it is, however, possible to model conditions required to initiate the precipitation of an immiscible sulphide phase. The results of theoretical and experimental work on sulphur solubility systems undertaken as part of a PhD and postdoctoral year at Imperial College are given in Buchanan (1988).

The results of the experimental modelling of silicate–sulphide systems at constant temperature demonstrate that the sulphur-carrying capacity of a silicate melt can be increased by adding iron or a reductant. Clearly a magma contaminated with banded ironstone and organic matter would have a high sulphur-carrying capacity. The possibilities of an immiscible sulphide forming in these circumstances is further enhanced where additional sulphur is introduced into a mafic magma such as the Bushveld-type.

Although the Platreef represents the product of primary crystallisation from an original Bushveld magma, contamination from floor rocks played a significant role in its petrogenesis. The horizon therefore provides a superb natural laboratory for testing and applying the results of the experimental work. The author mapped a 25 km stretch of the Platreef outcrop in the early 1980s, which provided the basis for developing the system of zoning for the Platreef that is still used. The author was then involved with the first geostatistical resource estimations of those parts of the Platreef where Anglo America Platinum established their Mogalakwena mine, currently the world's largest open pit PGE mining operation.

High background levels of PGEs of between one and three grams per tonne are present along most of the 25 kms strike length of the Platreef, but the effect of contamination often obscures the primary trend of mineralisation. Although there are sectors along the Platreef where background levels of PGEs rise to significant concentrations with grades of up to 56 grams/tonne recorded in the Zwartfontein South area, the key to delineating areas of mineralisation that can be successfully mined lies in distinguishing between erratic value and that which displays some degree of geological continuity. The task is aided by the recognition of several petrographic facies along the strike length of the Platreef, each with its characteristic style of PGE mineralisation. These facies can in turn be correlated directly with changes in floor rock geology.

The Extended Case Study of the Platreef shown in Appendix C demonstrates the synergies that arise from esoteric scientific research when applied to mineral deposits. The principles were applied to other geological settings where similar conditions are present, notably the Nkomati mine, also in South Africa (see Fig. 5.3).

The style of mineralisation at Kevitsa in Finland, where an immiscible sulphide melt in a mafic magma acts as a collector for the metals, is similar to that of the Platreef, which of course also hosts PGE, Ni, and Cu mineralisation, albeit in different proportions. There is also clear evidence of an open system with contamination of the original magma by country rock, which may have acted as a trigger of the immiscible sulphide phase.

Nickel is associated with both silicates (olivine) and sulphides (pentlandite and millerite). Only the sulphides will be recovered by flotation, which might contain no more than two-thirds of the total nickel in the rock. The silicates olivine and pyroxene have undergone alteration to serpentine and amphibole, respectively. Serpentine contains talc, which interferes with froth flotation used in the recovery of sulphide, while amphibole reduces the efficiency of the grinding stage. Grade control must therefore take into account both the concentration of the metals and the variability of the silicate mineralogy.

The extractive metallurgy after the mineral processing stage is also fundamental to an understanding of the operation at Kevitsa, with smelting and refining directly impacting revenue assumptions. Boliden has a major commercial advantage due to its capability of handling concentrate, which was a key factor in the financial modelling of the Platreef scenario.

5.5.4 *Nickel laterites*

Olivine-rich magmatic rocks such as dunite and peridotite present in ultramafic volcanic rocks provide an important potential source of nickel. These are widespread in the Archaean of Western Australia. When immiscible sulphides form at liquidus temperatures, nickel will partition strongly into the melt forming high grade deposits such as those found in Kambalda. A sulphide not only acts as a powerful collector of metals, once liberated from the matrix of gangue rock the technique of froth flotation ensures a highly efficient mechanism for its collection and concentration. Release of the metals from the primary mineral association also takes place as an exothermic reaction in the subsequent downstream pyrometallurgical process.

For sulphides to form requires specific chemical conditions to be present but for most of these types of ultramafic volcanic rocks, nickel will partition into olivine as it crystallises, with concentrations of up to 0.6% in the mineral. This nickel is present in solid solution in the olivine and forms part of the crystalline lattice. Cobalt is often found in association with nickel laterites. Where metals partition into a silicate phase in this manner, release from the mineral phase involves an endothermic reaction. This effectively represents an energy barrier that must be considered in any evaluation of a project.

In geologically stable terrain such as Western Australia, the surface weathering process can extend down to depths of 100 metres resulting in the dunites and peridotites undergoing alteration to laterites comprising hydrated minerals such as goethite. As laterites are present in the surficial environment and are softer and less competent than their precursor primary rocks, they are amenable to open pit mining techniques where the ore can be broken using mechanical ripping rather than the more expensive drill and blasting methods.

The alteration also results in partial release of nickel from primary olivine with this natural process representing a precursor stage as indicated in the reactions given below. There is still an energy barrier that must be considered in any evaluation of a project. Primary olivine undergoes an oxidation and hydration reaction to form goethite as indicated below.

$$(Fe^{2+}, Ni^{2+})_2SiO_{4(\mathrm{Olivine})}$$

$$Fe^{2+} = Fe^{3+}$$

$$Fe^{3+} + 2H_2O = FeO(OH)_{(\mathrm{Goethite})} + 3H^+$$

$$FeO(OH) + Ni^{2+} + 2H_2O$$

$$= FeO(OH) \cdot (Ni)(OH)_{2(\mathrm{Nickeliferous\ Limonite})} + 2H^+.$$

Nickel recovery is then amenable to further hydrometallurgical processing of nickeliferous limonite where the slurry passes through a High Pressure Acid Leach (HPAL) circuit, Counter Current Decantation train and sulphide precipitation to produce a Mixed

Sulphide Product. This is then treated using the Sherritt–Gordon method to produce cobalt and nickel in its elemental form. A good example of this type of project is the Murrin Murrin operation in Western Australia where the challenges faced were during design and commissioning of the plant. Delays and significant operational problems led to the original capital cost estimate ballooning from US$1 billion to US$1.6 billion.

Alteration of peridotite and dunite can result in the formation of serpentinite and garnierite $(Ni, Mg)_3Si_2O_5(OH)_4$ which contain nickel but these lateritic associations are highly refractory and a conventional hydrometallurgical approach will not be appropriate. A key part of any evaluation of nickel laterite projects must take into account the complex mineralogy associated with these deposits.

5.6 Hydrothermal Precious Metals (Au and Ag) and Base Metals (Cu-Mo-Au)

5.6.1 *Epithermal gold*

It is generally accepted that the bulk of the world's primary gold deposits were formed through the action of hot aqueous (hydrothermal) fluids in the Earth's crust. Typical hydrothermal fluids responsible for base and precious metal deposits are Na-K-Ca-Cl-SO_4 brines, carbonated CO_2–H_2O fluids or mixtures of both. Ore metal concentrations are strongly dependent on the fluid composition, temperature and pressure, but are generally of the order of a few parts per million (ppm) to several hundred ppm for base metals and a few ppm to a few parts per billion for gold. Precipitation of the base and precious metals may take place in response to changes in the composition of the fluid either by mixing of two different fluids, by exsolution of a vapour phase (boiling) or by chemical interaction with the country rocks. Precipitation can also be caused by a drop in temperature or pressure.

Hydrothermal gold deposits were originally classified according to the likely source of fluid, the temperature and depth of emplacement; they include hypothermal, mesothermal and epithermal. Of these, epithermal has found a niche in the scientific literature and refers to deposits formed close to surface and usually of tertiary age and are the most important in terms of tonnage and contained gold. The type area is Carlin in Nevada.

5.6.2 *Porphyry copper*

Porphyry deposits are normally large tonnage (20 to more than 500 Mt) and low grade (0.4% to 0.8% contained copper). They are amenable to bulk mining techniques (e.g. open pit, block caving). These are usually disseminated deposits which are typically associated with tertiary or recent, high level, acid to intermediate, subvolcanic intrusions. An important metallogenic province is the Cordilleras of South and North America. The type deposit is Bingham Canyon in Utah. The magmas derived from the partial melting of a predominantly igneous source and of deep crustal or mantle origin. The host rocks comprise tonalites (quartz diorite) to granodiorite and tend to be metaluminous ($Al_2O_3 < Na_2O + K_2O$). They are relatively oxidised ($Fe_2O_3/FeO \geq 0.3$) and water-poor (2–3 wt.%).

Magma can reach shallow depths (2–5 km) before crystallisation and water saturation will occur. They tend to occur on the oceanic side of a subduction zone.

Porphyry deposits comprise both hypogene mineralisation consisting of a stockwork and disseminated mineralisation (formed beneath the surface at high temperatures $\sim$600–350°C). They can also be associated with secondary supergene and hypogene mineralisation enrichment due to acidified groundwater leaching which forms a surface blanket.

5.6.3 *Archaean greenstone gold deposits*

These deposits comprise structurally controlled vein, lode and replacement bodies associated with shear zones within Archaean greenstone terrains. These belts are composed of arcuate, greenschist-facies metamorphic volcanic or volcano-sedimentary units in association with large areas of granite. Notable examples are in Western Australia.

Individual deposits are small, of the order of a few million tonnes of ore. The grades are usually higher than those in other types of gold deposits. Gold is typically associated with iron sulphides. Intense localised hydroythermal alteration of the wallrocks adjacent to the mineralised lodes is typical.

In an operating mine, the forward planning process fully integrated into the extensive programme of exploration and evaluation drilling provides a superb example of how the mine life of projects associated with shear-hosted gold deposits (which are notoriously complex due to the pinch and swell nature of the mineralisation) can be extended. Spatial constraints have been addressed through dedicated underground drilling cubbies and directional drilling, permitting oriented deflections that are delineating new extensions to the mineralisation. This requires geological skills of the highest order.

5.7 Granitic-hosted Tin (Sn)–Tungsten (W) and Niobium (Nb)–Tantalum (Ta)

Host rocks to Sn and W mineralisation tend to be derived from the partial melting of a predominantly reduced sedimentary source with mid to deep crustal origin. These are often true granites, peraluminous ($Al_2O_3 > Na_2O + K_2O$) and reduced ($Fe_2O_3/FeO < 0.3$). They are water-rich (7–8 wt.%) and typically crystallise in the mid to lower crust ($\approx 12 - 40$ km depth). They tend to occur on the continental side of a subduction zone.

Pegmatites, coarse-grained zones within granites, also host the mineral "coltan" which consists of an intergrowth of minerals within the columbite-tantalite group $(Fe, Mn)(Nb, Ta)_2O_6$ for which a nearly complete solid-solution series exists. Tantalum (Ta) is widely used in mobile phones. A pure tantalite end-member could theoretically contain up to 86% Ta_2O_5. With specific gravities varying from 5.2 columbite to 8.0 for tantalite, the minerals are often present in alluvial deposits. Given that tantalite can reach a price of over \$200/tonne this encourages exploitation by artisanal miners in central Africa that is fuelling conflict.

5.8 Sedimentary-hosted (Sedex and Carbonate) Pb, Zn, Ba

Sedimentary-hosted Pb/Zn deposits are associated with Sedimentary Exhalative Pb-Zn (SEDEX) and carbonated-hosted deposits. The latter were first described in the scientific literature as Mississippi Valley-type but the style of mineralisation is also present in the Irish-type deposits. Mineralisation mainly occurred sub-seafloor by replacement of carbonates during diagenesis. The source of the mineralising fluids is considered to be evaporated seawater and the main depositional mechanism is considered to be the mixing of metalliferous ore fluid with low temperature bacteriogenic H_2 S-rich brines.

The term Stratiform Zn–Pb–Ba SEDEX deposits was originally introduced as a genetic term and refers to the ore-forming process that is found in local basins or depressions on the seafloor. Examples are: Sullivan and Howard's Pass (Canada); HYC or McArthur River and Mt Isa (Australia); Red Dog (Alaska, USA). They contain more than 50% of the world's reserves of Pb and Zn and more than 25% of global production. The dominant sulphides are galena, sphalerite, pyrite and barite, with lesser amounts of chalcopyrite. Silver can be present in minor amounts (mostly in arsenic and antimony sulphosalts or in galena). Ore minerals commonly occur in finely layered horizons, parallel to bedding, interbanded with clastic material and iron sulphides.

5.9 Geochemically Abundant Elements Cr, Fe

5.9.1 *Spinels in mafic magmatic rocks*

Ferrochromium and ferrovanadium production in South Africa is based on exploiting the chromite and magnetite deposits of the layered rocks of the Bushveld Complex. The compositional field of spinels defined by their atomic end-members is given in Fig. 5.6.

The use of Cr/Fe ratios to describe compositional characteristics of the spinels can be misleading as samples with the same chromium levels would have different molecular Cr/Fe ratios where

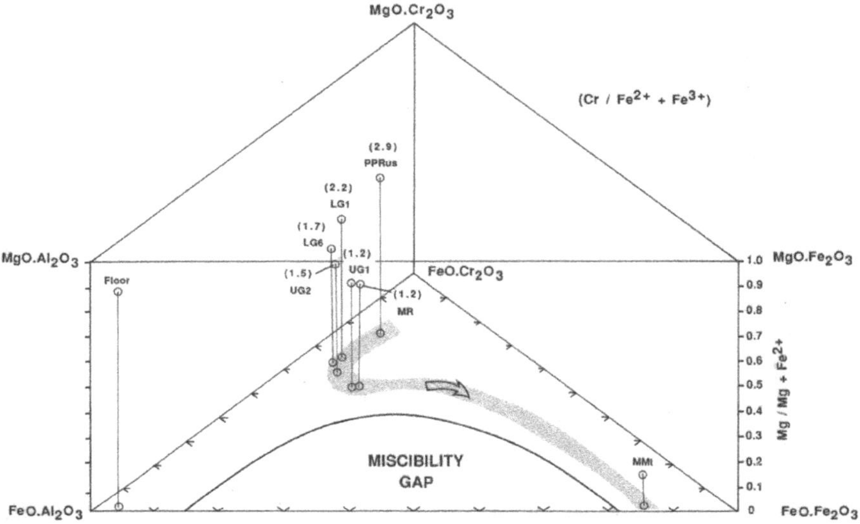

Figure 5.6. Compositional variations of spinel phases from the Bushveld Complex plotted within the spinel prism.

the proportion of MgO.FeO varied. Accurate comparison of the composition of different samples should also take into account atomic solid solution between the divalent (Fe^{2+} and Mg^{2+}) and trivalent (Fe^{3+}, Al^{3+} and Cr^{3+}) elements.

A solid solution can exist theoretically between chromite and magnetite, producing a continuous fractionation trend. The minerals spinel and magnetite will coexist as separate phases. A spinel phase is not, however, normally ubiquitous throughout a fractionated sequence of rocks. In the Bushveld, spinel is absent from the main zone rocks, which overlie the Merensky Reef. The reappearance of a spinel phase as magnetite is observed in the upper zone, 2,500 m higher in the sequence.

Numerous chromitite layers are present in the 1,500 m critical zone of the Bushveld Complex, which underlies the Meresnsky Reef. They are categorised, from the base upwards, into lower group (LG), middle group (MG) and upper group (UG). Chromite operations, which supply ore for the local ferrochromium industry, are concentrated in the LG layers, where the highest Cr/Fe ratios are found.

Normally only the most persistent and thickest layer in the group is mined. In the western and eastern parts of the complex, this is the LG-6, which is up to 2 m thick and has a Cr/Fe ratio of 1.6.

The Upper Group of chromitite layers is characterised by Cr/Fe ratios of 1.4 or less. The UG-2 would not be exploited for its chromitite alone, but it does yield chromite as a by-product of platinum mining, which is not normally utilised. The UG-1 occurs 20 m below the UG-2 and consists of a composite zone of alternating narrow chromitite and anorthosite layers (see Fig. 5.7). There have been many attempts to create a business case around the premise that as UG-2 is a by-product of platinum mining no cost can be assigned to extraction. The product needs pelletising and as ferrochromium producers are paid on chromium units the best that has been achieved is to blend UG-2 with LG-6.

Figure 5.7. View of the Dwarsrivier cutting in South Africa showing the UG-1 layers.

The LG-6 chromite produces charge ferrochromium with 54% chromium. The ferrochromium producers derive their revenue from chromium units in ferrochromium. As smelting costs remain the same, chromites with high Cr/Fe ratios command higher prices. Ideally, lumpy chromite ore should be used to produce ferrochromium as it creates a permeable charge.

Magnetite and ilmenite ($FeTiO_3$) are present as a discrete phase in nearly all the upper zone rocks of the Bushveld Complex, up to 21 individual layers occurring in the eastern limb. The thickest of these is the main magnetite layer, which is up to 2 m in width. Since vanadium partitions strongly into the first magnetite to crystallise and the magma becomes depleted in vanadium as crystallisation proceeds, the main magnetite at the base of the upper zone carries the highest vanadium values (up to 1.6% V_2O_5). These high levels, combined with its considerable thickness, represent a major resource of easily exploitable vanadium ore for the South African ferrovanadium industry.

The presence of Ti (see Fig. 5.8) means that magnetite associated with mafic magmatic layered deposits cannot be used as a primary source of iron ore.

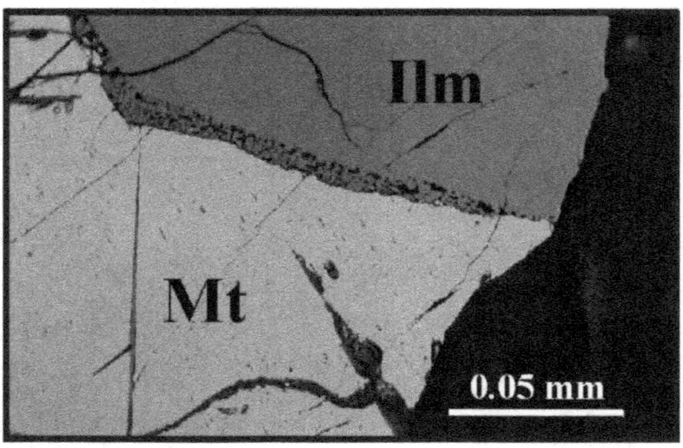

Figure 5.8. Reflected light micrograph from a Bushveld magnetite layer demonstrating the intergrowth of magnetite (Mt) and ilmenite (Ilm). The titanium mineral ulvospinel has exsolved from the magnetite which means that while magnetite can be separated from the ilmenite, titanium would remain associated with magnetite.

5.9.2 *Iron formations*

Iron ore is associated with both chemical sedimentary banded deposits where Fe^{2+} was transported in solution and chemically precipitated via oxidation to Fe^{3+} in haematite Fe_2O_3 or magnetite $FeO.Fe_2O_3$. Iron is also present in skarn deposits as well as carbonatite.

The Fe content of haematite is 69.94% and it has a density of 5. It is associated with Banded Iron Formations (BIFs) and accounts for most of world's production of Fe. These are very large deposits — in stratigraphic units hundreds of metres thick, hundreds to thousands of kilometres in lateral extent. They are characterised by fine layering, typically 0.5–3 cm thick alternating dark Fe-rich (most commonly haematite, more rarely magnetite) and light, silica-rich (chert) bands. Most BIFs were deposited in the Archaean and Palaeoproterozoic between 3500–1500Ma. Silica (SiO_2) precipitated from dissolved $Si(OH)_4$ in seawater and therefore there is a lack of associated aluminous and siliceous clastic particles. Where BIF undergoes secondary enrichment then ore grade iron deposits are formed via supergene and/or hydrothermal processes grading 62–65% Fe. This is known as "Direct Shipping Ore" because no processing is required but see Section 8.8.2 for discussion on grade optimisation.

5.10 Marine Minerals

The seabed is host to a range of minerals, including the diamondiferous gravels found off the west coast of South Africa and Namibia. "Marine minerals" in the context of this report relate to "polymetallic nodules" under the International Seabed Authority (ISA) nomenclature and are more commonly described in the scientific literature as "manganese nodules". These are not restricted to the Clarion/Clipperton Zone, where all the contracts are held. The recognition of "ferromanganese crust" associated with seamounts appears to represent a new class of deposit, but this appears geochemically to be very similar to conventional manganese nodules.

"Polymetallic sulphides" under the ISA nomenclature are more commonly recognised as "seabed massive sulphides". The most advanced of all the proposed marine mining projects was the Nautilus Minerals *Solwara 1* project, which lies in the territorial waters of Papua New Guinea (PNG) and aims to exploit polymetallic sulphides. The company went out of business in February 2019. The major, unresolved flaw is in the lifting of the material from the seabed. Airlift technology is not practical from deep water, while the stages of pumping stations as formerly proposed by Nautilus Minerals are likely to be impractical.

5.11 Gemstones

Gemstone projects, which include diamonds, ruby (a red variety of corundum), sapphires (also a variety of corundum but blue), emeralds (a green variety of the mineral beryl), and lapis lazuli (a feldspathoid), are by far the most challenging to evaluate out of the wide range of deposits which form part of the minerals and mining business. The key technical factor for gemstones is quality, which involves the field of gemmology, a sub-specialisation of mineralogy. The approach used in obtaining a final opinion on the value of an individual gemstone is an art as much as a science. Inaccurate price assumptions mean that the financial model used for making an investment decision is going to be fundamentally flawed. This, when combined with the huge uncertainty associated with any grade estimation, results in instabilities during sensitivity analysis that render most financial models useless. An appropriate business model must take into account the almost insuperable requirement to retain the best-quality stones in the supply pipeline, starting with remote informal mining sites (which are often unsafe sites, tied to criminal activity, where it is impossible to prevent theft and which carry reputational risks for large jewellery brands). The only way to de-risk gemstone projects is to undertake trial mining under tightly controlled conditions. Typically, some 10% of the deposit needs to be mined before it can be evaluated to determine if it is able to support a commercially viable operation.

5.12 Conclusions

Each mineral deposit type will have its own unique geological characteristics and earth scientists and exploration geologists will usually specialise in a particular sub-set of a mineral deposit type. No matter how proficient the conventional engineering, or innovative the financial engineering, an operator cannot create a single additional ounce of precious metal or kilogram of base metal that nature did not provide. This is why a basic understanding of mineral deposits is needed for anyone involved in the natural resource sector.

Chapter 6

Petroleum and Coal

6.1 Introduction

In organic chemistry, a hydrocarbon is a compound consisting entirely of carbon and hydrogen. Petroleum and coal are hydrocarbons and both are derived from life forms (living organisms). These are present as alkanes with the general formula C_nH_{2n+2}. The major gaseous hydrocarbons comprise CH_4 methane (also described as natural gas), C_2H_6 (ethane), C_3H_8 (propane) and C_4H_{10} (butane). Petroleum refers to hydrocarbons from C_5 to C_{17} that are in a liquid state. Hydrocarbons from C_{18} to C_{40} make up waxes.

When the gas is removed from the reservoir during production, it cools and pressure is lowered; some of the C_{5+} molecules condense out as a liquid phase known as condensate which is a valuable product in itself. It is essentially a light crude oil.

Clathrates have water-based molecular structures that capture methane under appropriate high pressure and low temperature conditions and are common in permafrost environments.

The coalification process of precursor accumulated plant material is illustrated in Fig. 6.1. Preservation of plant material is initially achieved because the conditions are anaerobic and this is also associated with the presence of hydrogen sulphide. As the geological conditions are typically deltaic, there are regular influxes of fine sediment which then seal in the precursor coal-forming plant material. Initially, the main influence is biochemical activity followed by burial and then subsequently thermal and confining pressure. When combined with geological time, anthracitic coal is formed which

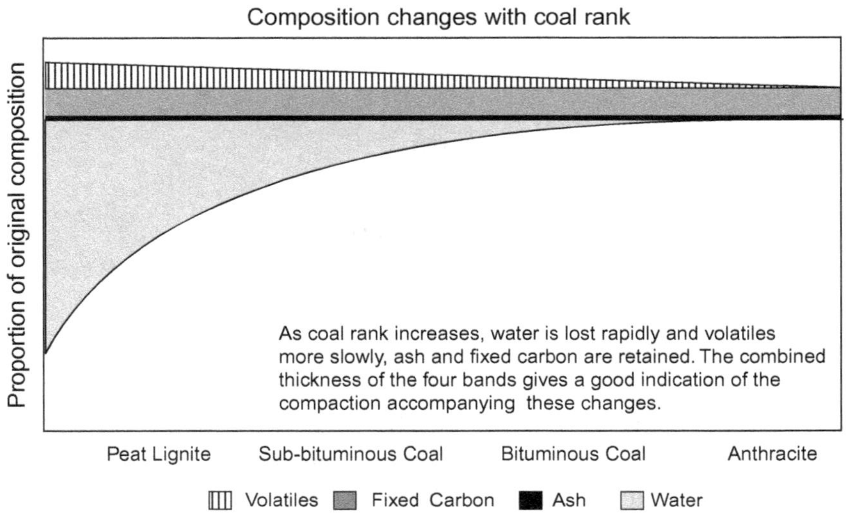

Figure 6.1. Diagram demonstrating the transition from transformation of vegetable matter in peat through to coal.

comprises mainly amorphous carbon and some pyrite. Coal has complex physiochemical characteristics that need to be determined when considering end use. This includes a range of different qualities such as feed for electrical power generation, injection of pulverised coal into a blast furnace during steel production and conversion into coke.

The range of chemical and physical properties determined as part of the evaluation process includes the following:

- *As Received (ar)*: includes Total Moisture (TM)
- *Air Dried (ad)*: includes Inherent Moisture (IM) only
- *Dry Basis (db)*: excludes all Moisture
- *Dry Ash Free (daf)*: excludes all Moisture & Ash
- The Proximate Analysis of any coal i.e. the % content of Moisture, Ash (A)
- Volatile Matter (VM), Fixed Carbon (FC) — also Sulphur (S)
- *Calorific Value (CV)*: can be expressed on any of the above bases.

Calories are metric and are also known as Le Système International d'Unités (the SI, or the International System of Units).

The alternative measure is the British thermal unit which is widely used in the United States. Coal heating units are as follows:

- kcal/kg: Kilocalories per kilogram
- MJ/kg: Megajoules per kilogram
- Btu/lb: British thermal units per pound.

Gross & Net Calorific Values are used to determine the price of coal. Gross CV or "higher heating value" (HHV) is the CV under laboratory conditions. Net CV or "lower heating value" (LHV) is the useful calorific value in a boiler plant. The difference is essentially the latent heat of the water vapour produced. Sulphur, normally present as pyrite, will burn adding to the heating value but also resulting in the emission of sulphur dioxide and contributing to acid rain unless scrubbers are installed. The associated costs are reflected in penalties which means that producers need to design coal washing plants that remove pyrite.

Typical heating values for coal are as follows:

- Bituminous coal (CV 6,000 kcal/kg)
- Brown coal (CV 2,250 kcal/kg).

To convert from kcal/kg to MJ/kg multiply by 0.004187.

Bituminous coal must meet a set of criteria for use as metallurgical coal in steel production, determined by particular coal assay techniques. These include moisture content, ash content, sulphur content, volatile content, tar and plasticity. Coking coal must also have low phosphorus content. Coke itself is produced by heating the coal in an anaerobic environment to produce a hard, porous carbonaceous material which is used in steel production both as a source of heat and a reductant. While petrographic characteristics of coal can be used to predict its suitability for coke production, confirmation of this has to be established using laboratory testing. Coal used for pulverised coal injection (PCI) reduces the consumption of coke per ton of pig iron as it replaces coke as a source of heat and, at high injection rates, as a reductant. Anthracite is often used as PCI. PCI coal tends to trade at a premium to thermal coal depending on its ability to replace coke in the blast furnace.

Methane is an important constituent of coal and while representing a significant hazard in an underground coal mining operation, can be extracted ahead of mining by drilling wells into the coal seam. Through different applications of borehole technology, methane is extracted from coal seams both for the purpose of providing safe underground mining conditions in coal mines, and as the source of unconventional natural gas as a cleaner fossil fuel energy. Pressure is reduced by dewatering and the desorbed methane flows to surface, compressed and used as an energy source. Unmined coal beds are also targets for carbon dioxide sequestration as this can be used to enhance coalbed methane recovery.

During coalification, the matrix shrinks, creating orthogonal fractures called cleats. Face cleats tend to be continuous; butt cleats are at right angles to face cleats. Typically, water fills the void spaces of the coal matrix. As the water is produced and the formation pressure decreases, methane — adsorbed on the surfaces of the coal matrix and stored in the micropores — is liberated. The gas then diffuses through the matrix, migrates into the cleats and fractures and eventually reaches the wellbore.

Coalbed methane is also known as Coal Seam Gas (CSG) and is different both from conventional upstream and combined conventional gas-field–LNG plant projects. The upstream CSG part operates under a different fiscal and ownership regime to an LNG operation. As the LNG plant is already built, an investment study focuses on future value. Production depends on number of wells drilled and their average performance. As already indicated in Section 4.7.1, engineering challenges related to the subset of geological heterogeneities will need to be considered within the context of their financial implications.

The precursor to petroleum formation is considered to be preserved high molecular weight dead organisms known as kerogen in an evolving sedimentary basin where anoxic conditions are present. Because of its high molecular weight, kerogen is normally insoluble in organic solvents. Type I kerogen forms mainly from algae, Type II kerogen from a combination of marine and plant organic matter, and Type III kerogen from land plants.

Clearly for hydrocarbons to accumulate a source rock is needed. As with the coalification process, moderate temperature combined with pressure is required. Hydrocarbons need to be heated in the range 80–150°C under lithostatic pressure (the oil window). Over geological time, this will result in the precursor complex organic chemical molecules being broken down as a consequence of cracking into simpler molecules comprising mainly the alkanes. At lower temperatures, conversion is incomplete and at higher temperatures pure methane is formed up to the phase boundary with graphite.

Type I and Type II kerogen are considered to be the more likely sources of petroleum while Type III kerogen is more likely to produce gaseous components, mainly methane. Under more extreme pressure and temperature conditions, hydrocarbons derived from Types I and II kerogen will also revert to gaseous components. Coal is formed from preserved plant material and is classified as Type III kerogen.

Chemical engineering through the Fischer–Tropsch process is able to reverse the natural coalification processes and convert a feedstock of coal, when reacted with steam and methane, into alkanes to produce synthetic fuels and a range of complex organic chemicals. Sasol in South Africa operates the Secunda coal-based synfuels manufacturing facility which converts mixtures of carbon monoxide derived from coal and hydrogen into liquid hydrocarbons. Sasol are actively seeking to promote their technology in which development of gas resources will enhance the gas to liquid capabilities in Sasol's core Fischer–Tropsch process, while seeking to utilise carbon dioxide generated to recover residual hydrocarbons from mature oil reservoirs. There is also an angle on securing carbon credits.

Any consideration of energy derived from hydrocarbons needs to recognise that the chemical systems, whether formed in a geological setting or in the controlled environment of an industrial process, are therefore constrained by the same basic thermodynamic considerations.

6.2 Wessex Basin Petroleum System

The type area for a petroleum system is located in Southern England where the full sequence of sediments from the Permian through to the Cretaceous (see Figure 6.2) can be seen in coastal exposures.

The sediments dip to the east successively so that younger rocks are encountered in a traverse from Exeter in the west through to Kimmeridge Bay in the east. The basin contains the largest onshore accumulation of oil in north west Europe at Wytch Farm with a Stock Tank Oil Initially in Place (STOIIP, see Section 4.5) of 800 million barrels (MM bbls) of oil and a total recoverable reserve of about 450 MM bbls. Directional drilling from the site extends up to 30 kms offshore.

The Permo–Triassic rocks were deposited in continental desert environments and are shown in Figs. 6.3 and 6.4. Both the Exmouth sandstone and the Sherwood sandstone make excellent reservoir rocks due to their high permeability and porosity. The former is the reservoir rock for the southern North Sea oil field and the latter for the Wytch Farm oil field.

Porosity, usually abbreviated to Φ, is a measure of the storage capacity of the reservoir. It is defined as the ratio between pore volume, Vp, and bulk volume, Vb, and expressed as a percentage:

$$\mathrm{Vp/Vb} \times 100.$$

The most common porosity range is 10–20%; the highest recorded porosity value is 37% and the maximum theoretical porosity value is 47%. Permeability measures the ability of fluids to flow through rock (or other porous media). The darcy is defined using Darcy's law and typical values of permeability range as high as 100,000 darcies (mD) for gravel, to less than 0.01 microdarcies for granite. Sand has a permeability of approximately 1 darcy.

An example of a potential reservoir rock is present at Orcombe Rocks shown in Fig. 6.3. The rock is poorly cemented with high porosity and a permeability of around 100 mD. This unit is the equivalent of the Rotlegend reservoir in the North Sea oil field.

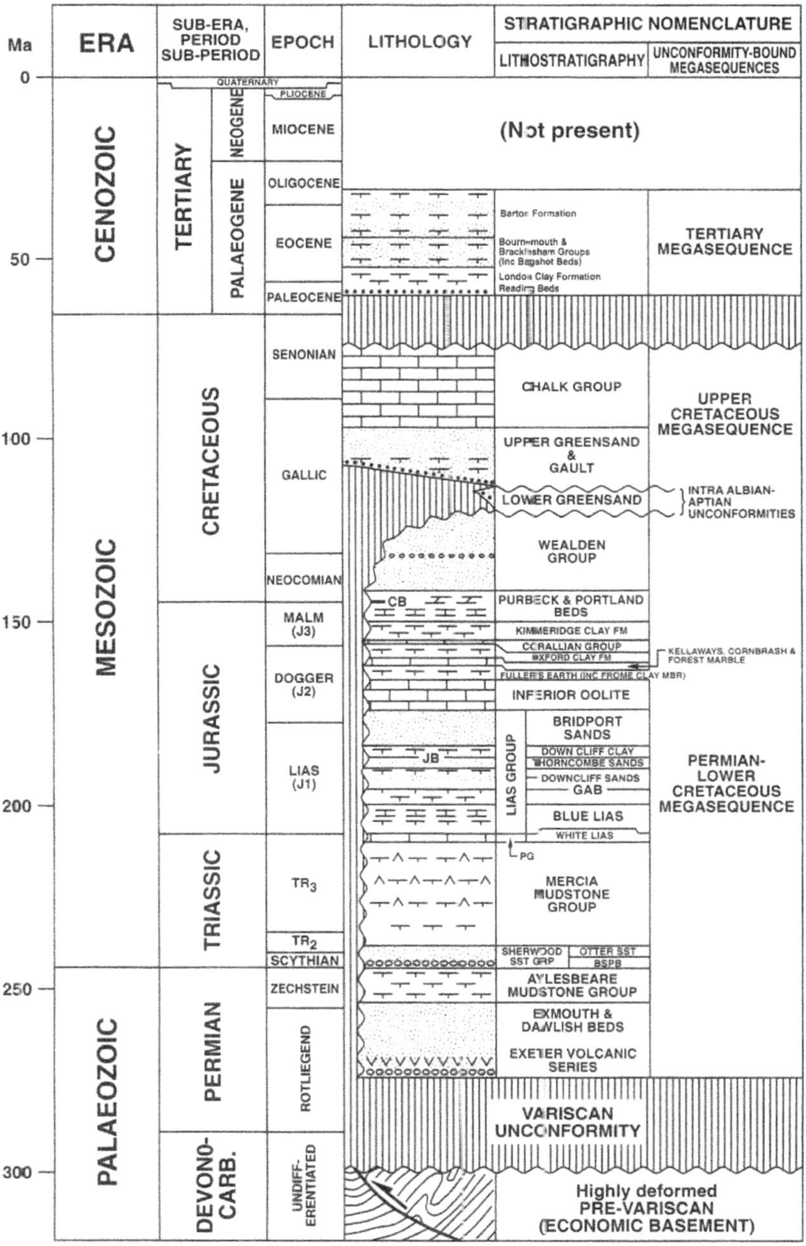

Figure 6.2. Stratigraphy of the Wessex Basin taken from Underhill, J. R. and Stoneley, R. (1998).

Figure 6.3. Orcombe Rocks. View of large-scale Aeolian cross bedding in Permian-aged Exmouth sandstone comprising medium sand-sized rounded grains.

A further example of a reservoir rock is present at Budleigh Salterton and is shown in Fig. 6.4. Here the Sherwood sandstone is located at the top of the Permian and base of the Triassic. High porosity of 15–20% and permeability in the range 10–100 mD are observed. This unit is the main reservoir for the Wytch Farm oil field with a STOIIP of 300 MM bbls (million barrels).

For a petroleum system to form an impermeable cap, rocks need to be present immediately above the reservoir rocks. The Mercia mudstone provides this feature for the Wytch Farm oil field and the contact is shown in Fig. 6.5. Note that the transition between Sherwood and Mercia is gradational over tens of metres — at the base of the cliff is a thick sandstone with thin mudstone, above that is thick mudstone with very little sandstone present. There is uncertainty as to the position of the boundary which would have implications for defining the top of a reservoir. Permeability in the Mercia is 10–20 mD providing a suitable cap rock for the Wytch Farm oil field.

Figure 6.4. Budleigh Salterton. View of interbedded matrix-supported conglomerates and sandstones at the base of the Sherwood sandstones group with channel structures present indicative of a fluvial braided river environment.

Clearly for petroleum to accumulate there must be a source and the organic-rich Lias (Fig. 6.6) is considered to be a candidate for the Wytch Farm oil field but in the North Sea burial was too deep and both temperatures and pressures were outside the oil window. Implicit in this model is the requirement for the hydrocarbons to migrate from the source rock into a suitable reservoir with a seal. Three rock types are present at Charmouth: limestone–marl–black shale. It combines the characteristics of both marine and fresh water depositional environments but predominantly marine and is highly fossiliferous. The black shales contain between 3–4% total organic content. This is probably the source rock for hydrocarbons for the Wytch Farm oil field.

The heterogeneity that can be present in a reservoir is best illustrated by the exposure of the Bridport sandstone at West Bay (Fig. 6.7). Differential calcite cementation forms harder beds more resistant to erosion. These discontinuous layers have a significant

Figure 6.5. Sidmouth. View showing the top of the Sherwood sandstone (see Fig. 6.4) and the transitional contact with the overlying Mercia mudstone.

impact on fluid movements in the subsurface. Porosity in softer beds is 10–100 mD and much lower in cemented beds. These were the reservoir rocks for the first discovery at the Wytch Farm oil field before the larger underlying Sherwood sandstone-hosted reservoir was discovered.

This was the first reservoir to be discovered at Wytch Farm and contains 150 MM bbls of STOIIP, smaller than the underlying Sherwood sandstone-hosted reservoir. As would be expected, lateral migration of oil would be relatively unimpeded but although the harder resistant beds are persistent, vertical migration would be restricted. As a consequence, recovery from the reservoir is about 20%. These sedimentary features would not be imaged by a seismic survey and even if a well log did identify the presence of bedding with different hardness characteristics, the lateral characteristics would be a matter of speculation. There is an inherent uncertainty

Figure 6.6. Charmouth. View showing the Lias, a finely bedded succession that includes some organic rich mudstone located at the base of the Jurassic.

associated with this type of reservoir that should be considered at the investment stage. The heterogeneity would also influence the performance of the reservoir during production as water injection aimed at sweeping oil towards a well system would not retain a simple interface but fingering would take place and pockets of oil would be isolated.

Migration of oil from a source rock can be seen at the Osmington Mills exposure (see Fig. 6.8). The well sorted sandstone is interbedded with bioclastic limestones and has a porosity of 200 mD. Heavy oil is seeping from the beds at the base of the cliff suggesting that this is an exhumed reservoir. The original oil has probably been biodegraded.

The Wessex petroleum system reflects the dynamic tectonism that started with the Hercynian orogeny and resulted in the local north–south stress regime that produced the graben structures.

Figure 6.7. West Bay. View of Bridport sandstone which lies above the Lias in the Jurassic comprising fine- to medium-grained sandstone suggested to be shallow beach deposits.

This permitted basin development and the deposition of the Permian and Jurassic rocks. The subsequent Alpine orogeny which started at the end of the Cretaceous and remains active produced north–south compression and resulted in the folding of the earlier basin sediments. This folding and faulting created the spatial relationships that permitted hydrocarbon source rocks such as the Lias to enter the oil window and oil to migrate and then to become trapped in suitable structural traps. The impact of the Alpine deformation can be seen from the Lulworth crumple (Fig. 6.9). The deformation has been caused by the Alpine orogeny and reflects the dynamic tectonism present in the Wessex Basin.

Tectonism also provides the mechanism for reservoirs to become over-pressured as oil trapped in suitable structures is then subject to lithostatic pressure.

Figure 6.8. Osmington Mills. View of the Bencliff grit which is part of the Corallian Group present towards the top of the Jurassic, showing an oil seep.

Burial of sediments during basin development will also result in compaction of sediments and migration of both water and hydrocarbons.

Chalk is also present in the Wessex basis (see Fig. 6.10). This rock is normally characterised by micro-porosity but is the main reservoir rock in the EkoFisk oil field in the southern and eastern North Sea oil field where interconnected fractures result in high permeability.

A view of Kimmeridge Bay and the production facility is given in Fig. 6.11. At its peak, the well produced 100 bbls per day and was originally estimated to have a STOIIP reserve of one million bbls. Actual recovery has been some three million bbls suggesting that oil is leaking from a breached trap, or hydrocarbon is still being generated in an underlying source or the original estimate of the size of the reservoir was incorrect. Currently producing 15 bbls per day.

Figure 6.9. Lulworth crumple, Stair Hole. View of the folded and faulted alternating hard and soft Purbeck beds overlying the Portland limestone of the Upper Jurassic dipping at 45° to the north.

A more comprehensive treatment of petroleum systems is given in the book *Introduction to Petroleum Geoscience* by Michael Ala (2017).

6.3 Unconventional Hydrocarbons

Unconventional hydrocarbons consist of unconventional petroleum (essentially alkanes with chain length up to C30+) and unconventional gas which is methane. These include tar sands, shale oil and oil shale derived from Type I and Type II kerogen. Unconventional gas includes shale gas which, although mainly methane, is also derived from Type I and Type II kerogen. Coal bed methane can also be considered as an unconventional gas albeit derived from carbonaceous shales formed from plants not from marine organisms. The

Figure 6.10. Lulworth Cove. View of an outcrop of the Chalk present at the base of the Cretaceous and formed from the accumulation of Coccoliths, the individual plates of calcium carbonate formed by algae.

main product is methane, chemically indistinguishable from coalbed methane and formed in the same terrestrial geological environment as coal. Coalbed methane is an important source of gas from the southern North Sea. While the petroleum industry is considered as a separate business from coal, geologically and technically there are more

Figure 6.11. Kimmeridge Bay. View of pumpjack on the apex of an anticline. Seismic target drilled in the 1970s below the Kimmeridge clay that acts as the seal intersected the Cornbrash reservoir.

similarities than differences. Both are essentially industries exploiting fossil fuels that provide most of the world's energy needs.

The characteristics of unconventional hydrocarbons are given in Table 6.1.

Shale oil is oil trapped in shale formations, usually organic-rich, but with ultra-low porosity and permeability. It is formed by the typical mechanism of "*in situ* saturation reservoiring", where shale is both the source rock and reservoir.

Tight Oil versus Shale Oil. Tight oil (or tight-sandstone oil) is conventional oil (light oil with low sulphur content) found within reservoirs with very low permeability. It is considered "unconventional" since to access it advanced drilling and completion processes such as horizontal drilling and hydraulic fracturing are needed. "Tight oil" is

Table 6.1. Classification of unconventional hydrocarbons.

Type	Geological setting and rock type	Hydrocarbon characteristics and reservoir type	Type area	Extraction and processing method
Unconventional petroleum				
Tar sands	Shallow exhumed conventional reservoir in which light fraction has been lost	Viscous bitumen present in sand and clay	Alberta, Canada	Open pit mining or *in situ* production involves injecting super-heated steam. Energy intensive. Syncrude
Shale oil	Deep sea (anoxic) marine environment. Organic-rich black shales that have reached the "oil window" pressure and temperature field of 60°C to 80°C	Liquid oil present trapped in pores of the shale. Some oil may migrate into a conventional porous sandstone reservoir	Bakken and Barnett shales of North America	Tight oil requiring horizontal drilling and hydraulic fracturing (fracking). Water, sand and chemicals are injected to induce porosity
Oil shale	Organic-rich black shales (organic content reaches 15–20% by weight — exceptionally high) that have not reached the "oil window" and necessary pressure and temperature field due to insufficient burial	Immature, comprises kerogen: Type II (mixed plant and marine material)	Lothian area of Scotland, Kimmeridge Bay — plays no part in the Wessex petroleum system	Mining. When pyrolysed (heated and retorted) at 500°C the shale will produce oil. Energy intensive. Produces high quality, low sulphur, sweet crude

(Continued)

Table 6.1. (*Continued*)

Type	Geological setting and rock type	Hydrocarbon characteristics and reservoir type	Type area	Extraction and processing method
Unconventional gas				
Shale gas	Organic-rich shales. The gas is both produced and trapped within the shale	Methane (natural gas) which is trapped in impermeable shale. Can be derived from mixed marine and plant material (Type I and II kerogen)	Barnett shales. North America	Tight gas. Fracking required
Coalbed preserved carbona-ceous rock methane formed from plant material		Methane (natural gas) which is trapped in the coal seam	Worldwide	Through different applications of borehole technology

not the same as "shale oil", which has risen to fame in recent years thanks to the "shale revolution" coined and spread widely by the mass media. Major tight oil plays include Eagle Ford, Bakken, Niobrara and the Permian Basin. This is a mature oil producing region that encompasses west Texas and southeastern New Mexico.

It has been known for a long time that vast amounts of oil and gas exist in tight reservoirs, but it was the greatly improved drilling and completion technologies born during the success of the U.S. "shale revolution" that finally unleashed this potential. Without assistance from advanced drilling and completion processes, the hydrocarbon contained within these reservoir rocks will not flow to the wellbore at economic rates. Horizontal drilling followed by multi-stage fracturing is used to induce permeability in these reservoirs from which it would otherwise be difficult to produce oil.

The key to the valuation of tight oil is in the complex interplay with the technical operational factors:

- *Exact nature and variability of the type well decline curve*: itself a result of advances in well placement and fracking techniques.
- Tight control of drilling and per-well Opex costs.
- *Achievability of accelerated drilling schedules*: this might depend on availability and cost of rigs.

Tight gas is held in low permeability (deep or "basin-centred") reservoirs. Production of tight gas also largely relies on natural or induced fractures which allow fluids to flow to the well bore.

The idea that hydrocarbons are produced by heating sedimentary organic matter was developed from the technique of pyrolysis. This is thermochemical decomposition of organic material at elevated temperatures in the absence of oxygen which produces a petroleum-like product. This industrial process was undertaken at Kimmeridge Bay on the organic-rich sediments (oil shales) see Fig. 6.12. The oil shales were extracted as a mining operation worked on various occasions from the 17th century to the 19th century. While the sediments did not reach the oil window in the type location, they are the source of petroleum in the North Sea oil field. At the type location, it is classified as an Oil Shale and when pyrolysed will produce oil and

Figure 6.12. Kimmeridge Bay. View of Kimmeridge clay which has a high organic content and, as is evident from the abundant ammonites, formed in a marine environment.

was mined at the site for this purpose. This is an example of an unconventional petroleum resource. Heating oil shales in a hydrous environment generates products that are physically and chemically closer to natural petroleum products.

The Athabasca tar sands (also called oil sands) are large deposits of bitumen or extremely heavy crude oil, located in northeastern Alberta, Canada, centred on the town of Fort McMurray. These oil sands, hosted primarily in the McMurray Formation, consist of a mixture of crude bitumen (a semi-solid form of crude oil), silica sand, clay minerals and water. Where they are near to the surface extraction is undertaken as an open pit mining operation. As will be noted, there is convergence between the petroleum and mining industries at the extraction stage.

When more deeply buried, steam-assisted gravity drainage is used to extract the hydrocarbon. The heavy bitumen then has to be upgraded to light sweet and medium sour synthetic crude oil. According to Suncor's website, this involves the following stages:

- Hot water is used to separate the bitumen from the sands. This step is called extraction and is not required for *in situ* bitumen.
- Bitumen is heated and sent to drums where excess carbon (in the form of petroleum coke) is removed.
- The superheated hydrocarbon vapours from the coke drums are sent to fractionators where vapour condenses into naphtha, kerosene and gas oil.
- The end product is synthetic crude oil. It is shipped by underground pipelines to refineries across North America to be processed into jet fuels, gasoline and other petroleum products.

6.4 Coal

For a bulk commodity such as coal, the concept of grade used for base and precious metals does not apply. The whole volume of material will be extracted and in some cases shipped directly without preprocessing. Setting up the financial model therefore has to take this into account. IC-CoalEval automates this process and the application includes the following scenario:

It is proposed to establish a Longwall Section on an underground coal mine to mine out an area of the coal reserves 2,500 m by 5,000 m. This portion of the mine has a coal seam 2 m thick on average, so there is a reserve of 25,000,000 m^3 of coal available in the area. The mining layout will be parallel advancing longwalls with 10 m gate protection pillars being left between them. The longwall section will have a called for production capacity of 10,000 tons of mixed quality coal per day. The longwalls will be 231 m wide, gate road to gate road, and the block of coal to be mined is estimated to be 2.5 km long. Taking each gate road as 4.5 m wide the block of coal being cut by each longwall is then 24 m wide by 2500 m long. At a seam width of 2 m with the average density of the coal at 1.35 t/m3 then there is a resource of 1,620,000 tons of coal to be mined by each longwall with an estimated quality of 90% steam grade, 5% coking grade and 5%

anthracite. It is estimated that the dilution will be 5% and the mining recovery will be 90%. The life of each longwall is therefore expected to be some 154 days and moving the equipment to the next longwall is expected to take 16 days, with the longwalls being worked on advance and retreat alternately.

The key form is that which handles volumetrics and the variables that need to be considered are shown in Fig. 6.13.

We have been told the project has an *in situ* resource of 25 million cubic metres of coal seam. The *in situ* resource is what is in the ground and will be more than what we are actually able to mine. Based on the geology we can calculate that, given a specific gravity of 1.35, the total tonnage of coal is 33.75 million tonnes. We can now determine how much of the *in situ* ore is mined. To do this, we enter the estimated loss of resource due to the selected mining method, in this case we are using 10%. This is as a result of the fact that some pillars of coal are usually left *in situ* for support reasons,

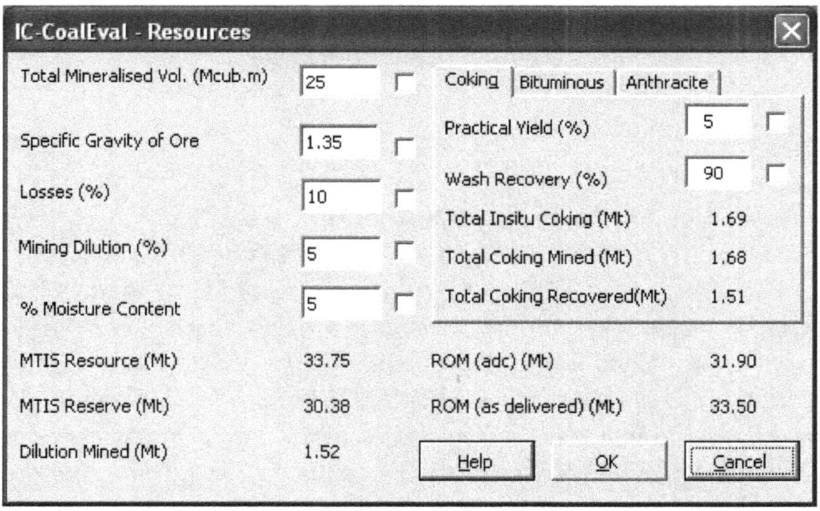

Figure 6.13. Form taken from IC-CoalEval.

often between adjacent longwalls, as is the case in this example. Also the full thickness of the seam may not always be mined for rock mechanics driven safety reasons, or to reduce surface subsidence problems. The result will be that not all the resource in the ground will be able to be mined and sent to the washing plant.

Next we can enter any dilution factor, in this scenario 5%, which means that every 9.5 tonnes of coal sent to the washing plant will also contain 0.5 tonnes ash (waste rock) i.e. the rock bordering on the coal seam. Having some dilution is normal, as it is often caused by mining conditions, but the key is to keep it to a minimum as it is often also caused by poor horizon control on the coal mining equipment.

In coal mining too, the moisture content of the coal is important as it affects both the percentage of the material shipped that is actually coal and the net calorific value of the coal so shipped, as the moisture will need to be boiled off before the calories are available for other use. Here we are using a moisture content of 5%. This is a multiproduct deposit so extra tabs are displayed for each variety of coal, to enter the *Practical Yield* (the percentage of the total coal mined that is of that variety) and *Wash Recovery* (the percentage of that variety of coal sent to the washing plant that reports as product). In this example, we are assuming there is 90% Bituminous (or Steam) coal, 5% coking coal and 5% anthracite. We have been given a plant recovery of 90% for each of these three varieties of coal.

So by clicking on the appropriate product tabs we can enter the percentages of each variety of coal to be produced. For Fig. 6.13 we have entered 5% as the *Practical Yield* for Coking coal and 90% for the *Wash Recovery* for Coking coal. Not seen in Fig. 6.13 we have also entered *Practical Yields* of 90% for Bituminous coal and 5% for Anthracite (not indicated in Fig. 6.13 as it is a static screenshot). The estimated *Wash Recovery* for each rank of coal is set at 90%. When the values for each rank are entered, the total *in situ* tonnage, total mined tonnage and total recovered tonnage for that rank of coal are calculated and displayed.

6.5 Coal versus Gas

When building an electricity power station fuelled by coal objections can be raised because it is perceived to be more "polluting" than one fuelled by natural gas (methane).

Taking the chemical thermodynamic approach, you get the following:

$$C + O_2 = CO_2$$

Coal

$$CH_4 + 2O_2 = CO_2 + 2H_2O.$$

Methane.

Based on enthalpy,

$$\Delta H^{o}_{reaction} = \Sigma\Delta H^{o}_{f(products)} - \Sigma\Delta H^{o}_{f(reactants)},$$

then both reactions each produce 44 g/mol CO_2 but coal produces 32.79 kJ/g of heat compared to methane which produces 50.14 kJ/g. So for the same CO_2 emission methane produces 1.5 times the amount of specific heat compared to coal. Methane is therefore "cleaner" in as much that more heat is generated per unit of CO_2 produced. It is nothing to do with "pollution".

There is a separate narrative around heat exchange efficiency during the generation of electricity which is greater for methane than coal. Gas fired power stations run a combined cycle, both a gas turbine and a steam turbine, from the heat rejected from the first process. Therefore, you use much less fuel input to produce the same electrical energy and have proportionately less CO_2 emission and therefore less greenhouse gas forming.

Furthermore, coal has inherent moisture so the overall specific heat will be reduced by the enthalpy of vaporisation of water. Shale is usually present so there is further energy loss due to the heat capacity of this material. Of course, pyrite is ubiquitous in coal so there is an exothermic reaction there, but SO_2 is a true pollutant and needs to be scrubbed, adding to operating costs.

If you introduce carbon capture and sequestration when considering coal, then you close the CO_2 gap significantly but not in full.

Project Evaluation

Chapter 7

Resource Evaluation

7.1 Introduction

Resource evaluation is a vital component of the project appraisal process. The financial modelling of the project depends on the amount and quality of mineral in the ground and the depth of overburden above it. If these variables are not correctly estimated to a satisfactory degree of certainty, then the subsequent economic evaluation will be inherently flawed. Resource estimation provides the foundation on which the principles of conventional and financial engineering are based. There will always be uncertainty attached to the estimation of the amount and quality of *in situ* valuable mineral, right up until production commences. However, it must be ensured that this uncertainty has been defined as accurately as possible before any investment decision can be made.

Experienced geologists, engineers and geostatisticians must undertake the technical resource evaluation, as the integrity of the subsequent economic evaluation depends on the reliability of their findings. There are three major techniques for collecting data on the deposit:

- geophysical techniques
- a drilling programme
- down-hole exploration.

Drilling provides the greatest resolution and is by far the most important tool in resource/reserve determination. Upon collection, data are processed by standard polygonal techniques and/or more complex geostatistical techniques, in order to construct isopach and isopleth maps. Isopach maps delineate mineralised strata and overburden thickness while isopleth maps illustrate the spatial pattern of other variables, such as resource grades. The following sections summarise the most common data processing techniques used to determine the extent of a mineral resource.

7.2 Sampling

The basic tool during exploration and evaluation is the diamond drill rig (see Fig. 7.1). Typical costs per metre would be around \$100. The cylinders of core produced are logged and mineralised zones split with a diamond saw and sampled. Preservation in storage of mineralised

Figure 7.1. Diamond drill rig, crowns, core and core storage. Preservation of core is essential to support resource estimation, process mineralogy and due diligence. Core diameters are normally produced in a range of sizes designated AQ (27 mm), BQ (36.5 mm), NQ (47.6 mm) and HQ (63.5 mm).

Figure 7.2. Views of a RC rig at Thabazimbi which is used for grade control aimed at ensuring that product specifications meet requirements. See Chapter 9. Drill hole spacing is around 10 metres, far closer than could ever be expected at the evaluation stage of a project.

sections of split core is essential for due diligence, particularly post Bre-X (Section 3.4.1).

Once the geological characteristics of a deposit have been identified from diamond drilling, evaluation can be followed up with reversed circulation (RC) drilling. Cost per metre can drop to $20. Features of RC drilling are given in Fig. 7.2.

7.3 Process Mineralogy

The Bre-X promoters described the mineralisation as being an epithermal gold deposit (see Fig. 7.3) yet independent mineralogical studies queried why the gold, identified in crushed samples

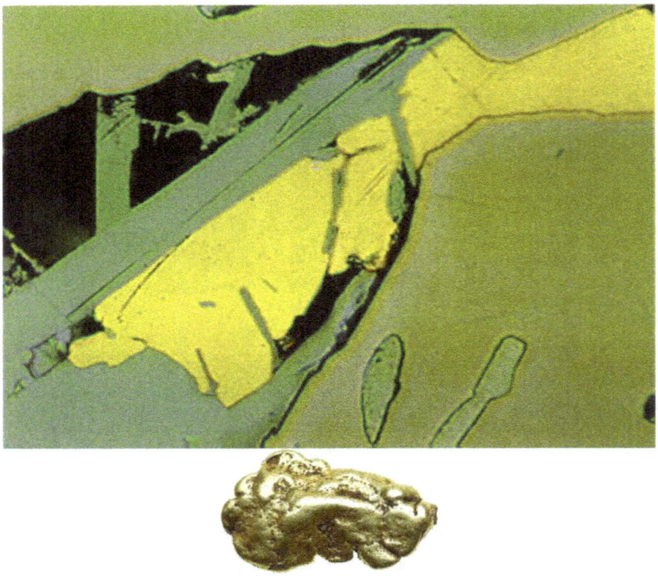

Figure 7.3. Reflected light view of gold inter-grown with pyrite from an epithermal deposit. Black areas are voids which were pathways of mineralising fluids. Horizontal field of view = 0.5 mm. Below, the characteristic appearance of a gold nugget formed in placer alluvial deposits.

used by the analytical laboratory responsible for the gold assays, was in the form of detrital gold with the characteristic morphology of placer gold. The obvious answer was that the samples had been salted with alluvial gold. Primary mineralogical associations were never preserved as all the core was crushed. It follows from this that diamond drill core should always be split down the centre with a diamond saw and only half the core sent for assay, thereby preserving a continuous representative section of core. Any sub-sampling should be on quartered core and only in exceptional circumstances should intersections through the mineralised zone be sacrificed.

7.4 Concepts around Geological Continuity

Fundamental to any approach to resource estimation is that there is geological continuity between sample positions. End member scenarios are illustrated in Fig. 7.4 with reference to the Merensky Reef and the type area for epithermal deposits in Carlin.

The continuity of the Merensky Reef is remarkable apart from local geological discontinuities caused by potholes and faults. The horizon has been traced for hundreds of kms on the surface and

Figure 7.4. View of the Merensky Reef (top left) and the Carlin epithermal gold deposit (bottom right). Continuity of the Merensky Reef is such that sampling is confined to raises that are 120 m apart. The Merensky Reef also has a clear visual marker which is the contact between the pyroxenite (brown) and the anorthosite (grey). Mineralisation at Carlin is associated with the bleached vein systems; it is impossible to predict distribution in the next face following blasting.

drilled down dip to more than 3 km. For Carlin-type epithermal deposits not only is continuity confined to carbon-rich rocks that may be 50 m thick, but also assays for high-grade samples such as that shown in Fig. 7.3 from two separate portions of split core are unlikely to provide reproducible results.

7.5 Polygons of Influence and Inverse Distance

The historical approach to estimating the grade and tonnage of a mineralised horizon is to divide it into polygons which each contain one drillhole sample (Fig. 7.5). This is usually generated by drawing perpendicular bisectors between samples or by expanding circular zones of influence. The variable value of the sample (e.g. grade of valuable element, thickness of mineralised zone, etc.) is then taken as the value of the variable for the entire polygon. The level of uncertainty in the results of this method is generally high, and the reliability of the estimates is predominantly a function of drill hole spacing. Sample variables (metal content in particular) tend to be more variable than block grades and the results for the whole mineral deposit should be used with caution when planning for selective mining.

The method is useful for volume-weighted global mean grade and tonnages. As sample grades tend to be more variable than block grades, it tends to overestimate the grade of blocks containing high-grade samples and underestimate those with low-grade samples. If using a cut-off grade, it reports too selectively (fewer tonnes at higher grades).

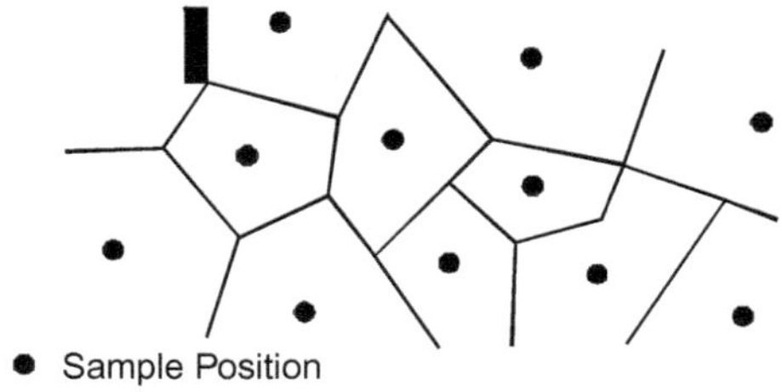

Figure 7.5. Polygons of influence.

7.6 Inverse Distance

In this method, the mineralised horizon is divided into e-mining resource blocks and the variable is estimated using a weighted combination of proximal samples, with those samples closest to the block having the greatest influence (Fig. 7.6). Samples are weighted by estimating their "inverse distance" from the mining block (or inverse distance squared, etc.). The choice of weights introduces a highly subjective element into the estimation procedure and takes no account of the geological structure of the mineral deposit, nor does the method provide any indication of the quality of the estimate (i.e. no quantitative measure of the inherent uncertainty).

Historically, complex polynomials were generated to reconcile sampling information available for a mining block which had been extracted and the metal content established. This has the following disadvantages:

- the choice of weights is subjective
- weighting does not reflect the geology of the deposit
- smooths data without reference to spatial variability
- point value set equal to block value
- the size and shape of the estimated block is not taken into account
- does not minimise the estimation variance
- there is no indication of the quality of the estimation
- there is no indication that optimum sample spacing has been used.

The industry was clearly ready to accept a more robust approach to resource estimation.

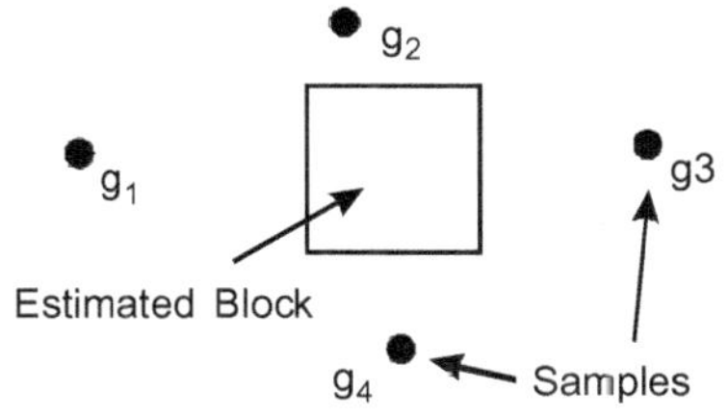

Figure 7.6. Inverse distance method of estimating grade in a block from proximal samples.

7.7 Geostatistical Methods

Geostatistics involves a more complex "moving average" technique, intended to provide the best linear, unbiased estimate of the variable in question (e.g. grade). Weighting factors are selected in order to give an unbiased estimate of the true value and to be as close as possible to the true value by minimising the mathematical variance of the estimation.

The field of Geostatistics was pioneered by Danie Krige (1919–2013), a South African Mining Engineer who worked on the paleao placer gold deposits of the Witwatersrand in South Africa; the technique of kriging is named after him. Krige's empirical work to evaluate mineral resources was formalised mathematically in the 1960s by French Engineer Georges Matheron. In 1968 he created the Centre de Géostatistique at the Ecole des Mines de Paris. The application of Geostatistics to the challenges of grade control in an active mining operation was promoted in a very practical way by Colin Dixon of the Royal School of Mines in the 1970s. The technique is now widely used and forms a standard part of degree courses in natural resources.

Geostatistical evaluation is a complex task and the assistance of a qualified, experienced consultant should be sought when interpreting geostatistical analyses reported in feasibility studies. The presence of a geostatistical evaluation in a feasibility study, however, is a positive sign and indicates the integrity of the reported resource and reserve estimation. Though not directly reducing the uncertainty of estimates, geostatistics quantitatively measures the level of inherent uncertainty and can also be used to determine the optimum drilling pattern for reserve estimation.

The principal tool in Geostatistics is the experimental semi-variogram. This is defined as follows:

$$\gamma(h) = \frac{1}{2N(h)} {}_{i=1}^{N(h)} [z(X_i + h) - z(X_i)]^2.$$

An interpolated variogram is then fitted to the experimental variogram generated from the primary sampling data base as illustrated in Fig. 7.7.

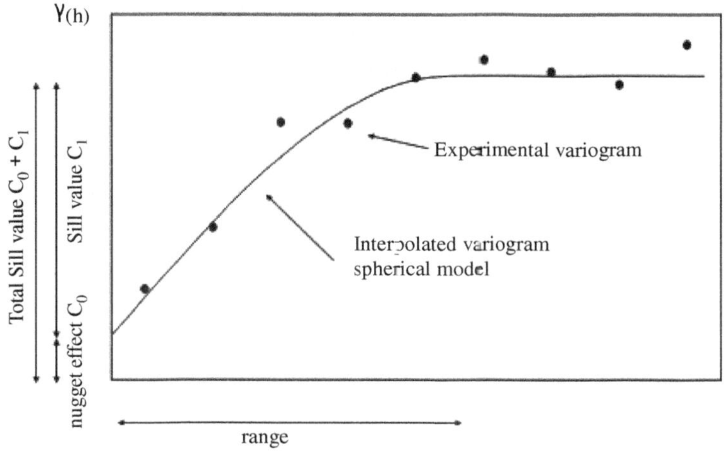

Figure 7.7. Variogram showing the relationship $y._{(h)}$ which relates the semi-variance of sample differences to distance between samples.

Where sample spacing falls within the range of the variogram, the resource can be classified as indicated (see Section 3.4.1). Close spaced sampling will delineate a measured resource. When outside the range of the variogram, this is classified as inferred. The allocation of the category is the responsibility of the geostatistician.

Resource blocks are superimposed on the mineralised unit and are then populated with grades derived from proximal samples determined from the application of the associated variogram. The dimensions of the resource blocks as indicated in Fig. 7.8 are determined by the geostatistician and at the evaluation stage would normally be much larger than the mining blocks established at the production stage. Clearly, communication needs to be monitored between the geostatistician and the mining engineer. In particular, the latter should not import the resource block model generated by the former and then reduce the dimensions down to the size of mining blocks for detailed mine design purposes. This corrupts the whole process.

A technical director or consultant working with the geostatistician would normally expect the estimation of grade and tonnage to be reported for the *in situ* resource. This would include internal dilution but definitely not mining dilution. This would be the resource used in the financial model. There would then be a separate conversation

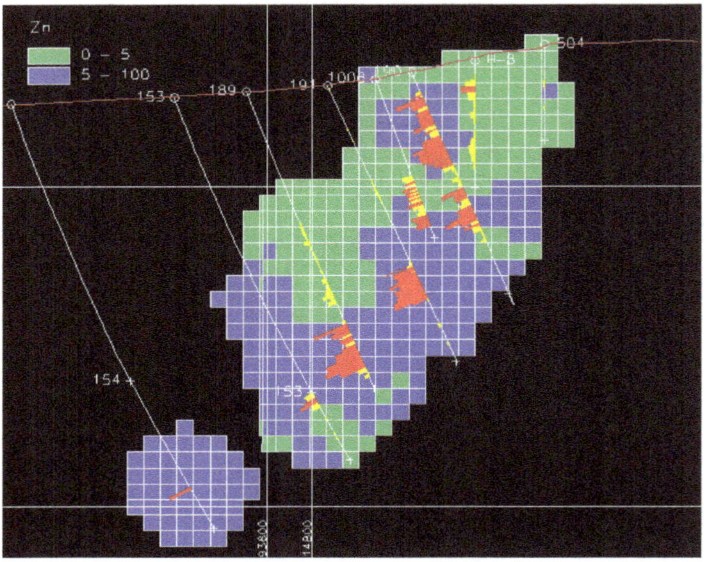

Figure 7.8. An initial unconfined estimation of the zinc grade variation from high-grade and low-grade ore samples is performed without geological control for subsequent comparison purposes. A 10×10×10 m grid data structure is employed. The above vertical view plane section displays the estimated zinc grade variation as a simple colour mapped display of green for values below 5% and blue for values above. The zinc samples relevant to the section are displayed in histogram format with yellow for values less than 5% and red for values above. As expected, the estimated variation exhibits high values in regions close to high sample values and vice versa. Reproduced with permission from EduMine.

with a mining engineer to get their opinion on likely mining dilution. There is also the constraint of mining recovery — part of the resource might be locked up in a shaft pillar, for example. If when the financial model is run with the other technical and financial variables and generates a positive NPV, the resource then becomes a reserve. This is not of course what is often reported — what might be described as a reserve by promoters is in fact a resource. A reality check is then needed.

Where a filter is imposed on a resource block model in which blocks with grades below a set cut-off are excluded from the global estimate, the characteristic set of grade–tonnage curves as indicated in Fig. 7.9 is generated. As resource blocks below the determined

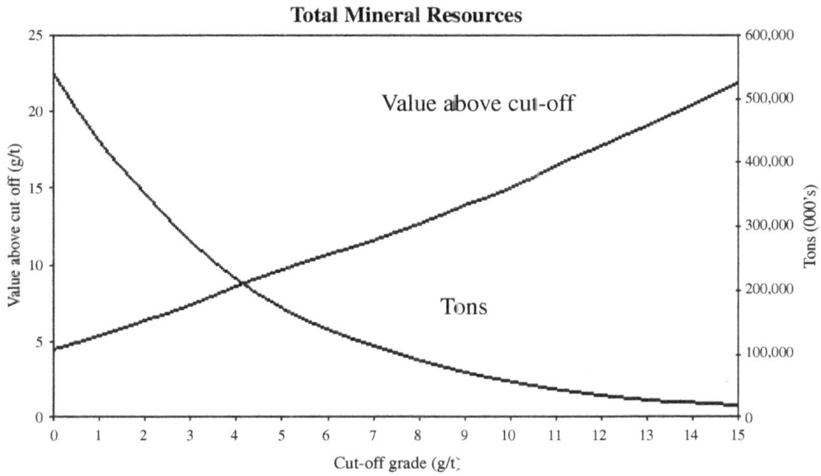

Figure 7.9. Grade–tonnage relationships.

cut-off are excluded from the resource estimate, the residual blocks will generate a higher overall grade, but there will of course be a corresponding reduction in the tonnage. The boundary condition for the cut-off grade in an underground mine would be the value where mining continuity is lost and the ore body breaks up into blocks that are no longer contiguous. In an open pit operation, where all mineralised material falling within the pit shell has to be excavated, there may be little advantage in attempting to extract preferentially the high grade zones within the deposit. Once de-coupled from the original resource block model used to estimate the *in situ* resource with kriged estimates of grade and associated uncertainty by putting in a cut-off boundary, you can no longer generate an uncertainty on the grade estimate of the residual blocks above the cut-off.

7.8 Reserve and Resource Definitions

The codes for reporting mineral resources (see Section 3.4) specify that the financial modelling should normally be confined to the Indicated and Measured categories. The results would provide a basis for a Preliminary Economic Assessment (PEA) or a Preliminary Feasibility Study (PFS) (see Section 8.3.1) which would be needed before a resource could be converted into a reserve, and then only if the exercise demonstrated that the deposit is capable of supporting a commercially viable operation. The results of trial mining should permit part of the resource to be classified as measured and therefore potentially a proved reserve.

If there is a component of inferred resource associated with a deposit (by definition, sample spacing is outside the range of the variogram), then further drilling could conceivably convert this to indicated and thereby allow a higher estimate of total metal/mineral content to be incorporated into the financial model. The wider the spacing, the fewer the holes needed.

There is therefore a direct correlation between expenditure on drilling and enhancing the valuation of the project. Considerable skill is needed to know when this in turn gives diminishing returns — adding to the indicated resource without simultaneously converting that to probable reserve is pointless.

Where evaluation drilling has resulted in the delineation of an indicated resource and where a PFS that includes a pre-funding discounted cash flow model has demonstrated economic viability, then considerable additional value may be added by converting any associated inferred resource into an indicated resource. Very often the inferred resource is much larger than the indicated at an early stage of the evaluation programme so a significant proportion of the potential value rests with the inferred resource. Provided there is transparency in the process a "what if?" scenario can be generated based on plausible assumptions on predicted grade, tonnage, capital and operating costs for a project with an expanded production capacity. The enhanced NPV that would often arise provides the justification for undertaking the additional evaluation drilling and can be a very convincing supporting narrative in an initial public offering.

7.9 Evaluation versus Production

There is a fundamental distinction between the point at which you get diminishing returns on drilling at the pre-development stage of a mineral project and grade control in an active mining operation.

Theoretically the financial performance indicators between the evaluation stage and re-running the original models with additional sampling should not be different. What is different is that on a day-to-day basis operating staff are making decisions on which benches are ore, waste or low-grade stockpile. The conclusion is that in making an investment decision, the promoters need to understand the production challenges involved in real mines.

We know from geostatistics that once drilling is in the range of the variogram and you have defined the nugget effect from close-spaced drilling in a selected representative area, "in-fill" drilling is not an intelligent use of money. The whole narrative around the Ivanhoe drilling and trial mining site focuses specifically on this issue. The photograph in Fig. 7.10 shows the three drilling rigs at 150 m spacing — agreed by their independent geostatistician.

Figure 7.10. Drill Spacing — Platreef Resources. The photograph shows three drilling rigs at 150 m spacing — agreed by their independent geostatistician, the qualified person under TSE regulations — which permitted them to "book" the resource as indicated.

The purpose of trial mining is to establish variability of grade on the scale of mining as well as to obtain bulk samples for detailed metallurgical test work. The minerals engineers (mining and processing) can only undertake detailed design studies on the back of this information. (Incidentally, the task of controlling trial mining must always be done by a mining geologist as detailed documentation of geological context is essential.) The resource reporting codes such as JORC, SAMREC, etc. were specifically set up for evaluation projects and in particular those seeking public funding through an IPO.

The role of the grade control people is to ensure that product specifications meet requirements. In Fig. 7.2 of an open pit, we see the close-spaced RC drilling. The challenges of blending through in-pit scheduling is discussed in Chapter 9. No end of confusion is caused by companies using the same JORC, SAMREC, etc. system of nomenclature in reporting their resources in their annual reports for their active mining operations.

Sampling "support" during mining far exceeds anything that we can expect to achieve at the evaluation stage and here there is a disconnect around evaluation versus operational grade control. Mining companies with active operations are well aware of this which is why in their annual reports they define their use of "probable" and "proved" reserves in terms of internal guidelines.

There was a sterile debate a decade ago when there was a move to incorporate the resource reporting in the annual financial reports with a value given to a reserve included as an asset on the Balance Sheet. This seemed to be the same meal ticket that consultants for the petroleum sector have in signing off annually Securities and Exchange Commission (SEC) reserve statements (see Section 4.6). It took an accountant to point out that if you used metal price in assigning a classification, then the proportion of the mineralisation allocated to a reserve could fluctuate year on year, creating wildly different tax obligations.

There is a lack of comprehensive guidance for mining companies under International Financial Reporting Standards (IFRS). The major issues relate to asset recognition and measurement in the treatment of reserves and resources. IFRS permits either historic cost or current value as a measurement basis for assets recognition. Historic cost is currently adopted by most mining companies since IFRS only permits use of current value if it can be measured reliably. The consequence of this is that the statement of financial position does not give a fair indication of the value of reserves and resources that the mining company has invested in. The alternative approach to asset recognition is based on a fair value measurement but this results in significant volatility in outcome as it is a function of metal price and operating costs. Historical cost is therefore the more appropriate method for asset measurement.

Chapter 8

Metals and Energy Project Appraisal and Finance

8.1 Introduction

The stages in the development of a mineral project are outlined in Chapter 3 and summarised in Table 8.1 against the corresponding supporting documentation that is needed. Different perspectives will arise around the timing of the stages of evolution from prospecting, say, six discovery holes drilled in the very early stages, funded with limited finance using venture capital, and the proposal to undertake evaluation drilling once more medium-term funding has been secured after an IPO. There would also be differences of opinion around the distinction between exploration and assessment drilling, but evaluation drilling should be seen within the context of defining the difference between "inferred" and "indicated", as determined by the range of the variogram in geostatistical modelling outlined in the previous chapter.

A preliminary feasibility study (PFS) must be based on evaluation drilling that has defined a resource at least up to the inferred category. A DCF requires the grade and tonnage of an indicated resource as the key input variables. The large resource, cited in some presentations, can only be determined after the evaluation drilling has been completed. A PFS and a full technical feasibility study are both based on the same resource estimation. Detailed conventional and financial engineering in the latter study will not generate a single additional ounce of precious metal or kilogram of base metal over that cited at the PFS stage (unless further drilling is undertaken).

Table 8.1. Nomenclature of documentation generated in mineral project development.

	Technical studies & contracts	Stock exchange requirements		Investment bank			
Stage	Format given by professional organisations	Toronto stock exchange	London stock exchange	Debt	Equity	Trading	Permits
Pre-IPO	Geological potential. Generated by competent or qualified person						Prospecting
Listing	JORC, SAMREC, etc. Codes, preliminary feasibility study. Generated by competent or qualified person	NI43-101 format technical report/ prospectus	AIM note for mining, oil and gas companies prospectus. role of NOMAD		Underwriting analyst reports		Exploration
Joint venture agreement	Due diligence based on data room. Geological potential. Generated by competent or qualified person				Preliminary information memorandum		Exploration
Funding	Full technical feasibility study. Front end engineering design. Environmental impact statement			Information memorandum, term sheet	Rights issue	Hedging strategy. Options	Mining
Construction start-up	Procurement, construction and management. Issued for tender/construction. Handover certificate			Construction monitoring, economic completion test. Production monitoring			Mining

For exploration companies, the best approach is to undertake the programme of work with funds being raised through venture capital funds or a private placement, as outlined in Chapter 3. This is not uncommon for early stage exploration and, of course, there would be no liquidity as changes in shareholding would be directly between two parties rather than exchange-based trading. As the exploration success allows the project to evolve, the original investors will want to take the company public. This process of bringing a project into production is inherently complex and promoters and investors get hopelessly confused about the interrelationships between the funding options and the stages in the technical evolution of their projects. Advisors add a veneer of mystique over the process to justify large fees. This chapter aims to provide a clear road map for the development of a mineral project, although the process is not that different for a petroleum project. AIM's guidelines incorporate mining, oil and gas companies in the same document.

8.2 Role of Stock Exchanges

There is a link between "liquidity" restrictions in selling shares in a natural resource company and what are classified as "Junior" or "Small Cap" and "Major". The argument is that once "Junior" shares are acquired by fund managers they would have difficulty disposing of a shareholding in these companies without there being a significant negative impact on share price (see Section 3.8). A more objective basis for considering liquidity would be the choice of stock exchange. Professionals understand that natural resource projects should be seen as part of the cycle from exploration through evaluation into pre-development, development and then production. Disposal of shares at the inflection points shown in Fig. 3.5 would be a perfectly rational decision to make, as there may well be a corresponding demand at that point.

The TSX is recognised as one of the leading natural resource markets and companies listed cover the whole spectrum from exploration through to production. It has a main listing for natural resource companies which, in general, share as a common feature projects that are in development and production.

The TSX Venture Exchange specialises in natural resource companies at the exploration stage and evaluation stage. Choice of listing is a decision the Board of Directors would take. Migration from the Venture Exchange to the main TSX would imply that projects are progressing toward the development stage. Failure to meet such market expectations would not help share price. Liquidity in the shares of a company is not related to size. An exploration company that has positive news flow would expect to see a rise in its share price and there would be a demand for these shares.

The share trading systems used by the TSX make no distinction between different categories of natural resource shares. The trading platform for the main market is exactly the same as that for the TSX Venture Exchange. Lack of liquidity will arise if market sentiment is depressed and sellers exceed buyers with the result that direct intervention by brokers may therefore take the place of online trading systems. Matching sellers with buyers in this type of market will obviously lower pricing and there may be a time delay before a sale is secured.

The main constraints on selling shares in an exploration company listed on the TSX Venture Exchange might occur where acquisition of the shares involved specific caveats against selling, such as when a director of the company has acquired a significant shareholding. The director would be expected to demonstrate confidence in the future of the company and maintain the holding regardless of the vicissitudes of the market.

The front page of a Preliminary Prospectus for an Initial Public Offering (IPO) of shares in a company to be listed on a major exchange with an advanced project in which evaluation drilling has been completed typically provides the following information:

[Blank] COMMON SHARES

[Blank] $ PER COMMON SHARE

The prospectus does not include the price of the share or the number of shares to be issued. In some circumstances, the prospectus itself does not go into the public domain in a timely manner let alone provide details of the share price. In these circumstances, the term prospectus is a misnomer — it does not offer a prospect of the future but simply a record of what has passed. It is published to obtain an indication of interest among potential investors in the new company. The preliminary feedback will then be used by the issuer (normally the underwriter, usually an investment bank) to price the new securities which is the reason the price and number of shares offered are not disclosed at this stage. Marketing strategy comes into play and the advisors would want to secure the support of a specialist commodity fund who would provide a cornerstone stake. They would be in a position to negotiate a favourable valuation that would be reflected in more shares at the proposed share price or offer a discount to the proposed share price for a fixed number of shares.

As outlined in Section 3.8.2, the issuer would then move on to the next fund manager intimating that a reputable mining fund is taking up, say, 20% in the IPO; this is a common approach in the private placement book building process. If there is a strong indication of interest, the price of the shares will be set higher and number of shares offered reduced. This would have less dilution impact for the original shareholders and project promoters.

Concerns have been expressed at the lack of clarity associated with the IPO process and as a consequence the UK's Financial Conduct Authority requires that the London Stock Exchange release the prospectus for an IPO in a timely fashion and place a valuation on the assets well ahead of the start of trading. The prospectus should also be available ahead of trading, but you do need to be close to the advisors. Timing can be very tight (just a day or two) between release of the prospectus and the start of trading. Technical reports are downloadable from company webpages but often not the original prospectus. To obtain this for TSX-list companies, it is often necessary to get onto the system for Electronic Document Analysis and Retrieval (SEDAR®) which is a filing system developed for the Canadian Securities Administrators.

An integral part of the prospectus will be the technical report outlining the features of the project. The TSX requirements are outlined in the Canadian National Instrument 43-101 — Standards of Disclosure for Mineral Projects, specifically referred to as Form 43-101F1 Technical Report and the role of the Qualified Person. This is now widely used as a template for minerals-related technical reports and is a codified set of rules and guidelines for reporting and displaying information relating to mineral properties of companies listed on Canadian stock exchanges. The technical report incorporates the following:

TITLE
CONTENTS OF THE TECHNICAL REPORT

Title Page
Date and Signature Page
Table of Contents
Illustrations
Item 1: Summary
Item 2: Introduction
Item 3: Reliance on Other Experts
Item 4: Property Description and Location
Item 5: Accessibility, Climate, Local Resources, Infrastructure and Physiography
Item 6: History
Item 7: Geological Setting and Mineralisation
Item 8: Deposit Types
Item 9: Exploration
Item 10: Drilling
Item 11: Sample Preparation, Analyses and Security
Item 12: Data Verification
Item 13: Mineral Processing and Metallurgical Testing
Item 14: Mineral Resource Estimates
Item 15: Mineral Reserve Estimates
Item 16: Mining Methods
Item 17: Recovery Methods
Item 18: Project Infrastructure
Item 19: Market Studies and Contracts

Item 20: Environmental Studies, Permitting and Social or Community Impact
Item 21: Capital and Operating Costs
Item 22: Economic Analysis
Item 23: Adjacent Properties
Item 24: Other Relevant Data and Information
Item 25: Interpretation and Conclusions
Item 26: Recommendations
Item 27: References

It is not unusual for a report to have the statement "This page has been deliberately left blank" under headings 13, 16 and 17 as notwithstanding the impressive scope of work implied by the contents page, the project may not have advanced much beyond the preliminary drilling phase. The obvious bias toward the resource estimation process and related geological models compared to the minerals engineering aspects is a legacy of the Bre-X fiasco. While the NI 43-101 format tends to be used as a convenient template for technical reports generated in support of an IPO regardless of whether or not the funds are to be raised on the TSX, this is not a requirement for markets such as AIM or the ASX.

The technical report needs to be prepared by or under the supervision of a Qualified Person (QP) who is an engineer or geoscientist with appropriate qualifications that include:

- At least 5 years of relevant engineering or geosciences experience
- Experience relevant to the mineral project
- Being a member (e.g. CPEng) in good standing with an acceptable professional self-regulatory association.

For an IPO, the technical report must be prepared by or under the supervision of a QP who is independent of the issuer. In regard to information disclosed relating to mineral reserves and mineral resources, it must use definitions i.e. a resource classification system set out in definitions standards approved by the Canadian Institute of Mining, Metallurgy & Petroleum Council (CIM).

8.3 Preliminary Feasibility Study

8.3.1 *Elements and characteristics*

An IPO prospectus must include a NI 43-101 Technical Report, which may include a substantial amount of the material information in a Preliminary Economic Assessment (PEA) or Pre-Feasibility Study (PFS). A full technical feasibility study (FS) may not be required if the funds are used for further evaluation drilling and exploration where, for example, the objective is to convert an inferred resource to an indicated.

A successful IPO will be expedited if the project has advanced to the point where an indicated resource has been delineated. This permits a PEA or a PFS to be undertaken. This usually takes around six months to complete and should cost in the range of \$250–\$500 K. It cannot be used for major programmes of capital expenditure and is not acceptable to banks for debt finance. For good projects, capital and operating cost estimates on an initial conceptual project design need not be more accurate than ±20%.

In addition to the resource estimation, the technical components of a PFS should also include the results of process mineralogical studies and metallurgical test work. Post Bre-X (see Chapters 3 and 7), the process mineralogical study is essential. A pre-funding DCF model should form part of a PFS which would include tax and royalty provisions. It would always be an advantage if as part of the exploration phase an environmental baseline study had been completed (Chapter 4). A PFS should normally be undertaken by an interdisciplinary team where good cross-communication is present. A range of different scenarios can be considered (as outlined below) and provides the basis for directors to conclude whether or not they should proceed with a project. A PFS also provides the baseline against which future investment decisions are made. It helps identify where further expenditure would add most value and often this shows up the need to add to the resource base.

8.3.2 *Cost estimation*

Estimation of costs is required at the PFS stage after ore reserves are determined, but before major capital is committed. At this stage, there is insufficient technical knowledge available for accurate estimation of costs. Estimates are based on calculated average costs of existing mine projects and ±20% accuracy will suffice.

There are two types of cost: capital costs (Capex) which are costs in a particular year that will produce benefits in later years, and operating costs (OpCosts) which are costs which only produce benefit for that year. The relationship between cost and capacity is given in Fig. 8.1. Capex increases with increased capacity but OpCosts generally decrease with increased capacity due to the economies of scale.

Even at the PFS stage, estimating costs do offer challenges. A starting point might be to use an analogue but there are online mining cost estimating systems such as CostMine available at: http://costs.infomine.com/.

Once a scenario is costed, then flexing of costs can be achieved by using the following empirical formula:

Cost 1 Cost 2 = Capacity 2 Capacity 10.6.

$$\frac{\text{Cost 1}}{\text{Cost 2}} = \frac{\text{Capacity 2}}{\text{Capacity 1}}^{0.6}.$$

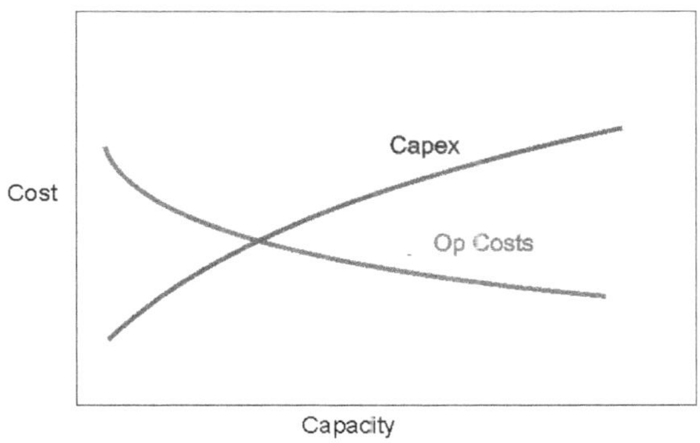

Figure 8.1. Relationship between cost and capacity.

For a base case mining operation with a production of 0.94 Mt/annum which is rampedup to the target that the mine feels they can achieve of 2.5 Mt, this then permits a commensurate reduction in OpCosts. If in the base case, it is given as $44/tonne run-of-mine, then the formula predicts a revised cost of $24.58/tonne run-of-mine. The approach was formalised by O'Hara (1980). It was developed based on the data gathered in Canada and provides a crude guide to capital costs of underground and open pit mines as well as operating costs of open pit, blast hole mining, cut-and-fill mining, shrinkage mining and room and pillar.

An example of the approach needed for more detailed cost estimates is given in Section 9.4.4.

8.3.3 *Asset optimisation*

A PFS and a FTFS play key roles in defining the transition from an indicated resource to a probable reserve, and form an integral part of the process of applying the codes for reporting mineral resources as discussed in Chapter 3. The most important difference between a PFS and a FTFS is that as there is more flexibility associated with constraining technical variables in a pre-feasibility study, it is much easier to undertake scenario analysis. This permits optimisation of an asset and therefore the NPV using a simple financial model based on a fixed discount rate. The size of a mining project can then be constrained by the time value of money, the choice of cut-off grade on reserve block models, and the impact of operating and Capex arising from economies of scale. This is demonstrated in Fig. 8.2.

The rate of production for very long life assets may be scaled up, thereby reducing OpCosts and allowing lower grade ore to be exploited. Conversely there will be a boundary condition when increasing the cut-off grade becomes self-defeating as mining continuity is lost.

Once the deterministic "sweet spot" has been selected based on a fixed metal price, then a MC simulation as outlined in Section 2.4 based on grade, plant recovery, operating and Capex would generate a probabilistic distribution of NPV that provides a more realistic

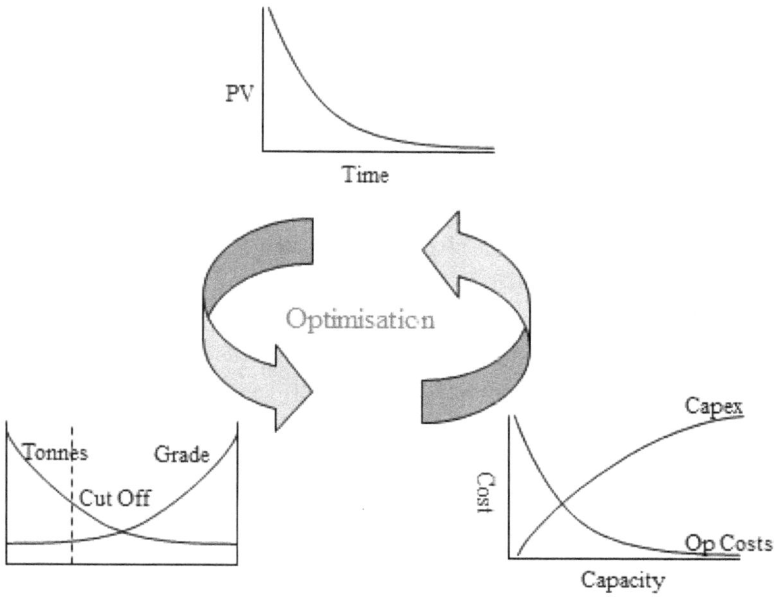

Figure 8.2. Size of a mining project is constrained by the time value of money, the choice of cut-off grade on reserve block models, and the impact of operating and Capex arising from economies of scale.

perspective of the robustness of the project. Changing metal price may allow the project to be re-optimised as, for example, open-pit design and the capital-to-operating-cost mix maybe revisited. Capital has to be spent on open-pit push back to provide access to deeper ore or the investment made in going from open pit to an underground operation.

Volatility in prices can cause difficulty in establishing a stable operating cost and capital cost mix at the PFS stage. The technique of ROV discussed in Sections 4.8 and 11.3 demonstrates how price volatility can be formally modelled using the principles of quantitative finance. Simply flexing price is a pointless exercise as it generates self-fulfilling outcomes.

Cut-off grade is far more likely to be determined by geological conditions and mining methods than what happens on the London Metal Exchange (LME) or currency markets. Reducing cut-off grade in a copper mine with the ore body coincident with the envelope of mineralisation (which is the case for most big porphyry deposits) does not "create" more copper.

8.4 Joint Venture

It can be a challenge for the Junior to secure the interests of a Major to enter into a JV and the investment banks can play a role by generating a Preliminary Information Memorandum. This includes due diligence on the legal and financial standing of a company. It incorporates description of licences and outlines the structure of local JVs. It also incorporates a technical report prepared by the Junior or independent consultant.

The structure of a JV is given in Section 3.8.4. In addition to the legal agreement that will be entered into, there has to be a process of due diligence: the guidelines are given in Section 4.3.

8.5 Feasibility Studies

8.5.1 *Introduction*

If a mineral deposit is classified as a reserve, then independent technical and financial studies must have been undertaken and have demonstrated that the deposit can support a commercially viable operation. Such a "Feasibility Study" under paragraph 40 of the JORC code is defined as:

> *a comprehensive technical and economic study of the selected development option for a mineral project that includes appropriately detailed assessments of applicable Modifying Factors together with any other relevant operational factors and detailed financial analysis that are necessary to demonstrate at the time of reporting that extraction is reasonably justified (economically mineable). The results of the study may reasonably serve as the basis for a final decision by a proponent or financial institution to proceed with, or finance, the development of the project.*

Feasible simply means possible, but a feasibility study (according to the *Collins Concise Dictionary*) is a study designed to determine the practicability of a system or plan. The technical guidelines for the term are therefore consistent with common usage.

For an engineer who has spent time with a nationalised industry, the connotation behind the term feasibility is to determine if mining is technically possible and that revenue generated covers OpCosts. The justification for the capital investment in the equipment needed for the task would not necessarily have been part of the remit. Honest differences in perspective then occur much to the frustration of operating staff who feel that mine development is being restricted by the business and finance divisions. Even when mine planning does take into account the need for return on investment in equipment, pre-production, underground development or pre-stripping in an open pit, the choice of discount rate in a financial model is often jealously preserved by the business and finance divisions who set the corporate cost of capital. The company's treasury department will usually calculate its WACC, which should be used for ALL projects that are financed by group funds (i.e. those not subject to non-recourse project financing). The WACC should not be adjusted for specific project risk if financed by group funds: project-specific risk should be handled by risking project cash flows instead.

To add to the semantic confusion, a company commissioning a "Feasibility Study" from a group of consulting engineers at a cost of up to a million dollars will not be best pleased if the conclusion is that the project is not feasible. Furthermore, there is a range of different types of engineering studies used in the industry and these are outlined below. This approach to conventional engineering needs to be seen within the context of the funding options available to the promoters that include a combination of debt and equity.

Any investment in a mining system needs to generate a revenue stream that not only covers the cost of extraction, but also a return that exceeds the discount rate selected. Based on these criteria (where the quantitative approach generates an IRR less than the discount rate), it must be concluded that it would not be feasible to proceed with the investment as mining is not a commercially viable option.

8.5.2 *Elements and characteristics*

An FTFS would typically take around 12 months to complete at a cost of around $1 million. The co-ordinating director would want to mobilise the advisory investment bankers, who, in turn, would want to alert their independent engineers. Estimates of the grade and tonnage used in an FTFS may well be derived from the same database used in a PFS. An FTFS would aim to undertake estimates of capital and operating costs and revenues to within an accuracy of $\pm 10\%$ and reduce other feasibility risks to low levels. In undertaking financial modelling, it would be prudent to base Capex assumptions on the estimate plus ten percent. This should not be confused with a provision for contingency, which should be a provision for the truly unexpected and unforeseen. To assign more than five percent to contingency will have a significant impact on NPV, as provision will need to be made for this cost in the capital structure. Essentially, it is only after construction is completed that the true cost of the project will be known.

Where a project under construction has to make an announcement that capital costs have been underestimated and that initial production would also be delayed by six months, this would have a dramatic impact on share price due to the dual negative effects. Not only would additional capital need to be raised for the project to be completed, but any delay also has a disproportionate effect on NPV, given the way in which DCF models work, with present value factors having the most impact at the start of the project life. Although the project cannot now achieve the performance indicators on which the original decision to develop it was made, there are clear incentives for existing stakeholders and shareholders to provide the necessary additional funding to bring the operation into production. If this is not possible, then the bank might foreclose on the promoters and invite new equity investors to provide fresh capital. The revised performance indicators could be attractive given that, from the perspective of a fresh scenario where significant progress was made, the construction time will have been reduced.

Detailed conventional engineering cannot create metal that was not formed from natural geological processes. Given that once sampling from surface drilling is within the range of the variogram, it may well be concluded that additional geological information on the scale of mining is needed. This provides justification for undertaking a programme of trial mining, which would normally be under the control of a mining geologist, as sampling should be undertaken in conjunction with meticulous mapping. This provides constraints on the approach to bulk sampling that can then be used for pilot plant treatment.

8.5.3 *Engineering design stages*

Given that a FTFS would seldom conclude the project is not feasible, it should be considered as essentially a framework for the engineering at the "procurement, construction and management" contract (EPC&M) phase or a "lump sum turnkey" contract. While the FTFS is likely to be associated with a pre-funding DCF model, this offers no guarantee that a project is commercially viable. The capital cost estimates will, however, provide the basis for determining the amount of capital needed for construction (both debt and equity).

For large projects seeking debt (also referred to as project finance), the loan will be repaid from cash flows generated by the project. Where there is no recourse or only limited recourse, then there are no tangible assets until the operation is in production. Banks are exposed to risk and will take a conservative view. Major mining companies have production experience not readily available to a Junior and a proven track record is a big advantage in securing both debt and equity finance.

The document the bank will generate is the Information Memorandum which outlines the terms of the loan. Protection will be sought against falls in metal prices and a hedging programme outlined. The presence of a hedging programme would of course limit the benefit for the company in the event of a significant increase in metal price. So a balance must be struck. The amount of metal hedged tends to be limited to no more than 40% of total production. The FTFS will be incorporated into the Information Memorandum as an appendix which is never described by investment banks as a

"Bankable Study" and when the term is used by a Junior, it does not inspire confidence.

Project finance allows further optimisation of NPV through gearing and the influence of WACC (see Chapter 3).

Actual construction requires the completion of front end engineering design (FEED). While this process could extend from 24 to 36 months and cost in excess of $10 million, it may well overlap with the start of construction. The construction phase involves the following contractual certificates:

- Issued for tender (IFT)
- Issued for construction (IFC) drawings/deviation to be authorised by client
- Handover certificate.

Even for a well-managed construction project, final Capex is unlikely to be better than within ±10% of the original estimates. This intrinsic uncertainty needs to be reconciled with provision for contingency in determining funding needs. Contingency should be used to cover unexpected circumstances and not the inherent uncertainty of the original capital cost estimates.

Construction monitoring will be undertaken by independent engineers who will report progress to the lenders based on management systems such as MS Project © used by the engineers implementing the EPC&M contract. These systems will be used to report actual costs to the lender. Banks must be aware of any cost overruns and ensure that the money provided by the lenders is spent according to the development plan. The bank's independent engineers therefore have the important responsibility of highlighting the potential for any overrun in time and cost.

After construction has been completed and the project commissioned, the bank's independent engineers will undertake the mechanical completion or economic completion test. This confirms that the project has been built as specified in the loan agreement and is capable of performing according to the development plan.

Once the project is in operation, the production monitoring will be undertaken by the bank's independent engineers to verify the ramp-up in production and OpCosts, and report progress to the lenders. If performance and OpCosts reconcile with those predicted in the original FTFS, then the corporate guarantees to the bank providing project finance may fall away and the lending goes non-recourse. Anecdotal evidence suggests that this reconciliation is achieved in around only half of new mining projects.

8.6 Project Finance Parameters

Input information is required to set up the financing structure of the project including the amount of debt and equity, interest rate and repayment schedule. This will include the following:

- *Capital structure.* The debt/equity ratio and the size of debt will be decided by the lender. It can be expressed as a percentage of the total financing requirements that will be funded as debt. The optimum draw-down period for the debt funding will be agreed between the project sponsor and the lender, and may be drawn out over as long as the first 5 years of the project.
- *Loan type and repayment schedule.* The schedule for loan repayment needs to be established in order to complete the cash flow model. The number and size of loan repayments will be negotiated between the lender and sponsor, as will the grace period, if any, before repayments must commence. Loan repayments can be made in equal instalments (straight loan) or made proportional to the production rate (production loan). There will be other cash flows associated with organising the project finance that must also be included in the early years of the model. These include an upfront fee by the bank for arranging the loan (a percentage of the total loan available), a commitment fee (an annual fee charged on the amount of the loan that has not been used), fixed charges (for agents' fees, legal documentation, independent reports, etc.) and contingency to act as a cushion against unexpected cost rises, etc. (a percentage of the total required funding).
- *Loan interest rate.* This is the annual rate of interest on the debt as set by the lender.

- *Return on equity*. This is the annual expected return on equity invested as funds. It can be calculated by a variety of methods including the CAPM and is often linked to the overall company gearing of the project sponsor.

IC-MinEval has a "Funding" tool which uses Goal Seek (an Excel© tool) that searches for a value which satisfies the conditions defined in the above scenario.

There are three types of financial ratios used in project finance, all of which analyse the project cash flow. These can be split into:

Annual cover ratios

- Interest cover ratio (available cash flow/interest rate)
- Principal cover ratio (available cash flow/principal) or (available cash flow − interest payment)/principal payment, or
- Debt service cover ratio (available cash flow − debt service)/debt service.

Present value (PV) cover ratios

- Loan life ratio (LLR). NPV of cash flows after funding during loan period, discounted by the interest rate, or
- Project life ratio (PLR). NPV of cash flows after funding during entire project, discounted by the interest rate.

The difference between LLR and PLR is a measure of the residual cash flow cover.

Overall ratios

- Debt: equity ratio projects with high market risk, typically 50:50 or 60:40, those with lower risk 75:25, or
- Residual cover PV of post-loan maturity cash flows/maximum loan.

As the only tangible asset is the unmined ore, the repayment schedule would be structured such that after the loan has been repaid there would be residual mineralisation, normally at least 30% of the original resource. This is known as the reserve tail. Before an investment bank provides project finance, they therefore need to convince themselves that the promoter of the project not only understands mining but has the human resources to manage production and implement grade control and metal reconciliation systems, particularly when dealing with heterogeneity in the ore body. This requires *esprit de corps*, experience, and dedication by the production team.

The application of these performance indicators is covered in Section 11.5.

8.7 Smelter Agreements

Processing at a base metal mine involves liberation and concentration and is always part of the ore extraction process. Often there is no conversion to metal end use which requires hydro- and pyrometallurgical chemical techniques. The process routes for metalliferous ores is given in Fig. 9.12. There is a boundary condition between physical processing in the plant and the pyro- and hydrometallurgical processing that is needed in order to extract metals from minerals. A smelting operation may be a separate business unit and analogous to the down-stream processing of petroleum products in the oil industry. It is only after smelting and refining that metals such as zinc and lead are produced in their pure elemental state so that revenue can be directly linked to market spot prices.

Nyrstar N.V. is a mining and metals business that specialises in zinc with mining, smelting, and other operations located in Europe, the Americas, China and Australia. Their business strategy was based on concentrate from their own mining operations being sent either to their own metals processing facility or sold on directly into the market. The company also sourced concentrate for metals processing from third party mines which permits flexibility. In 2014, 278 Kt of zinc in concentrate was produced from their own mines but almost four times that amount of zinc metal (1,097 Kt) was produced from their metal processing facilities.

Boliden has a similar business plan where concentrate from Tara, together with concentrate from other sources, is sent to smelters in Norway and Finland.

Smelters enter into two main types of agreements with suppliers of concentrate:

- Off-take Agreements — the supplier sells the concentrate to the smelter.
- Toll Smelting — the smelter processes the concentrate on behalf of the supplier. For toll smelting, there is a treatment charge, refinery charge (TC/RC) and price participation (PP). The implementation of PP allows the smelter to adjust the RC depending on changes in the spot price of the metal.

There is a narrative around the difference between toll smelting and net smelter return (NSR) and this is based on off-take agreements. A base metal mine would not expect to receive much more than 60% of spot price for the metals contained in the concentrate. There would also be penalties for impurities and moisture.

Both off-take and toll smelting agreements result from negotiation between the mine producing concentrate and the smelter and can be quite complex; parties would normally be reluctant to disclose details. This is understandable as the agreements are normally confidential documents. The typical off-take agreement may incorporate the level of detail given in Table 8.2.

Table 8.2. Smelter off-take agreements sample for a zinc lead project.

Zinc concentrate	Lead concentrate
Zn metal paid 85% Zinc smelters typically pay for 85% of the zinc contained in zinc concentrates (typically 54% Zn) valued at LME price averaged over the quotation period (QP) In addition, zinc smelters will pay for Ag content in concentrate if it exceeds certain threshold	Pb metal paid 95% Lead smelters typically pay for 95% of the lead contained in the lead concentrate (typically 60% Pb) valued at LME price averaged over QP In addition, lead smelter will pay for Ag, Au, Cu and Zn content in concentrate if it exceeds certain thresholds
Deductions Treatment charges Penalties and/or allowances Penalties depend on quality of concentrate, e.g. where the material contains impurities above the set thresholds the smelter is compensated	

Spot price has only a tenuous link to NSR. To have a perfect correlation assumes that TR, TC, penalties, PP mechanisms and delivery costs all remain static with the only variable being metal price. This is the way a spreadsheet might work but it is not how a real off-take agreement operates. At the very least, the price participation mechanism would generate quite unpredictable outcomes.

An example of how net revenue is determined in a base metal mine with a production of 1.3 million tonnes of ore per annum which produces two concentrate streams, one zinc and one lead is illustrated below. The silver reports to the lead concentrate and the mine has entered into an agreement with a smelter to undertake toll smelting. Key variables are given in Table 8.3.

The annual net revenue for each of the product streams is given in Table 8.4 as well as the NSR for the zinc and lead streams.

There is a strong incentive for the mine to incorporate into the plant design provision to recover the silver directly using lixiviation hydrometallurgical techniques such as the Merrill Crowe process. This is considered in Appendix B (Extended Case Study of the development of satellite deposits).

8.8 Case Histories

8.8.1 *Coal washing plant optimisation*

The major advantage of setting up a financial model of a coal project is that an alternative to where potentially all of the material mined

Table 8.3. Example of the application of the terms of an off-take agreement.

Metal	Head grade	Plant recovery	Spot price	Price participation	Treatment charges per tonne of metal	Penalty per tonne of metal
Zinc	14%	90%	\$2,000/tonne	90% of spot	\$300	\$50
Lead	3%	90%	\$1,000/tonne	80% of spot	\$200	\$70
Silver	60 grams per tonne	60%	\$10/ounce (one ounce = 31 grams)	50% of spot	zero	0

Table 8.4. Revenue distribution derived from the variables given in Table 8.3.

Smelter return values		Zinc	Pb	Ag
Ore mined tonnes per annum	830,000			
Head grade		1.80%	1.30%	
Plant recovery		90%	90%	
Zn produced tonnes		13,446	9,711	
Spot price $/tonne		$2,750	$2,500	
Paid under price participation		90%	80%	
Revenue per tonne		$2,475	$2,000	
Treatment charges per tonne of metal		$300	$200	
Penalty per tonne of metal		$50	$70	
Net revenue per tonne		$2,125	$1,730	
Net smelter return		77%	69%	
Annual revenue		$28,572,750	$16,800,030	
Head grade Ag grade grams per tonne				460
Ag content ozs/tonne				14.84
Plant recovery				80%
Ag produced (ounces)				9,852,903
Spot price $/oz				$20
Paid under price participation				70%
Revenue				$137,940,645
Total		$183,313,425		

is the product and so the run-of-mine "grade" would be 100% can be considered. Downstream processing can be designed to produce different product streams and a financial model is needed to optimise coal yields.

For example, an open-pit coal mine with a capacity of 200,000 tonnes mixed quality coal per annum might have a resource that has an estimated quality of 70% steam grade and 30% coking grade (also known as practical yields, see Section 6.4). If the first stage pre-treatment processing plant wash recovery is 70%, the cost of mining coal is $8.00/tonne, the cost of mining waste is $2.00/tonne and the stripping ratio of coal:waste is 1:6, the total cost of mining one tonne of coal would be $20.00 per month.

If the OpCosts for the first stage pre-treatment processing plant wash are $5.00/tonne, the additional costs of producing separate streams of steam and coking grade coal are $2.00/tonne and $5.00/tonne respectively in the downstream processing. Assuming 100% recovery, the overall processing costs per month are $210,000 and $196,000, respectively.

Based on price per tonne of steam coal of $50.00 and that of coking coal of $120.00, then the overall operating margin is $4,534,000 per month. If tests showed that when the first stage pre-treatment processing plant was operated such that only steam coal was produced then wash recovery would increase to 90%, and the potential operating margin drops to $3,640,000 per month. Running the plant to produce premium coking coal therefore improves the potential operating margin, notwithstanding the lower pre-treatment wash recovery, compared to producing only steam coal.

As the price of the different product streams changes, so will the need to adjust the product mix. Given that the market for coal is extremely complex, multiple scenarios may need to be modelled and the processing plant designed to allow the necessary flexibility.

A typical coal mine may have a dozen different product streams and balancing recovery with price to optimise performance in a coal washing plant is not a trivial task and impossible without a financial model.

One of the fundamental constraints on establishing a viable business in any mining operation that produces a low-value bulk commodity such as coal or iron ore is that the only way you can generate a material investment return for a holding company is through volume. AngloCoal's Zibulo Colliery room-and-pillar underground operation and their Landau open pit are both producing plus 3 million tonnes of coal per annum.

Operators get confused between an operating margin based purely on cash flow and return on investment. The moment any attempt is made to justify a significant capital investment in mining equipment the investment in terms of NPV cannot be supported. To make an investment in a processing plant would require reserves that would sustain at least 15 years of operation.

8.8.2 *Iron ore and steel production*

The processing of iron ore to produce steel involves the basics of reduction reactions. While this is mainly focused on blast furnaces in which coking coal is used as a reductant, there is now interest in the use of hydrogen as a reductant and direct reduction in terms of the future direction of the iron industry. The commercial impact of new technology applied (at an industrial scale) to the CO_2-free reduction of metal oxides to pure metals is being assessed. This is relevant to the energy transition and decarbonisation of natural resource industries. The final product is sponge ore, which is still only the precursor to steel manufacture. Essentially, it is the equivalent of scrap iron.

The basic mineralogical characteristics of iron ore are described in Section 5.9.2 with magnetite and haematite being the most common. The price of iron ore is quoted as "US cents per dry metric tonne unit (dmtu) × iron content". At a price of 80 cents dmtu and for a product containing 64% (the iron content of pure haematite is 69.94%, see Section 5.9.2), this would give a price per tonne of ore of $51.20/tonne. Magnetite based on stoichiometry has a higher iron content than haematite and in dmtu terms is therefore worth more per tonne than haematite.

The primary ore at LKAB's Kiruna iron ore operation in Sweden is magnetite, as is the by-product of copper mining at Palabora in South Africa. As both operations exploit deposits that are associated with the mineral-bearing phosphate apatite $Ca_5(PO_4)_3(OH,F,Cl)$ and given that phosphorus reduces the toughness of steel, it needs to be removed after grinding from the magnetite concentrate. While part of the process of producing a copper concentrate at Palabora, this detracts from the requirement of steel makers that the feed to their furnace should be lumpy not fines. The medium grade is sold as a dense medium separation product (used mainly in coal processing plants) and the coarse grade is sold as a blend feed to iron and steelmaking customers. Kiruna pelletise their fine-grained magnetite production using a rotary kiln with energy derived in part from the exothermic reaction of magnetite to haematite as follows:

$$4\,\mathrm{Fe_3O_4} + \mathrm{O_2} = 6\,\mathrm{Fe_2O_3}.$$

$$\Delta H_{OX} = -122 \text{ kJ/mol}.$$

While on a dmtu basis, the product has been degraded, pellets command a premium price over fines so value has been added.

As is the case with GREENIRON, Kiruna has also established a pilot plant designed to produce sponge iron in which the reverse (reduction) thermodynamic process, compared to the current (oxidation) method, is being tested. The precursor magnetite ($FeO.Fe_2O_3$) with a stoichiometric Fe content of 72% is reduced in a hydrogen environment to produce Fe° sponge, with an iron content of 94% and water being the by-product. This provides a massive price premium over the current product — fully oxidised iron pellets (Fe_2O_3) with a probable stoichiometric Fe content of 70% — while reducing CO_2 emissions. If sources of energy for sponge iron become hydroelectric, then LKAB will be at the cutting edge of "green" mining.

Setting up a financial model of an iron ore project conceptually involves the same approach as that used in a coal project (see Section 6.5). As can be seen in Fig. 8.3, dilution is inevitable during mining but there will be fixed mining costs.

Offsetting that are very stringent specifications established by the steel producers with penalties for SiO_2, Al_2O_3 and P. The maximum P content can be as low as 0.04%. As a consequence, iron ore operations need to implement a sophisticated grade control system starting from block modelling, in-pit blending and optimisation of plant recovery.

This would generate the revenue profile indicated in Fig. 8.4. In this scenario, there is a penalty for ore with an iron content that drops below 62.5% and ore below 60% is not accepted. To optimise performance in the plant, the recovery curves (Fig. 8.4) also need to be considered. The distribution of NPV based on a nominal capital expenditure for a push-back in an open pit is given in Fig. 8.5. This also takes into account not only the cost of capital, stripping ratios and mining dilution as well as the impact of penalties, notably phosphorus, but also the 62.5% boundary condition and the 60%

Figure 8.3. View of a working face at the Sishen mine in South Africa showing the outline of potential mining blocks. The dark brown horizon is high-grade haematite and the grey is quartz-rich BIF. The block on the left will include 50% dilution, that on the right 5%.

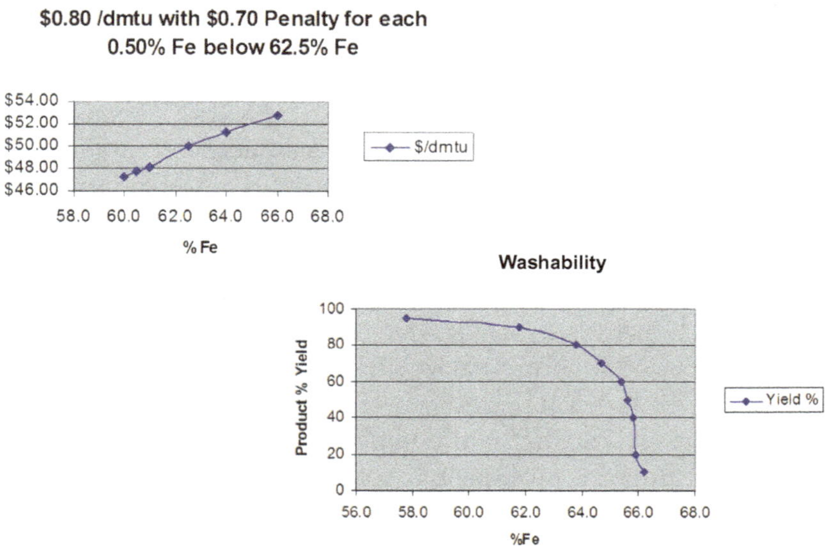

Figure 8.4. Iron ore revenue assumptions −6 to +1 mm Sishen ore recovery curves.

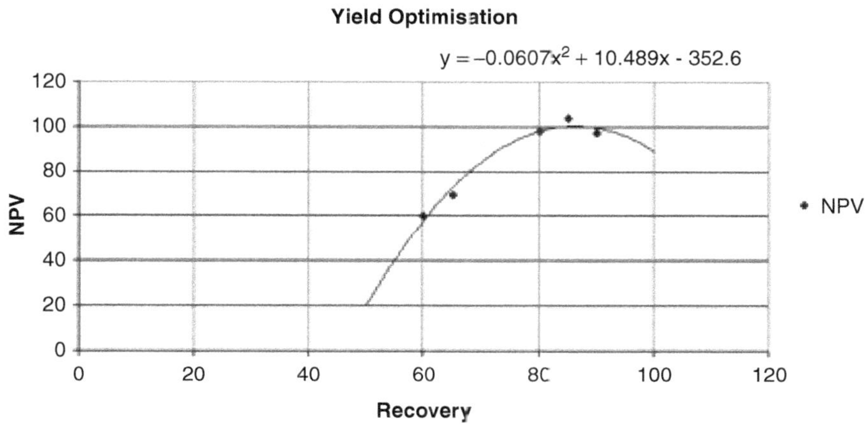

Figure 8.5. Yield optimisation curve derived from Fig. 8.4.

limit. There is also a separate issue around differential pricing of fines versus lumpy.

Optimum NPV is derived from a recovery of 85% which predicts a grade of 62.5% iron in the product. This is just on the penalty limit which is probably not coincidental.

The common quotation of iron ore per tonne is normally with reference to 64% iron. There is an analogue with the oil price which is based on West Texas Intermediate (see Section 4.7.2). Only a small proportion of oil trade includes this price benchmark. The reference price of 64% iron may not reflect the bulk of iron ore traded. As iron ore prices fluctuate, producers would adjust their operating conditions but these would need to be based on yield optimisation curves. The 64% benchmark may well be adjusted upwards under pressure from major consumers such as Chinese smelters concerned about environmental constraints. This will then impact on iron ore production cost models.

As is the case for coal, the commercial viability of developing an iron ore project depends on the availability of infrastructure. The dedicated Sishen rail system comprises 861 km of line. Each consignment comprises 216 × 100 tonne wagons/train with a travelling time in one direction of 18 hours. The port at Saldanha can handle 30 Mt per annum. Alternatives have been considered such as slurry pumping, particularly when magnetite-bearing ore has to be crushed and ground as part of a liberation process or where it is a by-product.

The primary ore at LKAB's Kiruna iron ore operation in Sweden is magnetite, as is the by-product of copper mining at Palabora in South Africa. Magnetite based on stoichiometry has a higher iron content than haematite and in dmtu terms is therefore worth more per tonne than haematite.

The magnetite associated with layered mafic intrusions is normally intergrown with ilmenite and has ulvospinel exsolved on the octahedral plane so is useless for steel production. It is, however, a source of vanadium (see Section 5.9.2).

LKAB produces magnetite from skarn and undertakes an oxidation stage on the fines and sintering that locks in a thermodynamic, and therefore pricing, advantage. Apatite $Ca_5(PO_4)_3(OH,F,Cl)$ has to be removed using flotation and the same occurs at Palabora which exports magnetite fines to China. In 2013, magnetite was as important a source of revenue at Palabora as copper. Industrial Development Corporation are investing in a pyrometallurgical process to produce metallic iron on site to enhance value.

The rare earth element (REE) resource associated with the Kiruna iron–apatite mineralisation is highly topical. The proposed extractive metallurgy strategy involves integrating the production of a REE oxide product with the existing magnetite-apatite product stream. Producing commercial levels of REEs implies that significant volumes of phosphoric acid by-product would be generated. Kiruna could then become the dominant fertiliser producer, which would rival its role as an iron ore supplier.

8.8.3 *Transition from open pit to underground*

The determination of the transition from surface to underground mining requires careful timing and integration of technical planning and development with a matching investment strategy. The process of undertaking PFS and full engineering planning studies should be

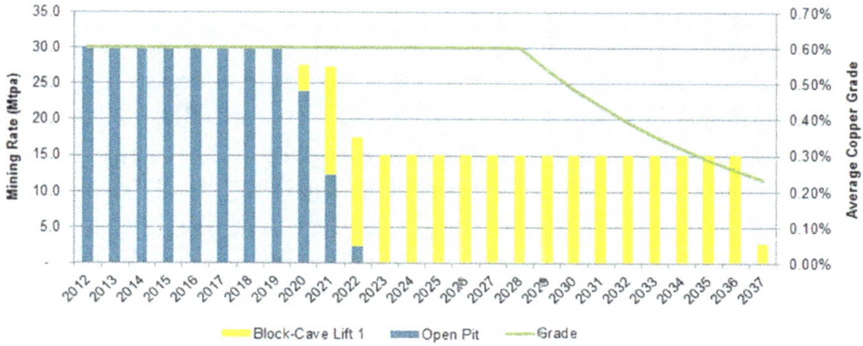

Figure 8.6. Production profile in the transition from surface to underground mining. As the pen-pit matures, the number of working faces becomes limited so production drops and this needs to be compensated for in the ramp-up of block caving. This is conceptually simple but technically challenging. It requires a large design effort, high quality construction and rigorously managed operations.

initiated in a timely manner, otherwise the sponsor will incur higher costs in attempting to speed up development once the investment decision has been taken. The consequence will be a serious dip in production on changeover. This is illustrated in Fig. 8.6.

Given the challenges in implementing block caving, there is a high risk of overestimating how much can be recovered from underground based on original ramp-up profile assumptions as caving is initiated. This has profound implications when planning matching investment needs and it is the interface between conventional technical engineering and financial engineering that forms part of this study. An integral part of this study was the development of models that consider the impact of unexpected delays in meeting production targets on the original financial performance indicators, such as NPV. These can be ameliorated through the use of innovative funding options aimed at reducing the cost of capital. The impact on reserve tail caused by dilution at underground drawpoints in block caving operations when the original open-pit side wall suffers failure needs to be built into the models, as it will influence the choice of repayment period (see Section 11.5).

8.9 Discussion

For an IPO, the prospectus must have a technical report prepared by an independent consultant (Competent Person's Report), which in turn may include all the elements of a pre-feasibility study. It may not be necessary to have a full technical feasibility study completed if funds are to be used for, say, additional drilling or trial mining.

A PFS can provide the basis for raising equity funding for additional evaluation drilling. It cannot, however, be used to raise enough funding for a major programme of capital expenditure and it is not, owing to the remaining project uncertainty, acceptable to banks for raising debt finance.

Project finance investment will be based upon an Information Memorandum, which incorporates a FTFS. Optimisation undertaken at the PFS stage is treated quite separately from the financial engineering that follows using project finance, which is essentially designed to optimise the capital structure. As the gearing changes, so does the NPV. The obvious reason why the NPV increases with increased levels of debt is because of tax relief on interest and because the cash flows are being discounted, reflecting the impact of cheaper debt finance.

Putting together a JV requires a valuation of the assets of the Junior as a basis for the determination of the vend-in conditions for the Major and a clear set of targets to identify when trigger points are reached. Usually this is linked to the delivery by the major of a PFS and a FTFS. These need to be defined with rigour if disputes are to be avoided. In the event that the Major decides not to proceed, a claw-back clause is often included in the terms of the original JV agreement.

Estimates of the grade and tonnage in the FTFS may be no different from those used for pre-feasibility but may well include the results of trial mining, bulk sampling and pilot treatment. This level of technical information would not usually fall within the scope of a pre-feasibility study. Permitting and EIA also need to be in place (see Section 4.1.1). A FTFS will also provide the verifiable cost and performance predictions. These are needed for the economic completion tests when operations funded from debt go from recourse to non-recourse.

In providing debt, a bank would also want to lock in revenue, so that the proportion of income needed to meet interest and debt repayment is secure. Of course, the amount of debt that a project can carry is dependent on performance indicators (debt service coverage and ratios such as loan life, project life, reserve tail, interest cover, principal cover and residual cover). The risk for the shareholders is that hedging imposed by the banks could lock them out of significant revenue from the project, because they receive less benefit from any major increase in metal prices.

This professional interaction is tracked through to the role of engineering, procurement and construction contracts within the context of financial engineering and optimisation of debt and equity at the funding stage. This in turn links back to the impact that delay has on financial viability at the construction and development phase, and reconciliation between initial design expectation and actual performance during production ramp-up. Finally, the role of the economic completion test becomes material before lending goes non-recourse.

Promoters with purely technical backgrounds however, often understand poorly the distinction between technical appraisal and financial engineering. Linking the sophisticated hedging strategies that are required when securing project finance to the technical appraisal and exploitation of the underlying assets, is highly complex. Correct structuring of the finance and hedging requirements does significantly enhance the value of mineral projects. For example, gaining access to funding may be value-additive in itself as it provides greater clarity over project timetables. A simple single year delay in moving forward at feasibility stage could erode 5–10% of value purely on a time value of money basis. Raising the finance itself may also be value-creating through the signal to the market that the project risk has been reduced significantly.

Antofagasta's strategy is to sell concentrate into the market under an offtake agreement rather than to enter into a hedging programme normally required when securing project finance. An offtake agreement would have a price participation clause so equity stakeholders then benefit from price volatility which would otherwise be capped under a straight hedging agreement. As described in the Platreef Extended Case Study 3 (Appendix C), given that this is a polymetallic deposit, there was merit in entering a streaming arrangement. Based on the conservative gold price of $1,200/oz the Platreef model generates a revenue of $670 million over the life of the mine. This has been used to reduce the capital need to build the mine.

Chapter 9

Minerals Engineering

9.1 Introduction

A mine open-pit blast as illustrated in Fig. 9.1 is just the visible manifestation of what is a complex process from *in situ* metal such as gold to a final Doré bullion bar.

It is quite an art for mining engineers to get blast-hole spacing and loading of explosives just right. You want to get optimum fragmentation of ore so most of that material goes through the grizzly at the primary crusher, while ensuring you do not waste explosives by breaking waste rock too small nor having to do secondary blasting on the waste rock. At the same time, you do not want physically to displace the rock mass significantly as grade control is based on ore remaining in its original spatial location.

The geologists have to delineate mineralisation and determine zones above cut-off grade that demarcate ore to be sent to the plant. There may be a low-grade component which may be suitable for heap leaching. The mining engineers have to ensure that after blasting there is no misclassification which in turn links to truck scheduling. The plant superintendent has to discharge minimum quantities of gold to the tailings constrained only by recovery curves. Plant recovery is among other things a function of head grade. Expertise is important at all levels from the operators upwards. In the plant, the complexity of the system's behaviour and associated relative lack of automation makes operator experience essential for achieving good recoveries and grades.

Figure 9.1. Open-pit blast at the Nkomati mine in South Africa. An explosion is a very rapid, self-propagating exothermic reaction. The main type of explosive used in the mining industry is ANFO. It consists of 94% porous prilled ammonium nitrate (NH^4NO_3) which acts as the oxidising agent and absorbent for the fuel oil. To initiate the explosive reaction, a detonator is required but this would not deliver sufficient energy to set off the low-sensitivity charge. However, it detonates the primary charge (the booster), which then delivers an explosive shockwave that is sufficient to detonate the secondary, main, high-energy charge.

Clearly to achieve optimisation of the production process the design of the project must take into account that each deposit will have its own unique characteristics. The best way to reduce technical risk is to undertake a programme of trial mining ahead of full scale production. Typical objectives would include the following:

- To visually observe the structural controls on the mineralisation
- To determine realistic modifying parameters to apply to move from resource to reserve
- To determine the optimal geotechnical parameters
- To determine the actual large-scale reagent consumption rates
- To gain understanding of ore material behaviour through the mill
- To verify bulk-sample/large-scale ore head grades

- To verify the total metal recovery
- To verify bulk densities used for resource estimation
- To provide bulk samples for low-grade testwork and assess waste rock acid rain susceptibility.

The management and planning of the underground layout design should be aimed at testing different mining methods. This also needs to take into account gaining access to different zones within the deposit so that inherent heterogeneity is identified. The key outcome of the study is determination of the probability of a significant positive net present value (NPV) for the base case assuming homogeneous ore and then re-running the simulation base case inclusive of heterogeneity.

9.2 Grade Control and Metal Reconciliation

In a modern mine, there must be a metal reconciliation system, and some really robust interdisciplinary exchanges can take place at the monthly planning meeting. The mineral process engineers attribute lower than expected ounces recovered to low grade in the plant feed. The miners say the geologists gave them the wrong information and that *in situ* grades were less than predicted, and in any event the mineral process engineers have let plant recoveries drop. The geologists say that excessive dilution took place during extraction which is why there was low head grade and ore was sent to the waste pile (and waste sent to the primary crusher). The geostatistician just smiles at the failure of his/her colleagues to understand the inherent uncertainty associated with initial drill-hole sampling.

A starting point in the process of metal reconciliation is often in the treatment of mining dilution. It is seldom if ever possible to mine only the ore. When recovering the ore, there will always be some waste rock (see Fig. 9.2). The amount of dilution is usually expressed as a percentage. External dilution is derived from outside the ore zone and internal dilution derives from waste bands in the ore zone. The volumetric impact is shown in Fig. 9.2.

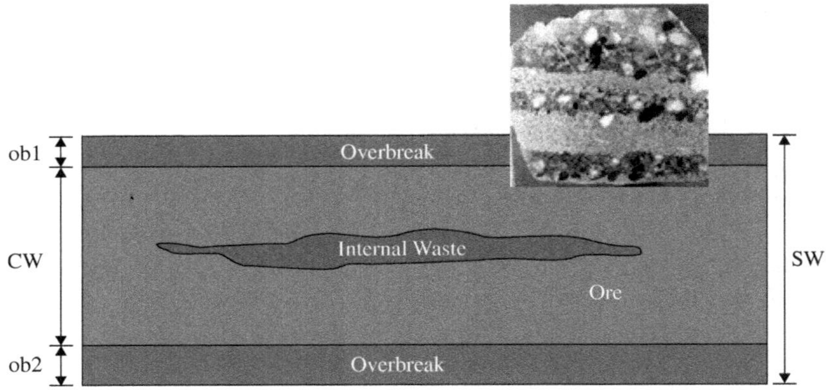

Ignoring internal dilution – averaged in when selecting CW

CW = Channel Width
SW = Stoping Width
ob1 = Hanging wall overbreak
ob2 = Footwall overbreak

CW	ob1	ob2	SW	Dilution
[illegible]	[illegible]	[illegible]	[illegible]	*
1000	100	100	1200	20.00
1500	100	100	1700	13.33

Figure 9.2. Calculation of dilution assuming the density of the ore and waste is the same. The inset picture is a section of Basal Reef from Free State Geduld Gold Mine in the Welkom Goldfield. Pebbles are around 3 cm in size and are associated with the gold mineralisation, while the brown sandstone is internal waste.

Table 9.1. Mass balance in a gold-mining operation.

Variables	Tonnes	Grade (g/tonne)	Content (grams)
Ore	100	10	1,000
Dilution at 10%	10	0	0
Total to plant	110	8.33	1,000

The object of the exercise is to send ore to the processing plant but, when mining, it is impossible to separate perfectly the waste from the ore. Inevitably, some waste gets mixed up with the ore and is sent to the plant. This is "dilution", usually expressed as a percentage and calculated as given in Table 9.1. Dilution material is usually assumed to have no valuable content (which is not always the case) and has the same density as the ore.

The impact of dilution needs to be accommodated in a financial model. For a scenario with a fixed capacity, annual production will determine project life. Dilution will extend project life and while all the *in situ* metal present will be recovered, it will take longer. Then, due to the impact of the time value of money, the NPV will be reduced based simply on the delayed benefit of the revenue stream. There will also be larger cumulative OpCosts albeit their impact will be ameliorated by the same low present value factors.

The break-even grade is defined as the grade at which revenue obtained is equal to the cost of producing that revenue. The selection of cut-off grade relates to the need to maintain mining continuity. There is an interrelationship between the two concepts and metal price which is treated in the classic study by Lane published in 1988 *The Economic Definition of Ore*.

When poor metal reconciliation takes place, the mine manager must have the wisdom and experience to recognise what is due to mathematical uncertainty and what is due to technical shortcomings. Lack of reconciliation may well fall within a defined envelope of uncertainty but people make mistakes and systems may need to be improved or re-engineered.

Selective mining must also compensate for the spatial disruption of mining blocks after blasting. Delivering feed to the plant that smooths out the inherent heterogeneity of the ore is achieved by blending this on the run-of-mine pad. The metal reconciliation system is designed to allow comparison of forecasts of metal in concentrate with actual achievements, which is undertaken on a weekly basis. This is the key mechanism, together with cost control, used for mine management and should always be implemented in a modern mining operation.

9.3 Management

Recent events in the South African mining industry have all the hallmarks of a major change in the political and commercial landscape. The concept of "cheap" labour-intensive mining was always an illusion. The Rustenburg-centred platinum mining industry based on underground mining of the narrow Merensky and UG-2 horizons is going to have to mechanise, train up well-paid teams of skilled operators, provide decent family housing and reduce underground shift numbers by a significant factor. The problem in the Rustenburg area is the narrow reefs that are just over a metre wide: if the stopes are going to be wide enough to handle even low-profile mining equipment, dilution will increase and head grades will drop. Reductions in OpCosts per tonne need to offset loss of head grade if the strategy is to succeed. If mechanisation is implemented, this will have social implications as unskilled labour makes way for skilled operators. These operational changes will inevitably draw attention to the potential of the Platreef (see Section 5.5.3) with high-grade zones which are at least 10 m wide and amenable to both open-pit and mechanised low-cost underground room and pillar mining operations.

It would seem that there is a limit to the relationship between cost and capacity illustrated in Section 8.3.2. The mining industry is now talking about "dis-economies of scale" which they consider to be a significant factor in mining's waning productivity. This is why there is a trend to spin off some of their operations into a separate company. If a company is too large, it cannot be managed effectively. Scaling up mines just makes them more complex to run while rapid staff turnover has left many mine managers without the people to monitor the increased complexity. There is also talk of how "silo mentality" has crept into management of a mining company as the large scale of the operations results in loss of perspective. Costs are being squeezed but may not be sufficient to make up for the fall in productivity.

With strong commodity markets and the focus on increasing output managers may take their eye off the ball with respect to production cost controls. The greater the output the less effective the management controls. It requires strong management to bring cost benefits back onto the economies of scale trend.

Advances in engineering design of equipment cannot over-ride poor operational management and strategic mine planning.

9.4 Mining Methods

9.4.1 *Open-pit mining methods*

The advantages of open-pit mining are that it is safer than underground mining; it is associated with lower operating costs and Capex per unit mined and higher productivities are achievable; there is less delay in starting mining in an open pit; and considerable flexibility can also be exercised in the design of an open pit as is illustrated in Fig. 9.3. This takes into account the relationship between topography and stages of development in relation to the orientation of the ore body as illustrated in Fig. 9.3. In surface mining, mining cost includes the cost of removing the waste overburden and waste side rock in the

Figure 9.3. A typical pit cross-section — Phases I–III are designed using increasing stripping ratios, thus increasing the volume of ore mined economically (after C.T. Shaw). Inset of Platreef at Overysel South, showing stable pit slope, ramp, blast-hole drilling and loading.

slopes of the pit. The ratio of the number of tonnes of waste that must be moved per tonne of ore mined is termed the Stripping Ratio (SR):

$$SR = \frac{Tonnes\ of\ waste\ removed}{Tonnes\ of\ ore\ mined}.$$

When the cost of removing waste exceeds the revenue generated by the ore, then the limits of the pit have been reached. This is the stage when surface operations are no longer economic and if deeper mineralisation is to be mined then underground methods must be considered.

The detailed relationship between blast-hole pattern and bench dimensions is given in Fig. 9.4 and as can be seen in Fig. 9.3, the relationship between the height of the benches and the distance between them determines the basic geometry of an open pit and its ultimate pit slope.

The pit slopes must be designed to be stable for as long as the pit is operating and to minimise the amount of waste needed to be

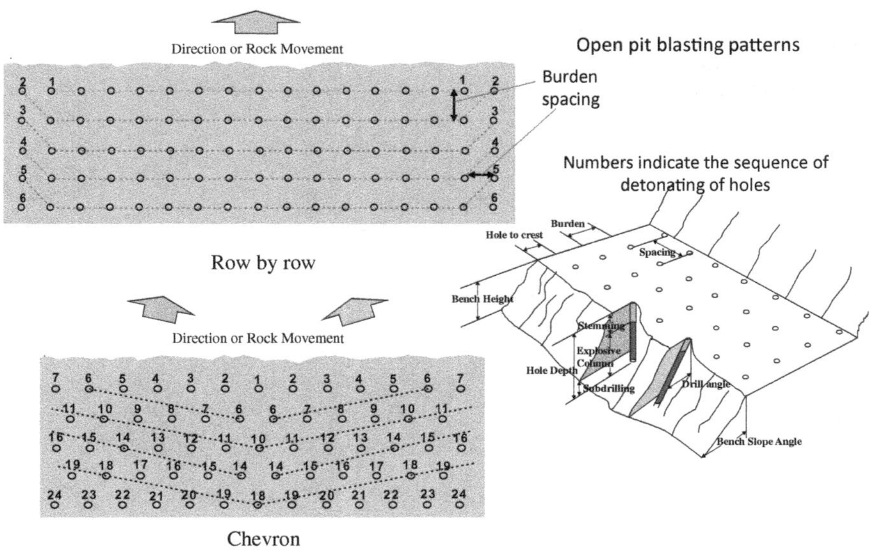

Figure 9.4. Open-pit geometry and terminology of benches (after C.T. Shaw).

extracted. Due to the varying directional properties of the rock, the acceptable overall pit slope angles may vary considerably around the pit perimeter. Commercial mine design software is available, which can illustrate the different phases of mine development and incorporate geostatistical and pit optimisation routines. Separate specialist software is available which focuses purely on each function.

The sequence of back-stripping can be adjusted to optimise NPV. The Lerchs-Grossmann algorithms are used in the surface mining industry to solve the pit limit problem and to generate an approximate solution to the extraction sequence problem. This is the basis for pit design software used to determine the ultimate pit that gives the highest possible undiscounted surplus between net revenue and total operating costs, without considering scheduling constraints or discounting. A nested pit shell analysis is then used to determine the discounted optimal pit. Nested pit shells are a sequence of ultimate pits generated by incrementing the commodity price across a range of values around the base price. See the Mine Scheduling Extended Case Study 7 (Appendix G).

The optimal pit gives the highest possible NPV, taking into account all operational scheduling constraints (annual mining and processing productivity), discounting and recurring capital costs. Pit optimisation algorithms have to assume a discount rate fixed by the parent company so the operation cannot use a gearing optimisation approach where the subsidiary cannot act as an independent company and raise fresh equity and secure debt from an independent investment bank. They must use the parent's corporate cost of capital. This must impact on stripping ratios and may even sterilise some ore — a source of some frustration to planning departments on mines.

The optimisation of pit design takes into account different geometric designs constrained by estimates of revenue assumptions in a financial model. For example, if an escalation in metal prices is assumed for the first 10 years, this will not be the same as using real versus nominal values as outlined in Section 2.2. There will be no distortion of NPV, but it will probably give a different outcome when pit optimisation scenarios are considered. If you do not assume metal price escalation in the model, then presumably you end up with a more conservative stripping ratio using identical scheduling. Assuming higher metal prices allows for a higher stripping ratio and as the open pit deepens, you may be able to neutralise the effect through different scheduling involving moving more waste in the early years with a no metal pricing escalation scenario. If the metal prices do increase after the back strip is completed, then there is a bonanza profit.

Surface mining involves the following operations:

- *Pit preparation — Pre-strip*
  - Orebody surface cleaning
    - Removal of vegetation
    - Removal and storage of top soil, subsoil
    - Excavation of overburden.
- *Mining*
  - Drilling and blasting of waste
  - Excavation of waste
  - Drilling and blasting of ore
  - Excavation of ore.
- *Haulage*
  - Loading
  - Haulage and dumping of waste
  - Haulage of ore to plant.

Pre-stripping includes removal of topsoil and subsoil and the equipment used includes scrapers, dozers, front-end loaders and trucks. This stage is treated as capital expenditure. Breaking rock requires drilling and blasting with the rotary blast hole rig the main item of equipment. Grade control sampling is undertaken using a reversed circulation drill rig of the type shown in Fig. 7.2.

The standard open-pit loading equipment comprises front-end loaders, hydraulic excavators and power shovels; key specifications are given in Table 9.2.

Figure 9.5 illustrates a power shovel. These are commonly used excavating machines both for overburden stripping and loading of

Table 9.2. Standard open-pit loading equipment.

Item	Capacity m^3	Capital cost \$ (million)	Radimiro tomic mine
Front-end loaders	2–40.5	0.35–4.5	$1 \times 20\,m^3$ $1 \times 15\,m^3$
Hydraulic excavators	2.5–50	0.45–50	$1 \times 33.6\,m^3$ $4 \times 26\,m^3$
Power shovels	7–80	5–50	$3 \times 56\,m^3$ $3 \times 44\,m^3$

Figure 9.5. View of a Bucyrus 495HR (later versions are branded Caterpillar 7495) electric rope power shovel. Photograph taken by C.T. Shaw 2013.

ore. Though pivot mounted on crawler tracks, the heavy-duty nature, fixed boom and trailing electric cable mean that the electric shovel is less mobile and flexible than a hydraulic excavator. However, the largest machines have bucket capacities well in excess of $50\,m^3$ and the shovels prove extremely productive in favourable pit conditions.

The shovel pictured is one of the largest models currently available with bucket capacity of over 60 m^3 over 100 tonnes and would cost in the order of tens of millions of dollars to purchase new. Cheaper, smaller-scale machines are often sufficient if used in combination with other excavation equipment.

The rate-determining stage in an open-pit production pipeline is the loading process and therefore consideration must be given to ensuring that the cycle of digging, swinging and tipping is optimised. Any waiting should be confined to the trucks and they in turn need to be positioned in mined-out areas to minimise shovel swing angles. Scheduling of truck movement in turn must be optimised to ensure that while an empty truck should be in place once a loaded truck has been despatched, having several empty trucks waiting is clearly not desirable.

Overburden, topsoil and subsoil is transported to a separate storage area for later use in reclamation. Waste country rock is transported to a dumping area — open pits have very large waste dumps.

Ore is delivered to a crusher for sizing either in the pit or at the plant — after sizing it will usually be on belt conveyors. Open-pit methods require haulage equipment to move the entire tonnage broken of both ore and waste out of the pit, which necessitates a combination of trucks and belt conveyors. Haulage costs are substantial and are often the critical component in the economic feasibility of a project.

The development of trolley equipment on the haulage trucks and plans for autonomous operation, described as autonomous haulage systems (AHSs), represent a major step-change in the approach to mining due to the advantages this offers. These include:

- No operator delays associated with shift changes with 24/7 operation
- No unnecessary travel
- Fewer trucks
- Constant speeds
- Greater safety with fewer people in the production area

- Virtual elimination of proximity conflict
- Less maintenance, as there is less equipment misuse.

There are also plans to introduce both remote and autonomous drilling, all of which will reduce operating costs. This provides a clear vision of the mine of the future.

Figure 9.6 illustrates one of the largest dump trucks used and, in modern big open pits, there may well be a fleet of five or more of these huge trucks. Smaller scale trucks will be used in most open pits moving smaller daily tonnages than in the giant pits. Smaller scale trucks may also be used in strip mines where haulage of the waste rock is not necessary.

Figure 9.6. The Liebherr T 284 is a two-axle rear dump truck with a payload capacity of up to 363 tonnes (400 US tons). This is one of the largest capacity dump trucks currently available. These trucks can cost in excess of US$3 million each with tyres costing US$100,000 each. Photograph taken at Minexpo 2016 Las Vegas by C.T. Shaw.

9.4.2 *Transition from open pit to underground*

The reasons for considering an underground mining operation include the following:

- Depletion of reserves economically accessible using surface mining methods.
- Stripping ratios become excessively high, as a rule of thumb when they exceed 1:10.
- Present value of developing an underground operation exceeds the present value of a further pushback.
- The availability of sunk capital in surface infrastructure including smelting and refining facilities present at an operation such as Palabora.

The determination of the transition from surface to underground requires careful timing and integration of technical planning and development with a matching investment strategy. Given the challenges in implementing advanced mining methods such as block caving, there is a high risk of overestimating how much can be recovered from underground based on original ramp-up profile assumptions as caving is initiated. This has profound implications when planning matching investment needs and it is the interface between conventional technical engineering and financial engineering that forms part of this study.

The production profile in the transition from surface to underground mining is given in Fig. 8.6. As the open pit matures, the number of working faces becomes limited so production drops and this needs to be compensated for in the ramp-up of block caving. This is conceptually simple but technically challenging. It requires a large design effort, high-quality construction and rigorously managed operations.

9.4.3 *Underground mining methods*

An underground mine consists of a carefully planned infrastructure of tunnels — shafts (vertical or inclined), declines (ramps), drifts (adits), raises and winzes. There are always two outlets to the mine and the failure to comply with this fundamental principle was the reason in October 2010 for miners being trapped with a cave-in at the Chilean San José copper–gold mine, located in the Atacama Desert. These are the access routes for the movement of the broken rock — but they are also for the movement of men, material, power supplies, air and water into and out of the mine — the mine services. An overriding consideration in all of this is safety.

Primary access to a buried ore body is through a vertical shaft which requires specialist service companies. A 7.25 m diameter shaft sunk to a depth of 1,000 m and with a capacity to hoist 6 Mtpa of ore could take up to 4 years to bring into production and cost around $2 billion if a spiral decline is being developed simultaneously. The cycle of shaft sinking involves a rock drill rig attached to the winder and lowered down the shaft where it is then hung on the stage and lowered to the shaft bottom. About 180 holes are drilled for every blast with each hole about 3 m deep. There are two drilling units, the one is active and the other one is used as a spare. You can drill the entire bottom in a matter of an hour to an hour and a half if everything goes well.

After drilling and blasting the bottom there is a mucking cycle during which two vertical shaft muckers, which are fixed on the stage, are lowered down the shaft where they muck the shaft bottom and fill the kibbles. In the stage are two holes — the kibble holes — through which two 10 tonne skips, which are used to bring out the blasted material, run up and down the completed part of the shaft from the shaft bottom to surface. Depending on the blast, it takes about 40 skip lifts to get the blast muck cleaned out. That will take about six hours.

A vertical shaft system not only represents the shortest distance between surface and the mine workings, but also once the shaft hoisting system is in place ore can be brought to the surface quickly in the skips. Double drum hoists allow the hoisting of two skips which are in balance and run on guides extending along the length of the shaft. With hoisting speeds of 10 m/s skips with 30 tonne capacity can be brought to the surface in less than two minutes. Raise boring machines are now standard technology in mining and the technique can be applied once the horizontal access is developed. These shafts can be used for ventilation.

Secondary access would be via a spiral decline developed on a gradient that would permit access by wheeled vehicles, typically around 11°. This means a spiral decline would need to be over 5 kms in length to reach the same depth as a 1,000 m shaft. This does, however, permit efficient operation of the mine given that modern underground operations are designed to be as highly mechanised as possible.

The main mining methods are derived from the geometric form of the ore bodies. While shaft sinking and putting in a spiral decline is always working against gravity, once the mining infrastructure is developed then by locating this below the ore body the design can use gravity to advantage to ensure that material flows down toward collecting points. By locating the pumping station near the base of the shaft, the mine can be kept dry. For horizontal or sub-horizontal narrow and wide tabular, low dipping ore bodies, the main mining methods are as follows:

- *Room and pillar*: Also called pillar and stall, this is a mining system in which the mined material is extracted across a horizontal plane, creating horizontal arrays of rooms and pillars.
- *Long hole stoping*: Uses holes drilled by a production drill to a predetermined pattern and is a highly selective and productive method of mining which can cater for varying ore thicknesses and dips (0–90°).
- *Longwall*: Form of underground coal mining where a longwall of coal is mined in a single slice. The method is also used on the ultra-deep gold mines of the Witwatersrand where the voids created by narrow palaeoconglomerates are expected to close behind the working faces as mining advances.

For vertical or sub-vertical ore bodies, the main mining methods are:

- *Sublevel stoping*: Involves vertical mining in a large, open stope that has been created inside an ore vein.
- *Shrinkage stoping*: Used for steeply dipping, narrower ore bodies with self-supporting walls and ore. It is an overhand mining

method that relies on broken ore being left in the stope to be used as the "working floor" and to support the walls.

- *Cut-and-fill*: Used for steeply dipping ore bodies in which the opened stope is back-filled with waste materials as each layer of ore is removed.
- *Drift and fill and Drift and bench*: Similar to cut-and-fill, except used in ore zones which are wider than the method of drifting will allow. In this case, the first drift is developed in the ore and is backfilled using consolidated fill. The second drift is driven adjacent to the first drift. This carries on until the ore zone is fully mined.

For massive ore bodies amenable to bulk mining, the main methods are:

- *Sublevel caving*. This starts at the top of the orebody and develops downwards. Ore is mined from sublevels spaced at regular intervals throughout the deposit. A series of ring patterns is drilled and blasted from each sublevel, and broken ore is mucked out after each blast.
- *Block caving*. A bulk underground mining method, which allows large low-grade deposits to be mined underground. This method involves undermining the orebody to make it collapse under its own weight into a series of chambers from which the ore extracted.
- *Panel caving*. A variation on block mining which divides the ore up into sections like block mining and extracts it in the same way, but production moves sequentially along the length of the orebody, so that only when one section of the ore is in production the next one is blasted. This saves in development costs.

The difference between block caving and other types of caving, such as sub-level or panel caving, is really the scale. In block caving, the entire orebody above the extraction level is caved all at once. In panel caving, the orebody is caved in sections (panels). The appropriate method for a mine will depend upon the rock properties and the shape of the orebody. The Venetia mine implemented panel caving, as this allowed underground mining to commence earlier than the original intention to use block caving mining methods.

While traditionally higher outputs were possible from an open pit compared to an underground mine, development using block-caving methods means that this is not necessarily always the case. In 2014, open-pit production at Chuquicamata, Chile, was 120,000 tonnes per day (tpd) (43.2 million tonnes per annum (Mtpa) of ore with the underground operation predicted to produce 140,000 tpd (50.4 Mtpa)). This is a reversal of the usual scenario where the transition from surface to underground mining results in a drop-off in production. This is achievable because the block caving mining method to be implemented will involve drawing from four separate levels simultaneously. The high rate of production from an underground operation is made possible because of the capacity of horizontal development compared to vertical shaft systems.

Palabora is now looking to develop Lift 2 in their block caving operation. Daily total tonnage at Palabora from the open pit in 1989 was 215,000 tpd (77.4 Mtpa) with ore tonnage achieving 91,800 tpd (33.0 Mtpa) at a strip ratio of 1:1.25. The predicted production from the underground block caving operation based on the shaft capacity was 25 Mtpa, although actual production reached a plateau at 12.5 Mtpa. The importance of rock mechanics in determining the viability of block cave projects became apparent. Multiple issues arising from the mechanical behaviour of the rock due to the alteration of the physical environment have a significant effect on the operation of block caves. Poor rock fragmentation has a large negative effect on the project value which arises owing to poor design of draw point layout and undercut size. This in turn results in a reduction of the extraction rate and an increase in the mining cost. In some cases, without appropriate geotechnical modelling at an early stage of project development, cave propagation may not occur. There have been cases where continued blasting is required, impacting on both the mining rate and mining cost.

When operating a block cave below an open pit, the draw rate must constantly be monitored and the cave propagation modelled to avoid direct dilution of the orebody and, in the worst case, sidewall failure in the open pit which eventually contaminates the ore and causes dilution. This results in lower head grade and reduction of the mine life.

Crucially, the ramp-up duration for any block cave is determined by rock mechanics. Ramp-up requires a parabolic increase in production which in some cases can last over a decade. This would have a major impact and significantly reduce the financial returns generated by the project compared to original projections.

9.4.4 *Mine operating cost estimation*

As outlined in Section 8.3.2, there are two types of costs, Capex and OpCosts. Capex are costs in a particular year that will produce benefits in later years and thus may be depreciated over the life of the mine. This impacts on the NPV in a DCF model as tax relief in later years is discounted (see Section 2.3.1). A tax model such as loss carry forward would enhance NPV as relief is applied in the early stages of a project.

OpCosts are costs which only produce benefit for that year and can be used to offset tax liability in the year they are incurred. This means they provide greater benefit in a DCF than Capex. OpCosts are composed of direct costs which are directly attributable to production and indirect costs such as administration. They are also fixed or variable depending on output. In a gold processing plant, cyanide will be consumed regardless of the grade of the ore but the cost of crushing would be directly proportional to the rate of production. In operating mines costs are reported as outlined in Fig. 9.7.

An insight into the process of cost estimation on a small open-pit gold resource is outlined below. The scenario assumes a small plant capacity of 500 tpd (around 150,000 tonnes per annum (tpa)). Entry-level mining normally starts at 250,000 tpa which at a grade of 10 g/tonne produces around 75,000 ounces assuming recovery of around 90%. A mid-sized operation would expect to produce 250,000 ounces per annum and head grade may be no more than 2 grams/tonne so the mine must produce 3.875 Mt of ore for processing. Waste rock movement may be five times this amount.

The actual process of mining comprises drilling, blasting, loading and hauling. The equipment required, performance and costs are given in Table 9.3. This provides the basis for generating the cost per tonne. It also demonstrates that the rate-determining stage

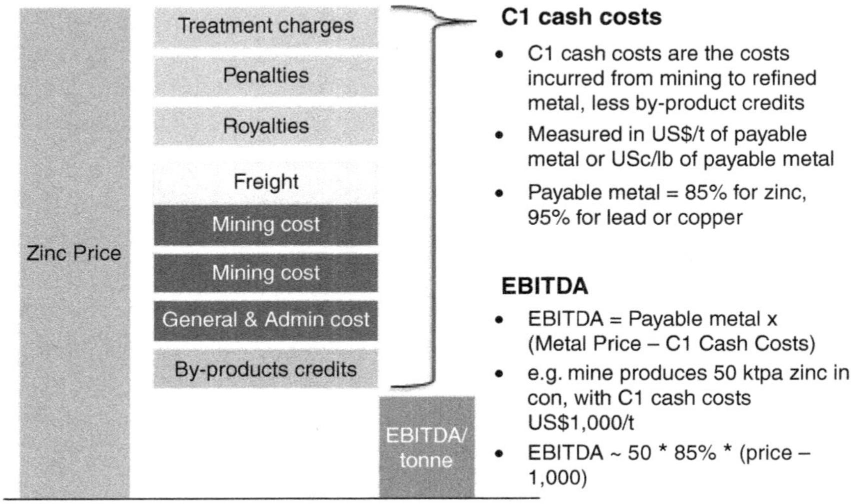

Figure 9.7. Breakdown of cash costs.

needs to be identified and this is normally the loading process. Performance of the preceding drilling process and the following haulage stage requires a selection of equipment that balances capacity with flexibility.

The process of compiling the technical parameters needed for the scenario given in Table 9.3 might take 30 person days and is entirely inflexible. Any change in the basic assumptions on capacity effectively means that the whole exercise has to be repeated from first principles as quite different specifications for the equipment would be needed. When this process is expanded to consider a mid-sized operation, as described above, the amount of work involved in undertaking the detailed engineering increases proportionately and the inflexibility is further entrenched. Scenario analysis is really only possible at the pre-feasibility stage and not at the FTFS stage. Small-scale mining of the type illustrated is not usually viable not only because of high unit costs but because the number of operators needed to run a small operation may be no fewer than that needed for a mid-sized operation.

Table 9.3. Cost estimates for benching.

Parameters		
Strip ratio	Waste:Ore	4
Plant capacity	t/day	500
Waste movement	t/day	2,000
Total movement	t/day	2,500
Rock density	t/m^3	2.75
Bench height	m	7

Unit cost summary		Ore	Waste
Drilling	$/t	0.43	0.20
Blasting	$/t	0.38	0.18
Loading	$/t	0.29	0.29
Hauling	$/t	1.48	0.23
Total	$/t	2.57	0.89

Drilling		Ore	Waste	Total
Burden	m	2.0	3.0	
Spacing	m	2.3	3.5	
Tonnes per hole	t	88.6	199.2	
Sub drill	m	0.6	0.9	
Metres per hole	m	7.6	7.9	
Tonnes per metre	t/m	11.7	25.2	
Metres per day	m/day	43	79	122
Holes per day	no./day	28	10	38
ROP	m/hr	20	20	
Drilling hours per day	hr/day	2.1	4.0	6.1
Working hours per day	no.	10	10	
Drills required	no.	0.2	0.4	0.6

Drilling costs		Ore	Waste
Bit	$/m	3	3
Rod	$/m	0.3	0.3
Stabiliser/ hammer	$/m	0.2	0.2
Rig	$/hr	30	30
Cost per hole	$/hole	38.0	39.5
Cost per tonne	$/t	0.43	0.20
Cost per hour	$/hr	100	100

(*Continued*)

Table 9.3. (*Continued*)

Blasting		Ore	Waste
Hole diameter	mm	108	108
Hole volume	m^3	0.070	0.072
Stemming	m	2.0	2.0
Charge length	m	5.6	5.9
Explosive density	t/m^3	0.8	0.8
Charge volume	m^3	0.051	0.054
Explosives per hole	kg/hole	41	43
Powder factor	kg/t	0.46	0.22

Blasting costs		Ore	Waste
Explosives	\$/kg	0.6	0.6
Detonator	\$/hole	3	3
Booster	\$/hole	3	3
Detonator cord	\$/hole	1	1
Delays	\$/hole	2	2
Cost per hole	\$/hole	33.6	34.9
Cost per tonne	\$/hr	0.38	0.18

Loading		Ore	Waste	Total
Bucket capacity	m^3	2.5	2.5	
Fill factor	%	0.91	0.91	
Cycle time	min	1	1	
Cycles per hour	no.	60	60	
Productivity	%	66	66	
Loose density (70%)	t/m^3	1.93	1.93	
Rate of production	t/hr	173	173	
Loading hours per day	hrs	2.9	11.5	
Working hours per day	no.	10	10	
Loaders required	no.	0.3	1.2	1.5

Loading costs		Ore	Waste
Cost per hour	\$/hr	50	50
Cost per tonne	\$/t	0.29	0.29

Hauling		Ore	Waste	Total
Capacity	m^3	12	12	
Cycle time	min	45	7	
Cycles per hour	no.	1.3	8.6	
Productivity	%	66	66	
Rate of production	t/hr	20	131	
Working hours per day	hrs	10	10	
Trucks required	no.	2.5	1.5	4.0

Hauling costs		Ore	Waste
Cost per hour	\$/hr	30	30
Cost per tonne	\$/t	1.48	0.23

9.5 Coal Mining

9.5.1 *Strip mining*

Strip mining (or opencast mining) is a surface method applied almost uniquely to the coal-mining industry. The principal feature of the method is surface land reclamation contemporaneous with overburden stripping and haulage. Rather than being transported to waste dumps for disposal as in open-pit operations, overburden is cast directly into adjacent mined-out panels. Excavation and haulage is generally combined in a one-unit operation (casting) and performed by a single machine. Uncovered coal is then mined by the conventional loader-hauler methods applied in open-pit mining.

Strip mining is a large-scale extraction technique, resulting in the lowest unit mining costs of any of the broadly used methods, high productivity, high recovery and greater safety records compared with underground mining.

Though expensive to purchase, the use of boom-type excavators such as draglines gives strip mining a major advantage over open-pit methods — the haulage (of overburden) component of the operating cycle is eliminated and contemporaneous surface rehabilitation is permitted. This results in more rapid uncovering of coal (and thus greater production levels) and lower unit OpCosts than a similar sized open-pit operation.

Depth constraints are the major limitation of strip mining, 100 m being the approximate technological and economic limit of the method. This translates to a maximum economic stripping ratio of approximately 40:1. The nature of the cyclic casting operation means that strip mining is a fairly inflexible mining method and is only feasible in the extraction of relatively flat-lying, regular coal seams. The initial capital investment associated with equipment purchase is considerable, though this is compensated for by reduced OpCosts as governed by the economics of scale.

9.5.2 *Longwall mining*

A series of longwall panels is laid out. Each longwall will be mined in turn with a narrow pillar left between it and the longwall next to it. The layout of the longwalls is dependent on the geology of the coal seams, the geology of the overlying rock strata, the geotechnical characteristics of the coal and the surrounding rock, any dislocations such as faults or folds affecting the seam to be mined, and any restrictions in force regarding the undermining of whatever is on the surface above the coal to be mined. Any unexpected faults in particular can severely affect the operation of a longwall — if the throw on the fault is large enough the whole longwall may have to be redeveloped.

The longwall shearer (or in some longwalls, a plough) cuts the coal from a face of 1,000 feet (300 m) or more between gate roads at each end of the face. In European practice, the gate road will be a single tunnel. In American practice, the gate roads are multiple tunnels mined on a room-and-pillar basis. On the longwall, the loosened coal falls onto an armoured face conveyor that takes the coal to another conveyor in the gate road. Longwall systems have their own hydraulic roof supports, called chocks or shields, which advance with the machine as mining progresses.

If the gate roads have been developed before starting the longwall and the longwall is mined back between these established roads, then it is called "retreat mining". If on the other hand, the gate roads are developed alongside the longwall as it progresses forward, then it is called "advance mining".

As the longwall mining equipment mines forward, the overlying rock that is no longer supported by coal must cave behind the line of shields in a controlled manner. This caving is essential for the stability of the system.

This is a highly productive underground mining method and is relatively safe as the operators at all times work under the protection of the powered roof supports.

9.6 Extractive Metallurgy

9.6.1 *Introduction*

When a mining project is brought into production and the quantity of metal produced does not reconcile with expectations, then the cause inevitably is associated with the processing plant not performing as predicted in the original assumptions. Correcting this involves delay and additional capital cost, yet consulting engineers are commonly asked to design a processing plant when no pilot test work has been undertaken.

Every ore deposit will have its own unique characteristics and a standard generic design for a processing plant does not usually have the flexibility to adjust to the inevitable departures from a hypothetical norm. Departures include such aspects as incomplete liberation of ore from gangue without a fine grind or incomplete separation of mineral concentrates in a polymetallic ore without appropriate controls in the flotation cells. Customisation is virtually always necessary when designing a processing plant.

While process mineralogical studies can provide important information on textural relationships on a microscopic scale, and bench-top tests on drill core can give indicative information on likely plant recoveries, there is no substitute for pilot scale test work. Bench-top tests would involve batch treatment whereas pilot scale testing mimics the dynamics of continuous processing. This allows overall recoveries to be determined and the characteristics of the concentrate to be established much more realistically. This ensures that realistic off-take agreements can be negotiated and revenue assumptions accurately predicted.

For the processing plant to incorporate in its design the flexibility to deal with heterogeneous feed requires pilot scale test work for which bulk samples on the scale of tonnes are needed. This will require trial mining and, if feasible, should always be considered. The instructions for the providers of a pilot plant testing services should be formulated by the consulting engineers designing the plant. There are specialist services that will undertake pilot scale test work on bulk samples. Typically, the facility will have an overhead gantry that allows different items of equipment to be dropped into different configurations and then key parameters, such as flow rates and mass balances, determined in a controlled manner. This permits much more reliable determination of overall recoveries that can be expected.

9.6.2 *Mineral processing*

It is said that mineral extraction starts at the stage after rock comes up the conveyor belt and into the processing plant. It is certainly true that a failure to understand the complexity of ores and to incorporate appropriate recognition into the design of the plant is a significant source of technical risk. The key stages are given in Fig. 9.8.

The key function of mineral processing is to achieve an optimum balance between what you want and what you don't want. Minerals are liberated using comminution, i.e. crushing and grinding, and this is a very energy-dependent stage which accounts for around 40% of the total energy used in mineral processing operations. It also accounts for 4% of the world's total electrical energy

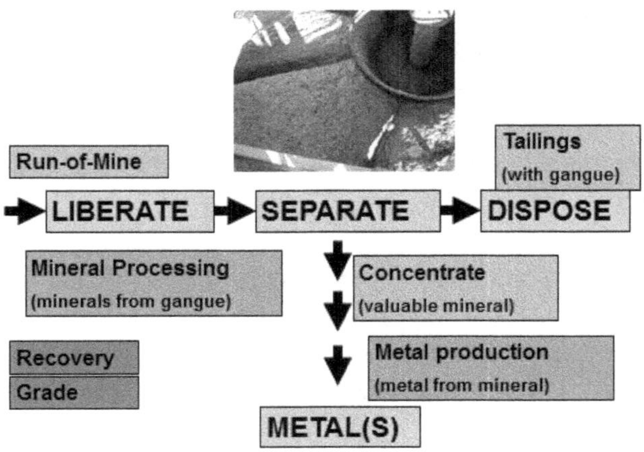

Figure 9.8. General process flowsheet and terminology (after J. Cilliers).

consumption, source: http://eex.gov.au/2013/11/crushing-energy-costs-in-the-miningsector/.

While pre-breaking takes place during blasting at the mining stage, explosives are a mixture of ammonium nitrate and fuel oil (ANFO) and so there is an energy cost at this stage. Overfragmentation during blasting complicates grade control and is less efficient than that which can be achieved using primary crushing. Run-of-mine (ROM) ore is crushed to a fine particle size and mixed with water to form a slurry, which is fed into the grinding mill where it is reduced to a very fine pulp.

Mineral separation uses differences in mineral properties. With flotation, the pulp is mixed with reagents (usually xanthate and a suitable frother) and agitated with compressed air. Air bubbles form and collect the hydrophobic sulphide particles. The sulphide-loaded air bubbles float to the surface and concentrate as a froth which is then collected (see Fig. 9.9). Flotation usually occurs at several

Figure 9.9. Flotation cells at DRD's Ergo gold operation. Reproduced with their permission.

stages, increasing the metal grade of the concentrate as it passes through each stage. Polymetallic sulphides can be recovered from the residual pulp by using suitable alternative reagents.

Inevitably, some of the metal in the initial ore feed is never recovered and around 90% recovery rate is the best that can realistically be expected. However, recovery rates may fall further, owing to attempts to produce a higher grade concentrate — 60–80% nickel metal recovery is not uncommon. In contrast, most copper by-products will normally be recoverable at higher rates.

For a copper scenario in which the plant is producing a copper concentrate, the higher the recovery the lower the copper content in the concentrate. This is illustrated in Fig. 9.10.

As can be seen, if the plant was operated such that 97% of the copper was recovered, the copper grade in the concentrate would be 20%. A feed of 1,000 tonnes of ore at a grade of 0.6% copper present as chalcopyrite (CuFeS2), which comprises around 35% copper, would contain 17.1 tonnes of the mineral in the feed. Of the 6,000 kg of copper processed, 5,820 kg would be recovered (16.63 tonnes of chalcopyrite).

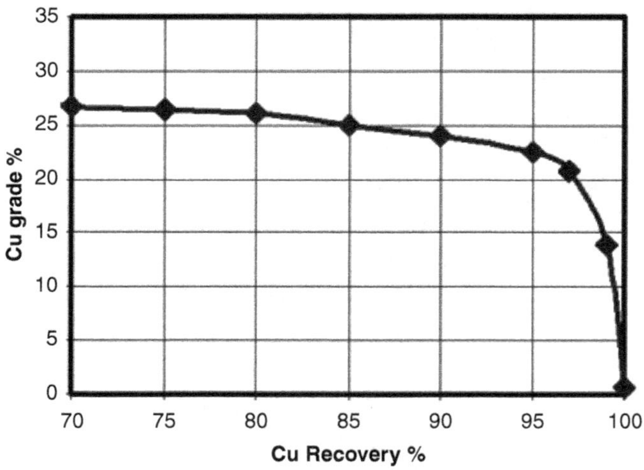

Figure 9.10. Grade–recovery relationship (after J. Cilliers).

Each tonne of concentrate, assuming it is made up entirely of chalcopyrite, would at a copper price of \$7,500/tonne be worth \$2,625. Transport and shipping costs would therefore be a small proportion of the overall contained value, allowing producers to enter into off-take agreements with smelters (see Section 9.5.2).

If recovery was reduced to 85%, then the copper grade in the concentrate would increase to 25%, but the overall copper produced would drop to 5,100 kg. As revenue is directly dependent on copper produced, there is clearly benefit from operating at the higher recovery rate. There are, however, diminishing returns on pushing recovery further as copper content in the concentrate would drop steeply. Transport costs increase for every unit of copper and as the copper content of the concentrate fell then the smelters would start imposing a penalty. Some smelters may reject the product completely if the grade is too low. At a 100% recovery, of course the grade of the "concentrate" is the same as the feed.

As some of the metal in the initial ore feed is never recovered and ends up with the waste material, usually in the tailings, controlled disposal is a key part of any mining operation. Residual sulphide minerals present in the tailings will oxidise in the presence of water and air resulting in acid mine drainage (AMD). The common mineral is pyrite that will react as follows:

$$4FeS_2 + 22O_2 + 14H_2 \rightarrow 4Fe(OH)_3(\text{solid}) + 8SO_4^{2-}(\text{aq}) + 16H^+(\text{aq}).$$

Iron oxides will be precipitated, giving the characteristic red colour to AMD while the high acidity means that other metal species will be dissolved and precipitated. The reaction can be halted by removing the presence of either water or oxygen, and this is achieved by initially keeping the tailings under water in an anaerobic environment and covering with soil after mining is completed. Long-term monitoring will be required. A raised embankment is the most common construction where tailings are put through a cyclone with the slime proportion discharged to the centre of the impoundment and the sand fraction to the beach behind the crest (see Fig. 9.11).

Figure 9.11. Wall of tailings dam from historical mining in the East Rand Witwatersrand gold-mining operation undergoing reclamation with the slurry being reprocessed through DRD's Ergo gold operation before being discharged onto a new tailings dam. This type of operation is rehabilitating land that can be utilised for industrial development. Reproduced with their permission.

9.6.3 *Extractive metallurgy*

Processing of a polymetallic ore involves liberation of constituent minerals and the physical concentration of the phases containing the valuable constituents will always take place near the site of open pit or underground mining operations. The conversion to primary metal requires hydro- and pyro-metallurgical chemical extraction techniques which may often be remote from the mine site. The process routes for metalliferous ores is given in Fig 9.12. There is a boundary condition between physical processing in the plant and the pyro- and hydro-metallurgical processing that is needed in order to extract metals from minerals. A smelting operation may be a separate business unit and analogous to the down-stream processing of petroleum products in the oil industry. It is only after smelting and refining that metals such as zinc and lead are produced in their pure

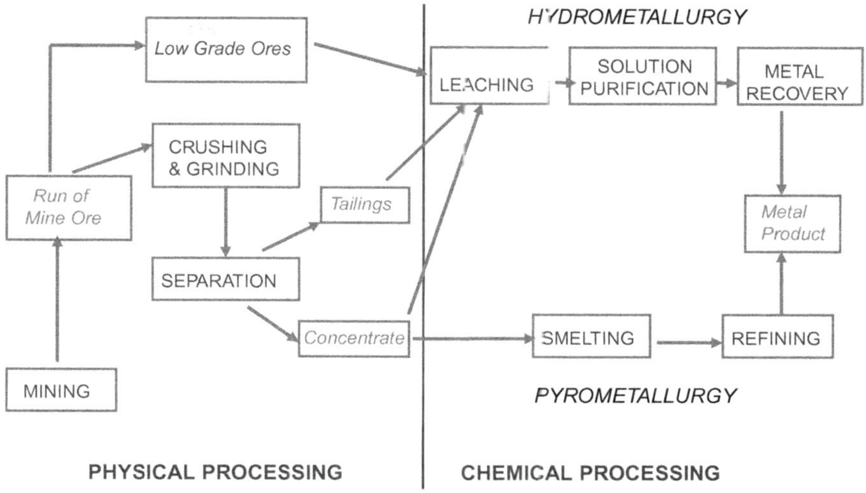

Figure 9.12. Process routes for metalliferous ores (after J. Cilliers).

elemental state so that revenue can be directly linked to market spot prices.

Once a concentrate has been produced, the contained metals need to be extracted appropriately using hydro- and pyro-metallurgical techniques. This is illustrated in Fig. 9.12. Where a mining company has an integrated down-stream metallurgical facility, then concentrate from their own mining operations can be treated directly but can or be sold on directly into the market under agreements described in Section 8.7.

In the case of nickel, metal concentrate is filtered and dried to a fine powder in preparation for the smelter. Smelters are not usually located on the mine site and may accept concentrate from a variety of individual operations. An off-take agreement is usually a confidential contract and it is often best to assume NSR and not spot prices in financial models.

The concentrate is exposed to a process known as flash smelting, which utilises energy from the exothermic reactions occurring when the iron and sulphur (contained in the powder) are burnt in an oxidising atmosphere The heavier molten metal sulphide sinks to the floor of the smelter while the lighter silicate melt floats to the top forming a slag.

The nickel matte is recovered and dried in preparation for further refining. Once again, some nickel is lost in the smelting process due to entrainment of the matte and as dissolved NiO. In general, the higher the matte grades, the higher the nickel losses. The slag is fed back into the smelter in an attempt to maximise nickel recovery. Flash smelting typically produces a granulated nickel matte containing approximately 75% nickel.

In South Africa, low sulphide PGE UG-2 concentrate is blended with high sulphide PGE Merensky Reef concentrate (see Section 9.5) to permit conventional (1,400°C) smelting. This means that the highly refractory chromite with a melting point of 2,200°C does not build up in the furnace. Chromium (Cr^{3+}) essentially partitions into the slag. The phase chemical systems and thermodynamic controls are identical to those outlined in Sections 5.5.2 and 5.5.3. The metallurgists are simply re-creating the conditions present in nature during the crystallisation of the Bushveld. In order to process a pure low sulphide UG-2 concentrate, enhanced chromium partitioning can be achieved by operating the furnace at a higher temperature, but this requires a design that incorporates graphite/copper cooling when operated at a temperature of 1,600°C. This system obviously provides a commercial advantage where an increasing proportion of the PGE comes from the UG-2 rather than the Merensky Reef. The high sulphide content of the Platreef provides a potential additional operational advantage as it ensures optimal proportions of matte and slag in the charge.

While PGE projects are a niche business, treatment of the extractive metallurgical issues is illustrative of the core theme for the "metals" part of this book. It is important that in evaluating a project the assessor looks beyond a product that comprises a concentrate of sulphide or oxide minerals to the associated contained metals. These can be directly linked to spot prices which allows for greater sophistication in financial modelling. NSRs usually imply fixed revenue assumptions, but if metal is produced as a final product and sold into a commodities market then the treatment of price volatility can be modelled using the principles of quantitative finance. PGE projects also demonstrate how financial modelling needed for an investment decision in down-stream processing must be constrained by the thermodynamics of smelting.

Refining facilities may be located at a distance from the mine and smelter as they have considerable power requirements and so seek to locate in a region where power is both readily available and cheap. Nickel refineries employ a technique known as the Sherritt–Gordon process in which the nickel matte slurry is treated to remove selectively unwanted metals, sulphur and finally copper. The resulting solution is then purified in a nickel reduction process, leaving a high-grade nickel metal product. Nickel is usually produced as marketable briquettes with a 99.8% Ni purity. Downstream refining can be considered a separate business unit.

The conclusion for many investors is that it is best to stick to gold as the operation will produce bullion on site. The only remaining stage is refining and a high grade non-refractory gold deposit may well be associated with low technical risk. If that logic is followed through, then diamonds are an even better option as all that is being produced on site is the raw mineral. The very low grades associated with primary deposits of kimberlite or alluvial gravels plus the challenges of determining price per carat, however, raise separate considerations that make these some of the most difficult projects to assess.

9.6.4 *Coal beneficiation*

Coal beneficiation is the stage of production when ROM coal is processed into a range of clean, graded and uniform products suitable for the commercial market (see Sections 8.8.1 and 11.7). Following extraction, coal usually requires crushing to reduce it to a usable and consistent size, while washing may be necessary to remove pieces of rock or mineral that are present and so improve the overall quality of the product. If ROM coal is of variable grade, blending may be required to ensure a consistent quality of coal to the end-user.

The extent of beneficiation carried out is dependent on customer requirements and the physical characteristics of ROM material. In some cases, ROM coal is of such quality that it meets user specification without the need for any treatment, in which case it is merely crushed and screened to deliver the specified product size. The capital requirements for developing a processing plant are generally low compared with the expenditure on mining equipment.

9.7 Capex Estimation

A typical Capex estimation at the PFS stage for a project that com prises an integrated mining and processing capability will normally also include provision for infrastructure. Capex estimates will be associated with an inherent uncertainty of ±20%.

Funding requirements at the FTFS stage must incorporate the cost of the EPC&M contract (see Section 8.5.3) which can be up to 15% of the total Capex. There is also the level of contingency that should be included as part of the overall funding requirement. No promoter wants to run out of money before the project is completed. This risk is compounded when the promotors insist that the independent engineers revise down Capex estimates. This fails to fully appreciate that the final costs under an EPC&M contract will only be revealed once tenders have been received. If initial estimates have been unrealistic, then the inevitable budget "blow-out" will occur during construction as reality sets in.

Unrealistic Capex estimates will probably be associated with inadequate provision for contingency. All construction stops and the operation fails to get into production on schedule and the start of revenue is delayed. The whole project then becomes fatally flawed, as the NPV on which the investment decision was made is never achieved.

The pragmatic approach is to accept that even at the FTFS stage Capex estimates will be associated with an inherent uncertainty of ±10% (see Section 8.5.3). Funding requirements should then assume that the final Capex would be the base case plus 10%. Contingency is then treated as covering the unexpected such as pre-production development encountering an aquifer which requires unprecedented pumping capacity. It should not be used to accommodate changes to the original design imposed by the promoter on the engineers implementing the EPC&M contract. Within that context, a contingency of 10% on top of the base case plus 10% should be adequate. Contingency can be as high as 20% but it is seldom clear how this is determined. If it is on top of the upper cost estimate it will be expensive if funded in part from debt. It also increases the challenge of securing the balance needed from the equity component.

Quantitative Finance

Chapter 10

Quantitative Finance

This book is based on the precept that mineral resource engineering and financial engineering are equally important aspects of project development. The latter includes use of "real options" based on the Black–Scholes formula, and other project risks including interest rate uncertainty and credit risk. This chapter provides a whistle-stop tour of the mathematical methods of quantitative finance that address these problems. Much more detail can be found in the textbooks listed at the end of the chapter.

10.1 Forwards and Futures

In the world of finance, a bank's discount rate is determined by its borrowing costs, which are derived from LIBOR, the short-term interbank rate. The exact construction is outlined in Section 10.4, but for now all we need to know is that at any time t there is a well-defined discount curve $D(t,T)$ representing the value at t of £1 delivered at T. Sometimes this is expressed in terms of a continuously-compounding rate r, so $D(t,T) = e^{-r(T-t)}$, or a time-varying rate $r(s)$ giving $D(t,T) = \exp\{-\int_t^T r(s)ds\}$.

For a financial asset, the spot price S_t is the current market price and a forward price $F(t,T)$ is an agreement between two parties, made at time t, to exchange one unit of the asset for £$F(t,T)$ at T. For an asset paying no dividends, the *unique arbitrage-free value* of the forward is $F(t,T) = S_t/D(t,T)$. This value can be perfectly hedged by, at t, borrowing S_t and buying the asset and, at T, handing over the asset and receiving $F(t,T)$ which is just enough to repay the loan. If any other forward price were quoted, then one party or the other could make a riskless profit by accepting the quote and then going long or short the hedging strategy just described; there is an "arbitrage opportunity". If the asset pays dividends, then the forward price will be less because the purchaser receives dividends before handing it over. When the "dividend yield" is q, meaning that dividends are paid in a continuous stream with $qS_u du$ paid in the interval $[u, u + du]$, then $F(t,T) = e^{-q(T-t)} S_t/D(t,T)$.

An important example is forward FX rates. Then there are two discount curves, the "domestic" one $D_d(t,T)$ and the "foreign" one $D_f(t,T)$. The formula is the same, with the foreign interest rate playing the role of the dividend yield q, i.e. $D_f(t,T) = e^{-q(T-t)}$, so the forward price of one unit of foreign currency is $F(t,T) = D_f(t,T)S_t/D_d(t,T)$ in domestic units, S_t being the spot exchange rate.

For non-financial assets such as commodities, the picture is completely different as forward prices for delivery of, say, Brent Crude at monthly dates are directly traded on exchanges, with significant volume out to 15 months and some specific later dates. So the prices are determined by supply and demand, not by some formula. The two concepts are linked by a "fudge factor" called the *convenience yield* y defined by $F(t,T) = e^{-y(T-t)} S_t/D(t,T)$ where F is the month-T delivery price and S_t is the nearest-month price. With this definition, F is equivalent to the forward price on a financial asset with dividend yield y. Factors such as storage costs influence the dividend yield, but note that a storage cost implies a negative "dividend yield" since such costs *increase* the forward price. If things are out of line, arbitrageurs can sometimes make profits by entering the buy side at an early date and on the sell side at a later date.

The main problem with a forward contract is *credit risk*. The buyer has *the right and the obligation* to pay the agreed price, say £10 per share. Suppose that when the exercise time comes around the market price is £9.50. Then the buyer would prefer to tear up the contract and buy in the market instead. This incentive is removed if trading is organised as a *futures market*. A futures market is an exchange where all participants are trading with the exchange, not with each other, and each participant maintains a "margin account". Contracts are opened with a range of expiry dates T. If we wish to participate in the T-contract, we

- enter the market (on either side) at no cost at time t_0, when the futures price is $f(0)$;
- on each day k our margin account is credited (debited if on the short side) with a payment $f(k) - f(k-1)$;
- at maturity *by definition* $f(T) = S_T$, the spot price.

The resulting change in our margin account (if on the long side) is

$$(f(1) - f(0)) + (f(2) - f(1)) + \cdots - (S_T - f(T-1)) = S_T - f(0),$$

all the intermediate terms cancelling out. Thus, aside from the payment schedule, the future is equivalent to a forward contract with forward price $f(0)$. It can be cancelled at any time simply by entering another contract on the opposite side. The commodities markets discussed above are actually futures markets.

Mathematical study of futures markets shows that, economically, forwards and futures are tantamount to the same thing; specifically:

- Forward and futures prices are the same when there is no interest-rate volatility
- They are *not* the same when interest rates are volatile, the future being higher if rates are negatively correlated with prices
- The difference is negligibly small except for long-term contracts in the interest-rate markets; see Section 10.4.

10.2 Options

Options are designed to get around the problem with a forward contract that one is obliged to go through with it even when it is disadvantageous to do so. A call option gives the holder the right *but not the obligation* to purchase an asset at a fixed price (the *strike*), either on a specific date T (a European option) or at any time up to T (an American option). A put option confers the right to sell. For the moment, we only discuss European options; the American case, which is more complicated, is covered at the end of the chapter.

A call option will be exercised only if the price S_T exceeds the strike price K; it is "in the money". Then, having bought it for K, the holder can sell the asset in the market, realising a profit $S_T - K$. If it is out of the money, $S_T < K$, then it expires worthless. In summary, its exercise value is $[S_T - K]^+ = \max(S_T - K, 0)$. Similarly, the put option has exercise value $[K - S_T]^+$. Often, options are cash-settled: the seller pays the buyer the exercise value in cash. Figure 10.1 shows the exercise value as a function of the underlying asset price. Being long a call and short a put results in a payoff $S_T - K$; the value of this payoff at time 0 is $D(0,T)(F(0,T) - K)$.

Both put and call have payoffs which are always non-negative, so to enter these contracts one should pay positive premiums C and P at time 0; otherwise there would be an arbitrage. Whatever these premiums are, they must satisfy the *put–call parity* relation $C - P = D(0,T)(F(0,T) - K)$, so we can concentrate on one of them, say the call option. To determine C, we need a stochastic model, i.e. a description of the random motion followed by the asset price S_t that will enable us to calculate quantities such as the probability that the option will end up in the money. The big breakthrough in this area was the Black–Scholes formula (1973), based on a model we describe now.

The basic random motion, or "stochastic process" in the Black–Scholes theory is *Brownian motion* W_t, characterised by the following four properties:

(i) $W_0 = 0$.

(ii) For any $0 \le s < t$, the random variable $W_t - W_s$ has the normal distribution with mean 0 and variance $t-s$; we write $(W_t - W_s) \sim \mathcal{N}(0, t-s)$. In particular, $W_t \sim \mathcal{N}(0,t)$.

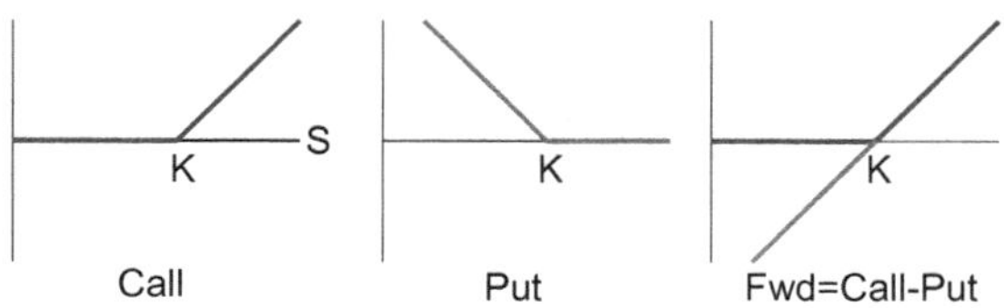

Figure 10.1. Exercise values of call and put options.

(iii) For any non-overlapping time intervals $s < t \leq s' < t'$, the increments $W_t - W_s$ and $W_{t'} - W_{s'}$ are independent.
(iv) The path $t \mapsto W_t$ is continuous.

The price model $S_t = S_0 + \sigma W_t$ was actually proposed by Louis Bachelier in 1900 but rejected later because for any $t > 0$ there is positive probability that $S_t < 0$, while stock prices are always positive. To counter this, in the 1960s economist Paul Samuelson proposed the model $S_t = A\exp(\sigma W_t)$ so that $\log S_t$ is normal or, as conventionally put, S_t is log-normal. The parameter σ is the *volatility*. A convenient way to parametrise the model is to take

$$S_t = S_0 \exp\left\{\left(m - \frac{1}{2}\sigma^2\right)t + \sigma W_t\right\}. \tag{1}$$

For a random variable $Y \sim \mathcal{N}(0, v)$, it is easily checked that $\mathbb{E}[e^Y] = e^{\frac{1}{2}v}$, so using (ii) above we have $\mathbb{E}[e^{\sigma W_t}] = e^{\frac{1}{2}\sigma^2 t}$. Thus, the mean or expected value of S_t is $\mathbb{E}[S_t] = S_0 e^{mt}$, so S_t has growth rate m and volatility σ. Another way to look at this model is to note that, for small x, $\log(1 + x) \approx x$, so the *return* over a short interval $[t, u]$ is by definition $R_{tu} = (S_u - S_t)/S_t$ and $\log(S_u/S_t) = \log(1 + R_{tu}) \approx R_{tu}$. Thus, Samuelson's model is essentially one in which *returns* are normal, rather than *prices*, and of course returns can be negative.

Black–Scholes showed that in a market containing an asset S_t with price model (1), paying dividend yield q, and a risk-free bank account paying a continuously compounded interest rate r, the unique arbitrage-free price paid at time 0 for a European call option with strike K and exercise time T is

$$C(S_0, K, T, r, q, \sigma) = S_0 e^{-qT} N(d_1) - K e^{-rT} N(d_2). \tag{2}$$

Here, N is the distribution function of the normal distribution $\mathcal{N}(0, 1)$,

$$N(x) = \frac{1}{\sqrt{2\pi}} \int_{-\infty}^{x} e^{-\frac{1}{2}y^2} dy,$$

and

$$d_1 = \frac{\log(S_0/K) + (r - q + \frac{1}{2}\sigma^2)T}{\sigma\sqrt{T}}, \quad d_2 = d_1 - \sigma\sqrt{T}.$$

An alternative form of (2) is the so-called *Black formula*. First, d_1 can be rewritten as $d_1 = (\log(S_0 e^{(r-q)T}/K) + \frac{1}{2}\sigma^2 T)/\sigma\sqrt{T}$ so, using the notation introduced in Section 10.1, (2) can be rewritten as

$$C(F, D, K, T, \sigma) = D(N(d_1) - KN(d_2)), \tag{3}$$

with $d_1 = (\log(F/K) + \frac{1}{2}\sigma^2 T)/\sigma\sqrt{T}$, where $F = F(0,T)$ is the forward price and $D = D(0,T)$ is the discount factor. This form of Black–Scholes is in fact much more widely applicable, because the interest rate parameter r is not market data, while D and F *are* market data. Formula (3) is correct without any assumption about existence of a continuously compounding bank account, using the method described below in Section 10.4 to determine discount factors from swap rates, and is also correct when F is determined by market trading, as for commodities, rather than the financial forward assumed in (2).

It turns out that the option value given by the formula (2) can also be expressed as

$$C(S_0, K, T, r, q, \sigma) = \mathbb{E}^{(r-q)}\{D(0,T)[S_T - K]^+\},$$

in which $\mathbb{E}^{(r-q)}$ denotes expectation with respect to a price model which is similar to (1), but with the growth rate m replaced by $r - q$. This is the so-called *risk-neutral* model and it was a puzzling feature when first discovered, but we will see in the next section why it has to be that way. A useful by-product is that the option value does not depend on the growth rate m — which it is practically impossible to estimate.

What is the basis for this formula? In their paper, Black and Scholes showed that it is possible to trade in the underlying asset and cash in such a way that the value of the resulting portfolio at T exactly matches the option exercise value (see Fig. 10.2). In other words, the option can be *replicated* by trading. It follows that the option premium must be equal to the initial investment in the replicating portfolio; otherwise there would be an arbitrage opportunity. The replication strategy is *delta-hedging*: at any time t the replicating portfolio holds a number of shares equal to $\Delta_t = \partial C/\partial S_t$, the derivative of option value with respect to underlying price, together with cash holdings such that the portfolio is self-financing. This is

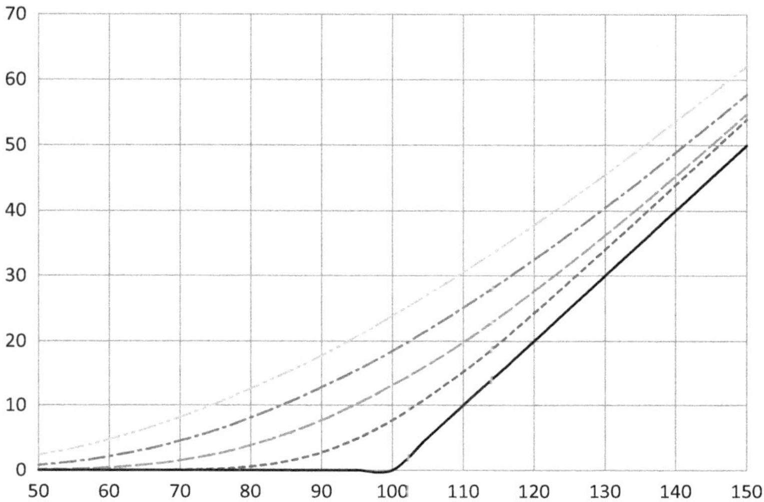

Figure 10.2. Black–Scholes option price for a 2-year option as a function of initial price S_0. Parameters are $r = 4\%$, $K = 100$. Volatilities are $\sigma = 0, 10\%, 20\%, 30\%$ and 40% (option value increases with volatility).

intuitive since it says that for small changes in the underlying price the change in option value is matched by the change in the value of the hedging portfolio. Δ_t can be calculated from the Black–Scholes formula and is equal to $N(d_1)$. The hedging argument will be clear once we have studied the binomial tree, the subject of the next section.

10.3 Binomial Tree

This model, introduced by Cox, Ross and Rubinstein in 1979, has played a decisive role in the development of the derivatives industry. Its simple structure and easy implementation have given analysts the ability to price a huge range of financial derivatives in almost routine way.

Start with a 1-period model for an asset whose price is S today and whose price tomorrow can only be one of two known values S_0 or S_1 where $S_0 > S_1$; see Fig. 10.3. This apparently highly artificial

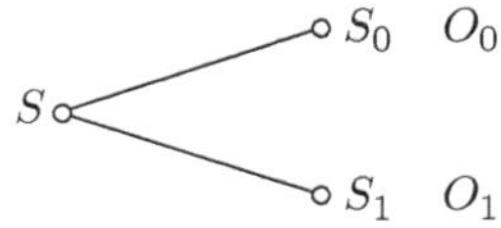

Figure 10.3. 1-period binomial tree.

situation is the kernel of the binomial model. We also suppose there is a bank account paying a daily rate of interest r_1, so that £1 today is worth $£R = £(1 + r_1)$ tomorrow. We assume that borrowing is possible from the bank at the same rate of interest r_1, and that the risky asset can also be borrowed (sold short, in the usual financial terminology). The only other assumption is that $S_1 < RS < S_0$. If $RS \leq S_1$, we could borrow $£B$ from the bank and buy B/S shares of the risky asset. Tomorrow these will be worth at least BS_1/S, enough to pay RB back to the bank. There will never be a loss, and will be a strictly positive profit if the price moves to S_0. This is an *arbitrage opportunity*: a strategy which involves no loss and a chance of positive profit. There is also an arbitrage opportunity if $RS \geq S_0$, realised by short-selling the risky asset.

An option is a contract that pays tomorrow an amount that depends only on tomorrow's asset price. Thus, any such claim can only have values, say O_0 and O_1 corresponding to "underlying" prices S_0, S_1, as shown in Fig. 10.3. Suppose that today we form a portfolio consisting of A shares of the risky asset and $£B$ in the bank (either or both of A, B could be negative). The value today of this portfolio is $p = AS + B$ and its value tomorrow will be $AS_0 + BR$ or $AS_1 + BR$. Now choose A and B such that

$$AS_0 + BR = O_0$$

$$AS_1 + BR = O_1,$$

solved by

$$A = \frac{O_0 - O_1}{S_0 - S_1}, \quad B = \frac{1}{R}(O_0 - AS_0). \tag{4}$$

The portfolio value tomorrow exactly coincides with the derivative security payoff, whichever way the price moves. Note that A corresponds to a discrete version of delta-hedging since it is just the ratio of the change in option price to the change in underlying price. If the derivative security is offered today for any price other than p there is an arbitrage opportunity (realised by "borrowing the portfolio" and buying the option or conversely). It is easily checked that

$$p = \frac{1}{R}(q_0 O_0 + q_1 O_1),$$

where $q_0 = (RS - S_1)/(S_0 - S_1)$ and $q_1 = (S_0 - RS)/(S_0 - S_1)$. Note that $q_0, q_1 \geq 0$, $q_0 + q_1 = 1$ and q_0, q_1 depend only on the underlying market parameters, not on O_0 or O_1. We can therefore write the price of the derivative as

$$p = \mathbb{E}_Q\left(\frac{1}{R}O\right),$$

the expected discounted payoff under the probability $Q = (q_0, q_1)$ defined above. Note that this probability, the so-called *risk-neutral* probability, emerges from the "no-arbitrage" argument. We said nothing in formulating the model about the probability of an upwards or downwards move and the above argument does not imply that this probability has to be given by Q. Note also that taking $O_0 = S_0$, $O_1 = S_1$ gives

$$S = \frac{1}{R}(q_0 S_0 + q_1 S_1);$$

today's price is the expected discounted value of tomorrow's price. This condition is enough to determine q_0, q_1. To summarise:

- There is a unique arbitrage-free price for the contingent claim.
- This price is obtained by computing the discounted expectation with respect to a certain probability Q.
- Q can be characterised as the unique probability such that the expected discounted underlying price is equal to the initial price.

Now we examine how to extend this simple model to multiple periods. First, consider the 2-period case of Fig. 10.4 and an option with exercise value O at time 2 where $O = O_0, O_1, O_2$ in the 3 states as shown.

Consider the situation at the intermediate time 1. By the 1-period argument, the no-arbitrage value of the option if the underlying price

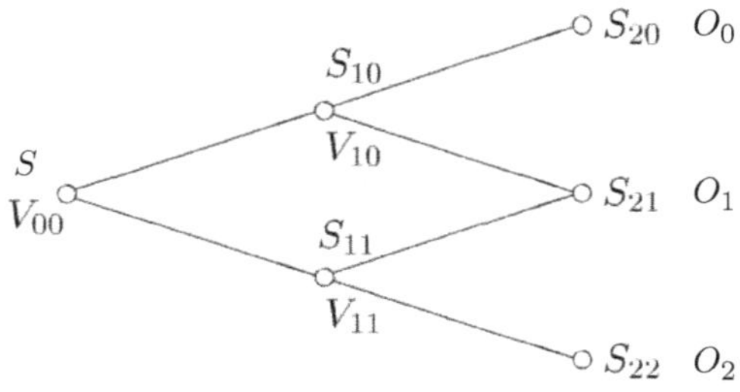

Figure 10.4. 2-period binomial tree.

is S_{10} is $V_{10} = (q_0^{10} O_0 + q_1^{10} O_1)/R$, and it is $V_{11} = (q_0^{11} O_1 + q_1^{11} O_2)/R$ if the price is S_{11}, where q^{10}, q^{11} are the risk-neutral probabilities at the two time-1 nodes. But now our option at time 0 is equivalent to a 1-period claim with payoffs V_{10}, V_{11}, so its value is just $(q_0^0 V_{10} + q_1^0 V_{11})/R$, where q^0 is the risk-neutral probability at time 0. We can write this simply as

$$V_{00} = \mathbb{E}_Q\left[\frac{1}{R^2} O\right],$$

where Q denotes the probability distribution for the whole tree defined by the node probabilities q^0, q^{11} and q^{12}. The argument extends in an obvious way to n periods, giving an option valuation $V_{00} = \mathbb{E}_Q[O/R^n]$. Things are particularly straightforward when, as in most implementations, the up and down moves are defined by factors $u > 1$ and $d = 1/u$, so that $S_{10} = uS$, $S_{10} = dS$, $S_{20} = u^2 S$, etc. Taking $d = 1/u$ ensures that the tree "recombines", i.e. $S_{21} = S$. In an n-period tree with this price specification, the risk-neutral probabilities at all nodes are the same, given by $q_0 = (R-d)/(u-d), q_1 = (u-R)/(u-d)$. The replicating strategy is still discrete delta-hedging, but the value of delta will be different at different nodes in the tree, meaning we need a "dynamic" hedging strategy in which the portfolio is rebalanced after each price move.

Finally, we want to look at tree-based models as a computational method for Black–Scholes. For simplicity, assume there are no dividends and the bank account pays interest at continuously compounding rate r. Then the Black–Scholes price model under the risk-neutral probability is

$$S_t = S_0 \exp\left\{\left(r - \frac{1}{2}\sigma^2\right)t + \sigma W_t\right\}, \quad 0 \le t \le T. \tag{5}$$

The price S_T satisfies $S_0 = \mathbb{E}[e^{-rT}S_T]$ — the risk-neutral property — and S_T is just a function of the underlying Brownian motion W_T. Dividing the interval $[0, T]$ into n equal-length pieces we can always write $W_T = X_1 + X_2 + \cdots + X_n$ where X_k is the kth increment, $X_k = (W_{kT/n} - W_{(k-1)T/n})$. The X_k are normally distributed, $X_k \sim \mathcal{N}(0, T/n)$, and X_k, X_j are independent for $k \neq j$. Now take independent random variables $Y_1, Y_2 \ldots$. such that $Y_k = \pm a_n$ with probability $\frac{1}{2}$ each, where $a_n = \sqrt{T}/n$. Then Y_k has mean 0 and variance a_n^2, just like X_k, and we define $W_T^{(n)} = Y_1 + Y_2 + \cdots + Y_n$. The discrete model is obtained by replacing W_T by $W_T^{(n)}$ in (5); this is called a "random walk" approximation to Brownian motion: at each time kT/n the process moves up or down by a fixed amount. We can represent the random walk as a path along a tree as indicated (for $n = 4$) in Fig. 10.5: at each time step the path move up or down an amount a_n with equal probability $\frac{1}{2}$.

As $n \to \infty$, the path takes a larger and larger number of smaller and smaller steps, and the distribution of $W_T^{(n)}$ approaches that of W_T, the normal distribution $\mathcal{N}(0, T)$. The argument for this is shown in Section 10.6. In most applications, $n \approx 100$ suffices. For option pricing in the discrete model, write (5) as $S_t = g(t)\exp(\sigma W_t)$ where $g(t) = S_0 \exp\{(r - \sigma^2/2)t\}$ and replace W_t by $W_t^{(n)}$. At the final

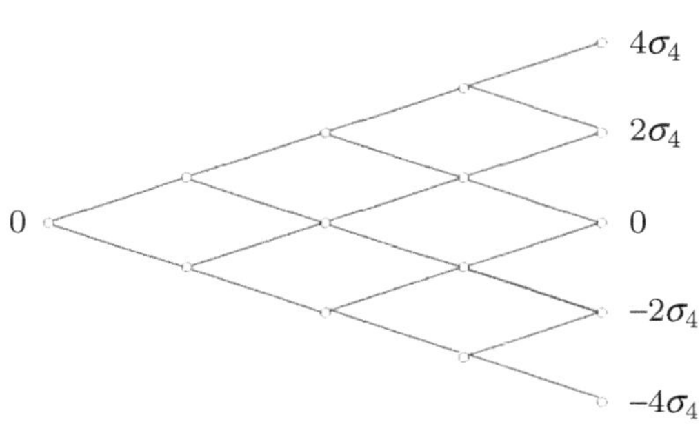

Figure 10.5. Random walk model with $n = 4$.

time T, $W_T^{(n)}$ takes the values $na_n, (n-2)a_n, \ldots, -na_n$, as shown for $n = 4$ in Fig. 10.5, and we can fill in the corresponding option exercise values $[S_T - K]^+$. Now we just take discounted expectations, starting at time $k = n-1$ and working backwards: at any node N the value is $e^{-rT/n}$ times the arithmetic average (recall the up/down probabilities are $\frac{1}{2}$) of the values at the two nodes to which N is connected on the right. Then the option price is the value at the initial time-0 node. In most applications, $n \approx 100$ suffices. For option valuation, it is not necessary to compute intermediate values of S_t, but they are needed to compute the hedge ratios that define the replicating trading strategy. For example at $k = 1$, we have two option values V_0 and V_1, so from (4) the number of units of the underlying in the initial hedge portfolio is $(V_0 - V_1)/(g(1/T)2a_n$.

A decisive advantage of tree models is their ability to price American options at a very modest computational overhead. Recall that in an American option the holder has the right to exercise at any time up to the final time T. The American option cannot be worth less than the European option since one possible strategy available to the holder is never to exercise before T. The extra "optionality" increases opportunity. It is a general fact, not restricted to the Black–Scholes model, that for call options on assets paying no dividends there is in fact no extra value in an American option: exercise at T is optimal. For put options, and for call options on dividend-paying assets (example: FX options) there is generally extra value. The theory of American options is complicated, and indeed was not fully worked out until more than a decade after the Black–Scholes paper appeared. However, the algorithm proposed by Cox, Ross and Rubinstein does indeed give the right answer. It applies in any tree model, for example, the one described above, which we consider here.

Option values are calculated in a tree by working backwards from the final time T. At T, the American option value is just the usual exercise value, $[K - S_T]^+$ for a put option. Now suppose we are at some node $\mathfrak{n}_{kj}$ at discrete time k in the tree, having computed the option values V^+ and V^- at time $k+1$ for the two nodes to which $\mathfrak{n}_{kj}$ is connected. If this were a European option, the value at $\mathfrak{n}_{kj}$ would be $V_C = e^{-rT/n}\frac{1}{2}(V^+ + V^-)$. Call this the *continuation value*. The *immediate exercise value* is $V_I = [K - S_{kj}]^+$ where S_{kj}

is the underlying price at $\mathfrak{n}_{kj}$. The American option value is then $V_{kj} = \max(V_C, V_I)$; if $V_I > V_C$ it is optimal to exercise, otherwise it is optimal to continue to the next time. Having assigned the values V_{kj} for all nodes j at time k we move backwards to time $k-1$ and repeat the procedure. The value finally obtained at the initial node is the American option value. The *stopping region* is the set of nodes for which $V_I > V_C$ together with all the nodes at the final time, while all other nodes comprise the *continuation region*. The algorithm only requires a few extra lines of code beyond the European version. In any sensible contract, the initial node will be in the continuation region. The optimal exercise strategy is to wait until the price hits the stopping region and then exercise.

In the Black–Scholes model, we have a formula (2) for the European option value. No such formula exists for American options and a numerical algorithm is always required. Technically speaking, we are solving a free boundary problem for a parabolic PDE. The tree method is by far the simplest algorithm that does the job. Figure 10.6 shows the typical form of exercise boundary for an American put.

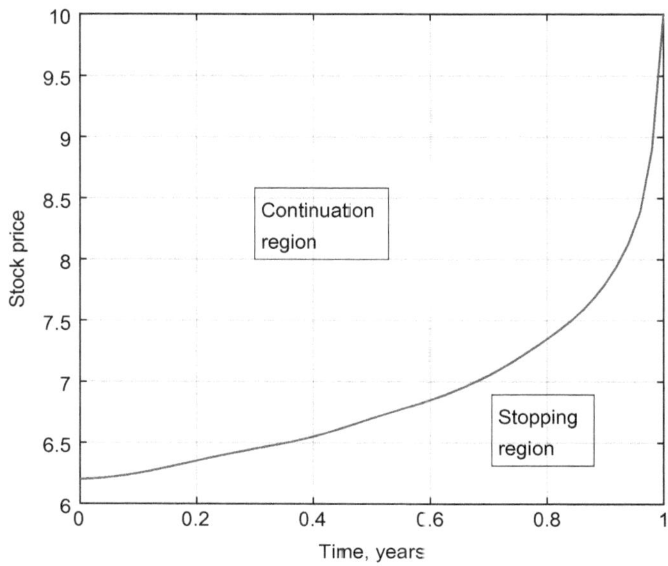

Figure 10.6. American put option exercise boundary, maturity = 1 year, strike = 10.

10.4 Interest Rates

There are many different interest rates "out there", but the ones most relevant to project finance are the LIBOR and swap rates since these form the basis for bank lending. The acronym LIBOR stands for "London Inter-Bank Offer Rate" and is an average, computed daily, for lending between one bank and another, so they represent a bank's funding cost. Commercial loans are often quoted in the form "LIBOR+x", meaning that the interest due is the current LIBOR rate plus a constant add-on x basis points related to the credit worthiness of the borrower. LIBOR rates are quoted for a range of maturities from overnight up to 1 or 2 years, the "benchmark" rate being 3-month LIBOR. Rates for longer terms are determined by interest-rate futures markets, which we will not cover here, and the swap market described below.

A key role in analysis of interest rates is played by the *zero-coupon bond* prices $p(t, T)$ representing the value at t of £1 delivered at T. In particular, $p(0, T)$ is the discount factor giving the current (time 0) value of future cash flows. Zero-coupon bonds are not market data but can be inferred from the data mentioned above. If $T = n$, an integer number of years, then the *zero-coupon yield* expressed on an annualised basis is the value y satisfying $p(0, n) = 1/(1 + y)^n$, the interpretation being that a bank account with initial investment $p(0, n)$ and receiving annual interest at rate y would have balance 1 at time n. One could also express the yield in, say, quarterly terms as $\hat{y}$ satisfying $p(0, n) = 1/(1 + \hat{y}/4)^{4n}$, or indeed in continuously-compounding terms $p(0, t) = e^{-\tilde{y}(t)t}$. The *yield curve* is a graph of zero-coupon yield against maturity; Fig. 10.7 shows a snapshot of the yield curves for three currencies. The curve moves randomly over time, and the challenge of interest-rate modelling is to represent these movements in probabilistic terms. It is instructive to watch these movements and there are websites[1] at which animations can be found.

[1] For example, https://stockcharts.com/freecharts/yieldcurve.php.

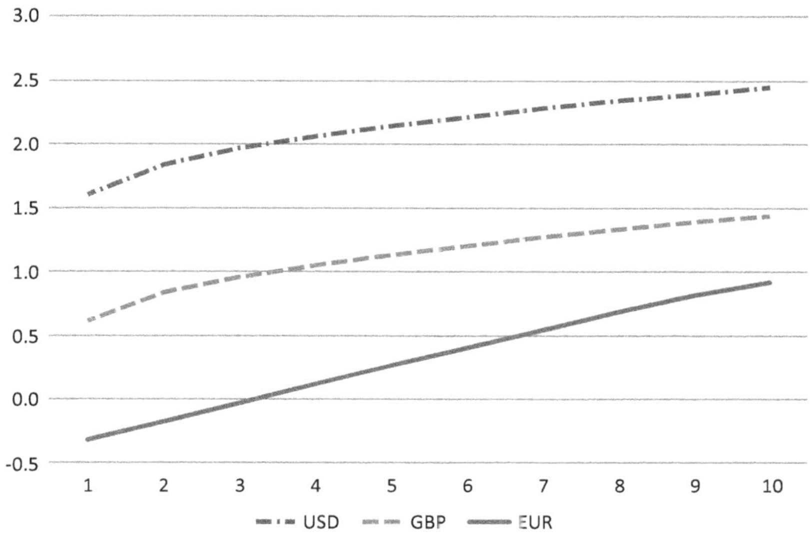

Figure 10.7. 1–10 year yield curves for USD, GBP, EUR, 25/10/2017.

For simplicity of exposition, we shall assume henceforth that all interest payments are made annually. Then the holder of a *bond* receives interest payments ("coupons") at rate c_k after k years on a principal amount, or "notional", M, and at the maturity time receives the final interest payment plus M. Since all payments are proportional to M, it is conventional to normalise to $M = 1$. Bonds are tradable assets with prices determined by supply and demand; if w is the price at a time when there are n years left until maturity, then the corresponding yield y satisfies

$$w = \frac{c_1}{(1+y)} + \frac{c_2}{(1+y)^2} + \cdots + \frac{c_{n-1}}{(1+y)^{n-1}} + \frac{(1+c_n)}{(1+y)^n}.$$

In a *fixed-rate* bond, all the coupons are the same, $c_k = c$, and the reader can check that $w = 1$, the bond is *at par*, if and only if $y = c$. Note the inverse relationship between yield and price. In general, bond prices move around in such a way that their yields are consistent with those of newly-issued bonds. Bonds can also be *floating rate* with coupons that depend on market conditions. An important instance is the *floating-rate note* in which c_k is the annual

LIBOR rate L_k for the period between years $k-1$ and k. Note that the rate is *set in advance* at time $k-1$ and *paid in arrears* at time k, so at each year the investor knows what the deal is for the coming year, but not beyond that. When discounting is based on LIBOR, the floating rate note is always at par at every coupon date, because the coupon and the yield are the same.

An interest rate *swap* is a contract in which two parties, payer and receiver, exchange payment of coupons on the same notional amount. The payer pays a fixed-rate coupon at rate c while the receiver pays LIBOR, up to an agreed maturity date n years. This is equivalent to exchange of a floating-rate note for a fixed-rate bond, since the final exchange of notional cancels out — hence the term "notional": it is the amount on which the coupon payments are based but is not itself in play. The n-maturity *swap rate* s_n is the value of the fixed-side rate such that the swap has value zero at inception. Since the floating-rate side has value 1, s_n is determined by the condition that the fixed side also has value 1. In terms of the zero-coupon bonds, this is equivalent to $1 = \sum_{k=1}^{n} s_n p(0,k) + p(0,n)$, i.e.

$$s_n = \frac{1 - p(0,n)}{\sum_1^n p(0,k)}. \tag{6}$$

In this equation, the left-hand side is market data since swaps are traded assets (in fact, the swap market is one of the biggest financial markets there is). Swaps are generally available with every maturity from 1 to 10 years and a more sparse selection of longer maturity dates out to 25 or 30 years. To construct the yield curve, we have to use the various values $s_1, s_2, \ldots$ together with equation (6) to "back out" the zero-coupon values $p_k = p(0,k)$ appearing on the right of (6). If there are no gaps in the data, a simple recursion does the trick. Suppose we have computed $p_1, \ldots, p_k$ based on data $s_1, \ldots, s_k$. Then, from (6), $\sum_{j=1}^{k} p_j = (1-p_k)/s_k$, so moving to $k+1$ we have

$$s_{k+1} = \frac{1 - p_{k+1}}{(1-p_k)/s_k + p_{k+1}},$$

and consequently

$$p_{k+1} = \frac{1}{1 + s_{k+1}} \left(1 - \frac{s_{k+1}}{s_k}(1 - p_k)\right).$$

In reality, there will always be gaps in the data so we need some interpolation to complete this algorithm. Values of $p(0,t)$ for t between coupon dates are also obtained by interpolation. In practice, this procedure is extremely accurate and different banks will agree on the discount curve to within fractions of a basis point. As mentioned above, the short end of the yield curve is not determined by swap rates but, out to 1 year, directly by market-quoted LIBOR rates and, between 1 and 2 years, also by interest-rate futures. However, for project finance, it is generally the longer terms that are relevant.

10.4.1 *Interest rate options*

Nothing we have discussed so far requires a model. The situation is similar to computing forward rates in the equity world where a simple hedging argument is all that is required. The same is true of forward LIBOR rates, which are defined in terms of zero-coupon bonds (ZCB) by

$$F(j,k) = \frac{p(j,k-1)}{p(j,k)} - 1. \tag{7}$$

The reason for this is as follows. The relationship between LIBOR L_k and ZCB is $1/(1+L_k) = p(k-1,k)$ (the ZCB is equivalent to discounting at the LIBOR rate), so $L_k = 1/p(k-1,k) - 1$ and the value at $k-1$ of the L_k, which is paid at k, is $L_k/(1+L_k) = 1-p(k-1,k)$. This amount is perfectly hedged at time j by a portfolio that is long $p(j,k-1)$ and short $p(j,k)$, with value $p(j,k-1)-p(j,k)$. Moving forward from j to $k-1$, this value becomes $1-p(k-1,k)$, exactly matching the LIBOR value. Thus, $F(j,k)$ represents the value at j of the LIBOR payment L_k.

When we turn to interest rate options, a model is required, as in Black–Scholes. The standard options *caps* and *swaptions*. A cap in an agreement under which scheduled LIBOR payments over n years will never exceed a fixed cap K, so at date k the value is $[L_k - K]^+$, protecting the investor against unexpected rises in rates.

A contract with this payoff is called a *caplet* and the value of the cap is just the sum of the n caplet values. A swaption, initiated at time 0 and defined by two dates $k < n$, gives the investor the right to enter, at time k, a swap with maturity n at a fixed-side coupon c agreed at time 0. It is a *payer's* [*receiver's*] swaption when the right to enter is on the fixed [floating] side. The main use of a swaption is to enable the investor to get out of an unfavourable swap. The swap contract requires payments right up to its maturity date. By definition, the value is 0 at inception and at maturity after the last exchange of payments, but it may move significantly away from zero at intermediate times. For example, if an investor is paying the fixed side rate c and swap rates fall to s then she is now paying too much to secure the LIBOR payment stream. She could at no cost enter a new swap on the opposite side, but the net effect would be an obligation to pay coupons $c - s$ until the end of the contract. The point of the swaption is to enable her to negotiate in advance for a better "get out" deal. A useful variant in this respect is the *Bermuda swaption*, which allows for exercise at any one of a range of future coupon dates. Like Bermuda, this option is somewhere between America and Europe, but closer to America.

Modelling movements of the yield curve is a complex subject. The oldest and most traditional approach is to model the *short rate*, in which a zero coupon bond is represented as $p(t,T) = \mathbb{E}[e^{-\int_t^T r(s)ds}]$ where the short rate $r(t)$ is a stochastic process. One of the best-known versions, the Hull–White model, assumes that $r(t)$ satisfies the equation

$$dr(t) = \lambda(\theta(t) - r(t))dt + \sigma dW_t, \tag{8}$$

where W_t is Brownian motion. Note that when $\sigma = 0$ and θ is constant, the solution is $r_0(t) = \theta + (r(0) - \theta)e^{-\lambda t}$, $r_0(t)$ is "mean-reverting". When $\sigma > 0$, $r(t)$ is a gaussian process with mean $r_0(t)$ and variance $(\sigma^2/2\lambda)(1-e^{-2\lambda t})$. Thus, $r(t)$ is asymptotically stationary with mean θ and variance $\sigma^2/2\lambda$. Hull and White showed that if we allow $\theta(t)$ to be time-varying, it is possible to choose it so that $p(0,t) = \mathbb{E}[e^{-\int_0^t r(s)ds}]$, where $p(0,t)$ is obtained from today's yield curve. We can then use the model to price caps and swaptions. The Hull–White model used to be frowned upon because the short rate, being normally distributed, can be negative with positive probability;

but now that negative rates do appear in some markets this feature is, perversely, an advantage.

Short rate models have several shortcomings. The first is that they need re-calibrating every day. We choose $\theta(t)$ at time 0 to match the prices $p(0, t)$, but the next day we observe a new yield curve that is not exactly matched by the model, so the parameters have to be adjusted to a new value. This shortcoming also appears in the Black–Scholes model for equities where we choose an implied volatility to match option prices today but will need a different volatility tomorrow. In both cases, the conclusion is the same: the model is not rich enough. To take this further, we need to examine the range of yield curve moves that occur in reality versus the moves the model is able to generate.

The standard way to study yield curve moves empirically is to collect a sample consisting of a year or more of daily yield curves and apply the statistical technique of Principal Components Analysis (PCA) which pulls out the main "directions" in which yield curve moves take place. The results are shown schematically in Fig. 10.8. The dominant move is a "parallel shift", Fig. 10.8(a), in which the curve moves bodily up or down. The next most important move is a rotation (b) in which the moves at either end of the curve have different signs, and finally, less significantly, a "parabolic" type of move (c) in which the central part of the curve moves up and the wings down, or conversely. In the Hull–White model, all zero coupon bond prices $p(0, t)$ are ultimately just functions of the initial short rate $r(0)$, implying that the only yield curve moves covered by the model are parallel shifts.

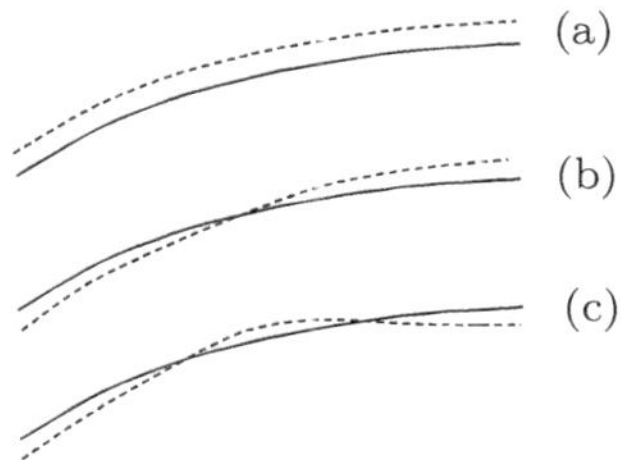

Figure 10.8. Yield curve moves (a) parallel shift, (b) twist, (c) hump. Solid line is original curve, dotted line is shifted curve.

A more sophisticated model allowing for a wider range of yield curve shifts is the Libor Market Model. The idea here is that the evolution of a swap or swaption depends only on the LIBOR rates $L_k, k = 0, 1, \ldots, n$, and their evolution is captured by modelling the set of forward Libor rates $F(t, k)$ defined as in (7) but with the current date being an arbitrary time t rather than just an earlier coupon date j. As pointed out above, these forward rates suffice to value and LIBOR payment in the future.

Either of the above models can be used to calculate prices of the standard interest-rate derivatives, caps and swaptions, in fixed-maturity or Bermuda form. A major use of swaps, and one reason for the huge size of the market in them, is as hedging instruments for these derivatives. The value of, say, a swaption at any time depends on the yield curve observed at that time covering the period up to the swaption maturity. Readily traded swaps depend on the same thing and so can be used to delta-hedge the swaption. The procedure in brief outline is as follows, referring to Fig. 10.9 in which T_4 is the maturity date of the swaption and we want to set up an initial hedge at time 0. Our hedging instruments are four swaps with maturities as shown in the figure. Each of the swaps depends on the yield curve up to its maturity, but not beyond, so we start with the T_4 and calculate the sensitivity of its value, and the value of the swaption, to F_3, the forward swap rate at T_3. By taking the ratio and trading that number of T_4 swaps, we form a portfolio that is insensitive to movements in F_3. Moving backwards to T_2, we calculate the sensitivity of that portfolio to movements in F_2 and cancel out that sensitivity by adding the right number of T_2 swaps. Continuing in this way, we arrive at a portfolio that is insensitive to any of the forward swap

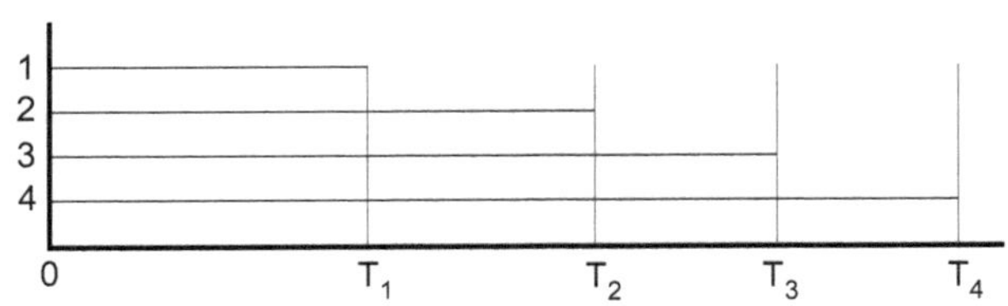

Figure 10.9. Maturity times for four swaps.

rates. Set up at 0, the portfolio will, of course, need rebalancing, with further trading in the swaps, as time goes on. Of course, there is much more to swaption hedging than this, but delta-hedging is the most basic ingredient.

10.5 Credit Risk

Credit risk is of course the risk that your counterparty will fail to come through with payments due. The traditional way to evaluate credit worthiness of a listed company is to look at the credit rating it is awarded by rating agencies such as Standard & Poors or Moodys.

These ratings are ranked AAA, AA, A, BBB, ... based on the company's accounts, trading position, performance in the market and any other factors deemed relevant. A company's borrowing costs, in particular the interest rate it needs to pay in order to launch a corporate bond, will depend on its credit rating, often being quoted as "LIBOR+x".

A new way of trading credit was introduced by J. P. Morgan in 1994 in the form of the *credit default swap* (CDS). From modest beginnings, the size of the market (the total face value specified in all open CDS contracts) mushroomed to $62 tn in 2007, but the CDS somewhat fell out of favour after the financial crisis and the size is now about a 10th of its maximum — still a huge number.

Figure 10.10 indicates the mechanics of a CDS contract. The contract refers to a specific entity, for example, a corporate bond issued by XYZ plc, and the objective is to insure the protection buyer

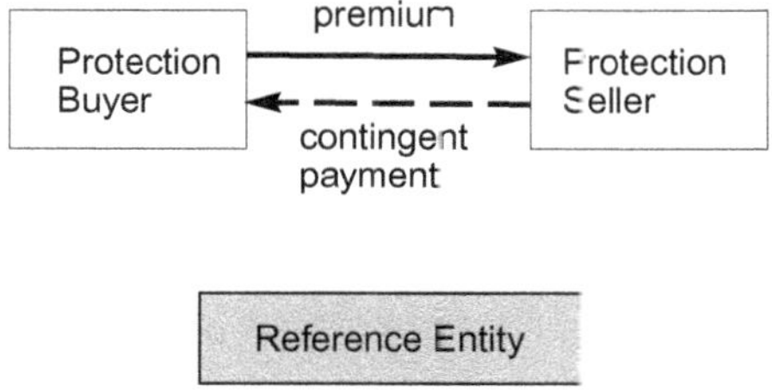

Figure 10.10. CDS transaction.

against default of XYZ in relation to coupon or principal payments due on the bond. Here "default" means any failure to pay moneys due in full and on time. This could include "technical" defaults such as paying a few days late. The buyer pays the seller premium payments in the form of regular coupons for the whole length of the contract or until a default is declared. In the latter case, the post-default market value of the bond is assessed, and then the seller pays the buyer the "unrecovered value" of the bond, the difference between its face value and the post-default market value. If the buyer owns the bond, the effect of the CDS is to make it essentially risk-free, since either it will make all payments as scheduled or the buyer will receive the full face value at the default time, so in effect the bond just matures early.

For this reason, the CDS premium must be close to the difference between the bond coupon and a comparable AAA bond. There is however — and this would be anathema in the insurance world — no requirement that the buyer should own the bond. From the seller's point of view, writing a CDS is economically equivalent to holding the reference bond: he receives the CDS coupons in exchange for taking the default risk. For this reason, CDS trading has to a large extent taken over from trading in the bonds themselves, which is one reason the market is so large.

Credit risk modelling is primarily concerned with modelling times of default, which are discrete events. In the case of a CDS, for example, a model should enable us to evaluate, at any time, the probability of default at subsequent coupon dates or at maturity.

As for other asset classes, credit risk models are required in two varieties, "real-world" models that statistically describe the evolution of prices as they are observed in the market, and "risk-neutral" models used for pricing à la Black–Scholes. Often, the primary model will be the risk-neutral one, the "real-world" model being the same but with an extra term reflecting the so-called *market price of risk*.

Research in this area was initiated — as were so many things in mathematical finance — by Robert Merton, in a 1974 paper whose influence lives on. It is concerned with corporate debt and instantiates the idea that a firm will default when its assets are insufficient

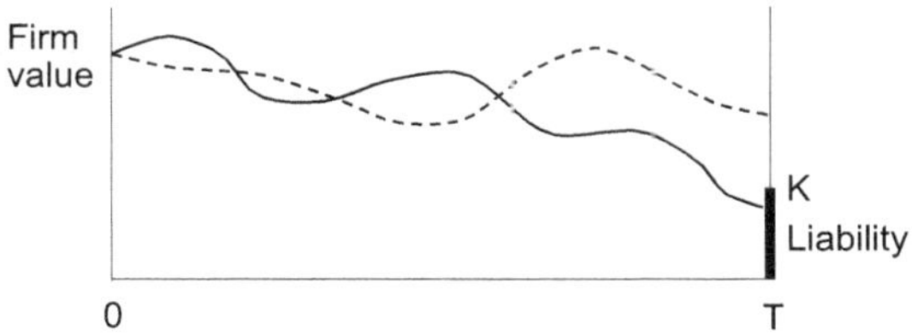

Figure 10.11. Evolution of firm value.

to cover a liability when the latter becomes due. Figure 10.11 shows this idea in the case of a single liability to be paid at time T; it shows two possible evolutions of the value of the firm's assets V_t, the solid line resulting in default as the end value is less than K, the liability.

It is apparent from the figure that the default risk is a *put option on the value of the firm*: at time T the amount of the liability that the firm cannot pay is $[K - V_T]^+$, the put option exercise value, and the liability will not be paid in full if this option is in the money. A cheap way to complete the model is to suppose that the firm value follows a log-normal diffusion — the Black–Scholes model — in which case the default probability is just $N(d_2)$.

Firm value models cannot directly be used in practice in any straightforward way because the value of a firm is not observable data. It is not the same thing as market capitalisation (the share price times the number of shares). Neither is it a traded asset, so it would be meaningless to build what is intended to be a risk-neutral firm value model whose growth rate is the riskless rate. Merton's idea is, however, valuable conceptually in isolating the essence of credit risk.

Practical structural form models drop the firm value interpretation and regard V_t as an abstract factor process. Following a 1976 paper by Black and Cox, default is deemed to occur at the first time t_D at which V_t reaches some low barrier level L as shown in Fig. 10.12 rather than just checking the value at some payment date as in the Merton model of Fig. 10.11. If we want to use this model for pricing a CDS, then the first task is to calibrate it, i.e. select model parameters in such a way that model-predicted prices match the current prices of CDS contracts traded in the market. In this case, the "price"

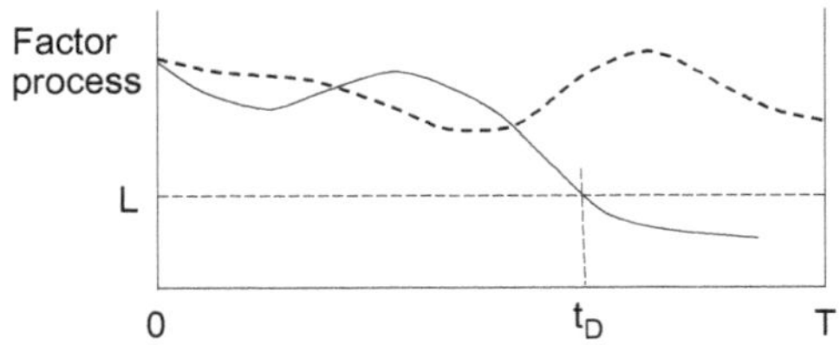

Figure 10.12. Barrier default model, with two trajectories of the factor process, one of which defaults at time t_D.

means the premium paid by the protection buyer (expressed as an annualised rate). The model is calibrated when the coupon rate is fair in the sense that the expected discounted value of the coupon payments exactly matches the expected discounted value of the post-default payment made by the seller. From the mathematical point of view, all these values are expressed in terms of the distribution of the random default time t_D, together with some model of the recovery rate, so the calibration task boils down to specifying a process V_t and a barrier level L such that t_D has a specified distribution. Several ways to accomplish this task have been proposed, and finding an optimal one is still a topic of active research. It can be quite complicated, particularly if default is correlated with the movement of interest rates. How to specify the recovery value is also contentious, but this is a statistical rather than mathematical question.

To clarify the calibration procedure, it might be helpful to consider a highly simplified example, as illustrated in Fig. 10.13. We suppose that two CDS contracts are traded on the same underlying bond of XYZ plc, with maturities $T_1 = 1$ and $T_2 = 2$ years respectively, the protection buyer paying coupons c annually in advance. Thus, for the 1-year CDS, the buyer pays a single coupon $c = c_1$ at time 0. If XYZ defaults within the first year, the buyer will receive a payment U_1, the unrecovered post-default value of the bond, paid at T_1. For the 2-year CDS, a coupon payment $c = c_2$ is made at time 0, and a second coupon, also c_2, is paid at T_1 if XYZ has not defaulted before or at that time. The buyer will receive U_1 if default takes place in the first year and U_2, the unrecovered year 2 value if XYZ defaults in the 2nd year. The coupon rates c_1 and c_2 are market data,

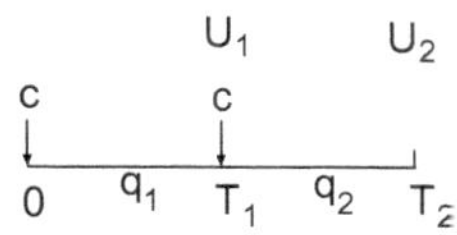

Figure 10.13. CDS calibration example.

set at time 0. We assume that U_1 and U_2 are known constants and that there is no interest-rate volatility, so we also have zero-coupon bond values $p_1 = p(0, T_1)$ and $p_2 = p(0, T_2)$. Our model will specify (albeit indirectly) the risk-neutral distribution of the default time t_D, but it is clear that in this example we just need to know q_1 and q_2, the risk-neutral probabilities of default in the first and second years, respectively. These probabilities are fixed by the requirement that each CDS contract the net discounted value of the cash flows is zero — the contract is a "fair game". For the 1-year contract, we pay c_1 at 0 and receive U_1 at T_1 if t_D is less than or equal to T_1, which happens with probability q_1. The condition for zero expected discounted value is $0 = c_1 - q_1 p_1 U_1$, fixing q_1 at $q_1 = c_1/(p_1 U_1)$. For the 2-year CDS, default happens in the first year, in the second year or not at all, with probabilities $q_1, (1 - q_1)q_2, (1 - q_1)(1 - q_2)$ respectively. In the first case, the cash flows are exactly as in the 1-year CDS only with coupon c_2. In the second case, we pay two coupons and receive U_2 at T_2; in the third, we just pay the two coupons. Writing down the net discounted value condition gives us an equation to solve for q_2; we leave it to the reader to work out the details.

Real cases are much more complicated, in particular because the recovery payments and interest rates will be stochastic and may be correlated with each other and with the default events. But the principle is the same.

Having achieved calibration, our model can be used to price new contracts and to calculate the sensitivity of prices to, for example, movements in interest rates — this kind of information is essential for hedging purposes. It can also be adapted to provide a "real-world" model for risk management purposes, bringing in statistical data such as default history and change of rating data provided by the rating agencies.

10.6 Convergence of the Binomial Tree to Black–Scholes

With the notation of Section 10.3, each increment of Brownian motion $X_k = W_{kT/n} - W_{(k-1)T/n}$ has normal distribution $\mathcal{N}(0, T/n)$ with characteristic function $\mathbb{E}[e^{iuX_k}] = e^{-\frac{1}{2}u^2 a_n^2}$, where $a_n = \sqrt{T/n}$. In model (5), we replace X_k by Y_k which has characteristic function

$$\mathbb{E}[e^{iuY_k}] = \frac{1}{2}(e^{iua_n} + e^{-iua_n}) = \cos(ua_n).$$

For independent random variables, the characteristic function of the sum is the product of the individual characteristic functions, and hence

$$\mathbb{E}[e^{iuW_T^{(n)}}] = (\cos(ua_n))^n.$$

Taking the logarithm and using the power series expansion of the cosine gives

$$\begin{aligned}\log((\cos(ua_n))^n) &= n\log(\cos(u\sqrt{T/n}) \\ &= n\log\left(1 - \frac{1}{2}\frac{u^2T}{n} + \frac{1}{4!}\frac{u^4T^2}{n^2} - \cdots\right) \\ &= -\frac{1}{2}u^2T + O(1/n),\end{aligned}$$

where $O(1/n)$ denotes a term or order $1/n$. This shows that as $n \to \infty$ the characteristic function of $W_T^{(n)}$ converges to $e^{-\frac{1}{2}u^2T}$, the characteristic function of W_T, i.e. $W_T^{(n)}$ *converges in distribution* to W_T.

Chapter 11

Financial Engineering

11.1 Introduction

Once the resource estimation and conventional engineering stages have been completed, financial analysis can be undertaken using the tools of quantitative finance. The inherent uncertainties present in technical assumptions have their analogues in the probabilistic approach used in investment and portfolio management and the pricing of a range of financial derivatives. These are considered in this chapter.

11.2 Decision Tree

Once net present value (NPV) optimisation at the pre-feasibility stage has been completed as explained in Section 8.3.3, commercial decisions need to be taken. This process is aided by the use of a decision tree as illustrated in Fig. 11.1 starting from an MC simulation of the primary technical variables outlined in Section 2.4. This is based on simultaneous treatment of grade, plant recovery, OpCost and Capex at the PFS stage (see Section 8.3.3). We select these variables as they do not change project life and therefore the base case model. Capacity and size of the reserve would change project life and therefore the base case model. An MC simulation on these variables would not be valid.

In undertaking an MC simulation to determine the robustness of a project, there is no merit in flexing metal or commodity price as this generates a self-evident outcome (higher price will always improve

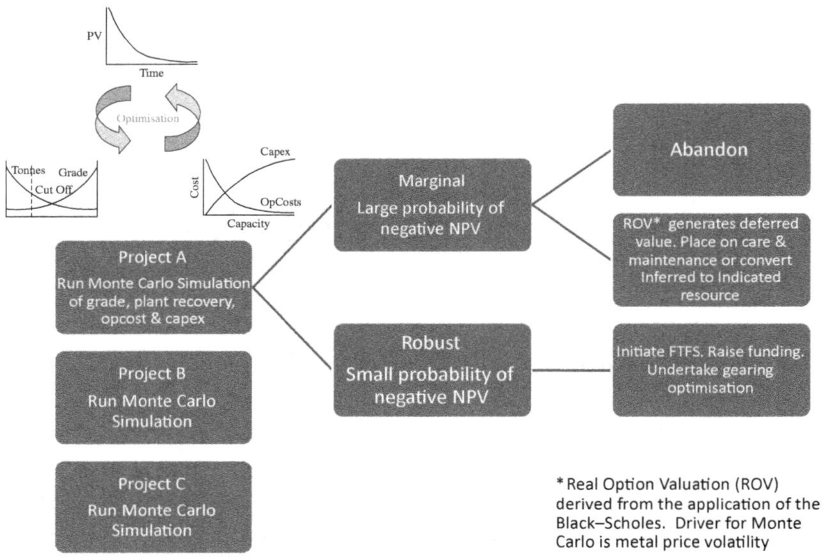

Figure 11.1. Decision tree at pre-feasibility stage after NPV optimisation derived from Fig. 8.2.

the NPV). The best way to take into account the influence of metal prices is through the technique of real option valuation (ROV).

11.3 Real Option Valuation

As outlined in Section 4.8, the application of ROV can be linked to practical considerations such as the duration of exploration licences. The steps that need to be followed in setting up a BS option pricing model for a ROV of a gold project (Extended Case Study 1, Appendix A) based on deferring the development in the expectation of more favourable metal prices involve the following:

- Determine the PV of the free cash flows during the operation period based on a cash flow model discounted by the CAPM (see Section 2.3.2) after removing the effect of financial gearing.
- Determine the strike price which is the PV of the development costs.

- Estimate the volatility of the PV of the free cash flow to the firm (FCFF) using as the driver to a MC simulation the forward metal prices and their volatility. The MC simulation will yield the volatility of the base case value (i.e. the PV of FCFF during the operating period).
- Time to expiration which is the time period in which to start development and could, for example, be the period after which a licence is either renewed or allowed to lapse.
- The risk-free rate.

The mean base case value from the output from the MC simulation will give the PV of the FCFF and the standard deviation (the volatility of the project) as shown in Fig. 11.2.

The values are applied to the BS option pricing model as outlined in Fig. 11.3. If this is treated as a European option which can only be exercised on the expiry date, then it is relatively simple to value. If this is significantly higher than the PV, then it is worth holding onto the licences. If not then the licence can be returned, as illustrated in Fig. 11.1.

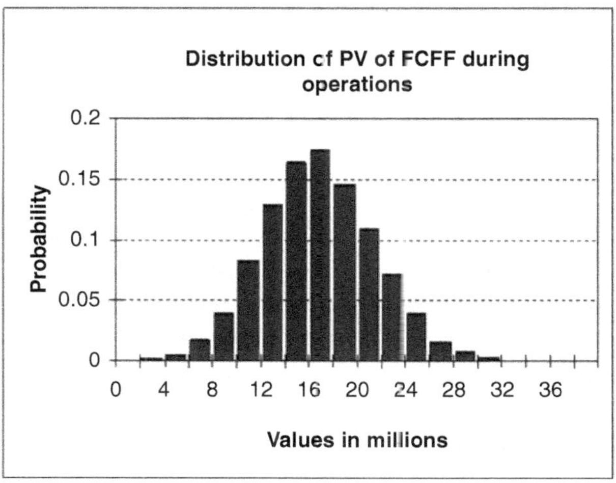

Figure 11.2. Output from an MC simulation.

Employ the Black & Scholes option pricing model, which is based on:

- The Base Case value (PV of FCFF during the operational period)
- The strike price (PV of the development costs)
- Volatility (of the PV of FCFF during the operational period)
- Time to expiration (time after which the Project is developed i.e. 3 years)
- The risk-free rate (the yield on 3-year sovereign debt)

The Black & Scholes equation for a Call Option:

$$V = N(d_1)A - N(d_2)Xe^{-rT}$$

Can be interpreted as follows:

$N(d_1)A$	the expected value of A if A > X at Expiration
$N(d_2)$	risk-neutral probability of A > X at Expiration
Xe^{-rT}	the Present Value of the development costs

Where:

- V current value of Call Option
- A PV of the FCFF during the operational period
- X cost of development
- r risk-free rate of return
- T time to expiration
- σ volatility of the PV of the FCFF during the operational period
- $N(d_1)$ & $N(d_2)$ are the values of the normal distribution at d_1 and d_2
- d_1 $[\ln(A/X) + (r + 0.5\sigma^2)T\} / \sigma T^{0.5}$
- d_2 $d_1 - \sigma T_{0.5}$

Figure 11.3. Application of the BS option pricing model to a hypothetical gold project. Reproduced with agreement from Chris Worcester See case study 1 (Appendix A).

The techniques of ROV can be applied to a range of different natural resource projects including oil and gas. Scenario analysis of an Athabasca Oil Sands Financial Model Steam-Assisted Gravity Drainage (see Section 6.4) is illustrated in Fig. 11.3 based on an unpublished dissertation by Bernard Guerbet, Imperial College London, in 2009 when oil prices were low and this type of project was considered to be commercially marginal (see Fig. 11.4). The scenario is based on the extraction of bitumen at a depth between 400

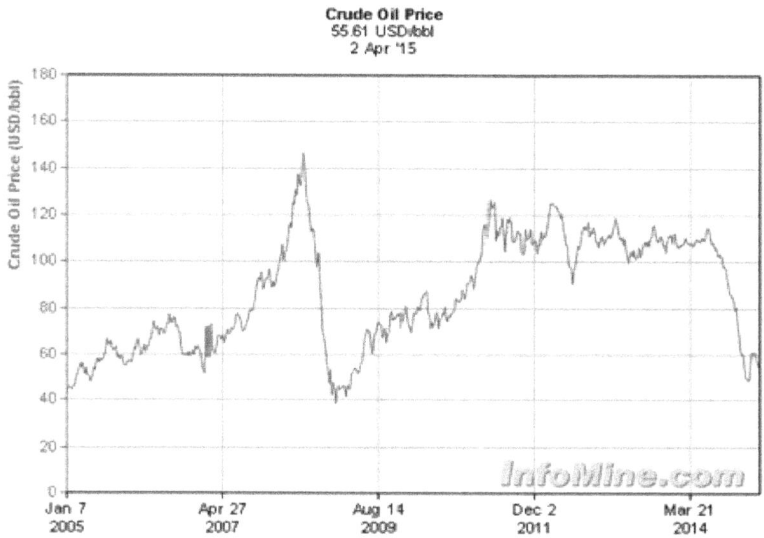

Figure 11.4. Crude oil price. Reproduced with the permission from InfoMine.

and 800 m below the surface. Each barrel of extracted bitumen will be upgraded into a barrel of synthetic crude oil (see Section 6.3).

The start of the Phase 1 construction period of 3 years was scheduled for the period 2009–2011. First oil production was in 2012, first peak oil production of 25,000 barrels per day (bpd) in 2015. The start of Phase 2 was scheduled for 2015 with an increase in production capacity from 2015 to 2022. Phase 2 was to be completed in 2019 with final peak oil production of 100,000 bpd in 2022. The plateau was reached from 2022 to 2045. A decline of production will start 2046 with end of production in late 2049. The results of the technique of ROV are given in Fig. 11.5.

As can be seen, the model demonstrated that deferring the development to 2012 would have coincided with the recovery of the oil price from \$70 in 2009 to \$110 in 2012 notwithstanding that a simple DCF model demonstrates declining NPV over the same period.

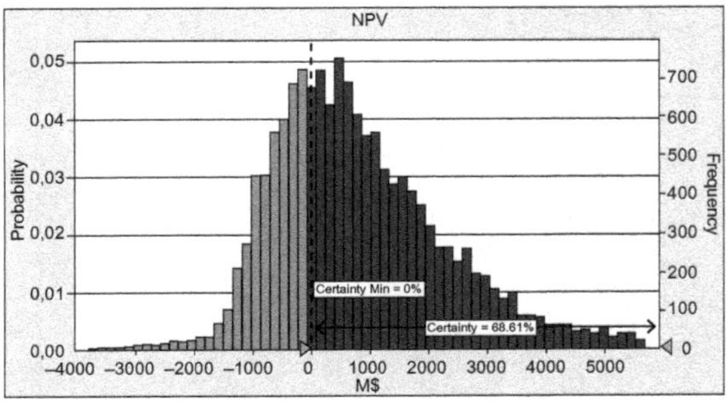

Real Option Valuation

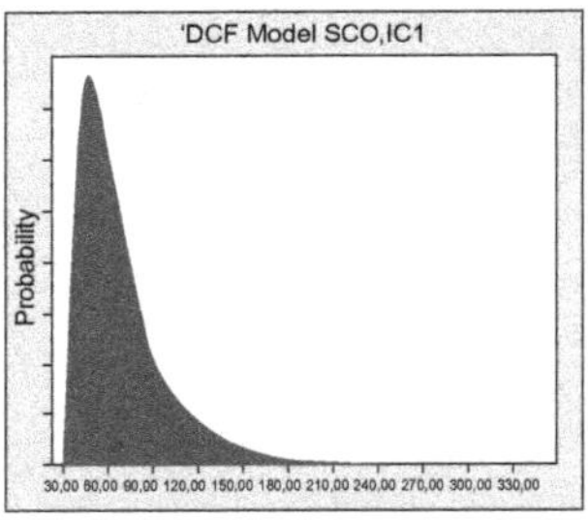

Lognormal distribution of oil price
Mean of $71, SD of 37.7

Time Delay (y)	Real Option Value (M$)	NPV (M$)
0	1,005	1,005
2	1,147	898
3	1,203	716
5	1,096	570

Figure 11.5. Diagram showing the distribution of NPV derived from the volatility of oil price and the ROVs generated from the BS model in 2009.

The correct decision would have been to retain the right to develop the project but defer the decision to invest.

11.4 Funding

11.4.1 *Tax and company structure*

The framework for a JV agreement is outlined in Chapter 3 (Fig. 3.6) and illustrates how the local JV company holds the mineral licence. This would obviously be geographically constrained but funding may well be sourced externally. It is not unusual for exploration to be funded by a high net worth individual via a private placement. Privacy issues can dictate that the holding company be registered in a tax haven and it is only when the project starts showing potential and follow-up stages of funding a development are considered that the tax implications of the set-up arrangements emerge. Unless there

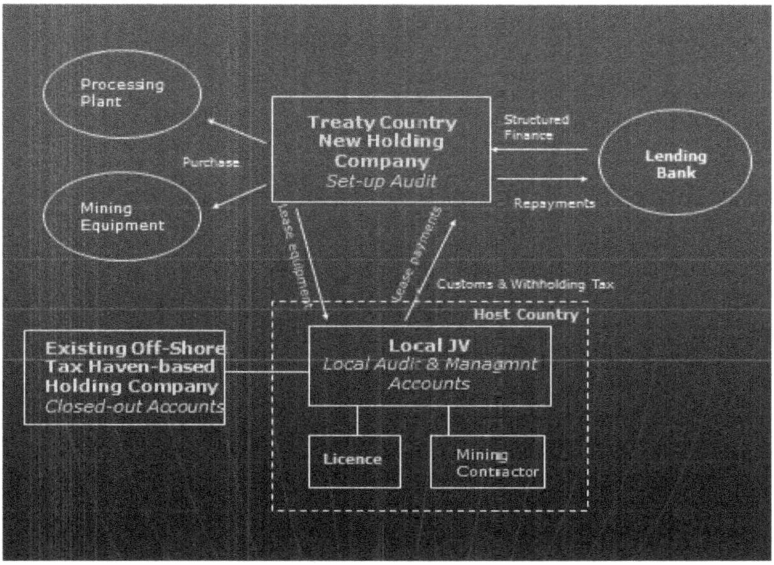

Figure 11.6. Company structure for a typical medium-scale mining project.

is a dual tax agreement between the country in which the project is located and the country where the company that will hold the asset is to be hosted, then there will be draconian withholding taxes.

These macro considerations would eliminate relatively subtle advantages arising from the tax relief on interest paid on debt and treatment of depreciation. This restructuring can be complex and IFRS need to be applied to local JV accounts which may have to be re-audited. Furthermore, there could be a need to prepare close-out accounts for the offshore vehicle through which the original exploration funding was provided. Then there would be the need for a set-up audit for the new company. This then allows more sophisticated arrangements to be put in place relating to leasing and payment of VAT, as illustrated in Fig. 11.6. While it is obvious that it would be best if the most tax-efficient company structure was put in place at the exploration stage, strategic considerations often take precedence (see Section 3.8.4).

Mineral taxation regimes can be complex, and each country will have a different regime. In an operating mine, attempting to have back stripping in an open pit allocated as an OpCost allows immediate tax relief compared to this being allocated to Capex, where relief is treated as depreciation. In a DCF model, the former scenario generates an enhanced NPV due to the effect of the time value of money. Where expenditure has to be allocated to Capex, a tax regime permitting a loss carryforward for depreciation would again generate an enhanced NPV.

A manager in an active operation must delegate his daily work and deal with multiple development scenarios which are an inherent part of mine planning. This includes the utility of applying the principles of discount cash flow modelling at the pre-funding stage, which allows comparison between development scenarios in an active operation based on the performance indicators of NVP, IRR, and pay-back. These would provide a snapshot of the value derived from a given period of production, where there is a simple relationship between the amount of ore produced and the capital cost. In an active operation though, an investment in a particular element (for example, footwall pre-production development and drill hole sampling) might be part of the normal cycle of mining as production proceeds. There is no fixed end point which can be incorporated into a DCF model. Other performance indicators, such as cash costs and tonnage of ore delineated, then become more relevant in ranking development decisions. The scenarios are seldom so inherently marginal that DCF modelling is unlikely to expose a feature that would not already be apparent from normal mine planning.

Consideration should be given to the boundary condition that applies to the normal allocation of sustaining capital in pre-production development on an active mining operation with a defined mine life, compared to the creation of what is essentially a new mine, albeit exploiting the same deposit. In the former case, this is part of routine mine planning with costs met from cash flow. There is no merit in setting up a DCF model if for no other reason than that the time span is seldom more than five years, whereas the optimum period for applying the technique at a 10% discount rate is about 15 years. The main flexibility is around the allocation of cost between Capex and OpCost. In accounting terms, it is best if this can be allocated to OpCost to allow immediate tax relief. Tax relief on Capex is obtained through depreciation where benefits are deferred.

In the hypothetical Extended Case Study 2 (Appendix B), the objective is to evaluate the different alternatives available to a mining company operating in the Peruvian Andes, following the discovery of an undeveloped deposit close to its operating mine. This grants them options such as the opportunity to extend mine life, increase annual production, and introduce a drastic change in the mineral processing method. Using debt also means that the full Capex of $460 million does not have to be met from the cash flows of the parent company generated from their existing operations. These can then be distributed as dividends. This in turn enhances the share price and allows the equity portion of the capital requirements to be raised through a rights issue. Equity investors also have the comfort that, in order to secure this level of debt, the bankers would have undertaken a rigorous technical review of the project. The role of independent engineers instructed by the banks ensures better planning and management at the EPC&M stage.

In summary, a medium-sized company considering developing essentially a new mine (albeit on the same deposit) at a cost of around $500 million should consider the use of project finance. The banks will be very comfortable, as operating cost estimates will be well constrained and production will be undertaken by experienced operators. Where the development of the new mine is going to cost more than $2 billion, then this is the domain of the large international mining companies that will use their corporate cost of capital for evaluation studies and act essentially as their own investment bank. Lending to subsidiaries on a rolling basis ensures they manage the corporate gearing that supports their share price and sets the corporate cost of capital. This does impact mine planning, where a major pit pushback is proposed.

Pit optimisation algorithms should assume a discount rate fixed by the parent companies outlined in Extended Case Study 7 (Appendix G). The operation cannot therefore use a gearing optimisation approach where the subsidiary cannot act as an independent company and raise fresh equity and secure debt from an independent investment bank. They must use the parent's corporate cost of capital. This will impact stripping ratios and may even sterilise some ore — a source of some frustration for planning departments on mines. In some cases, the discount rate they are required to use in mine planning is well above the corporate cost of capital, which means a much more conservative stripping ratio is generated.

Mineral taxation regimes are sometimes derived from petroleum fiscal models so some countries impose an excess profit tax (EPT), common in petroleum projects. It applies once the cash flows on the project generate a rate of return that exceeds a specified threshold. After that the additional tax is charged on a sliding scale up to a defined upper threshold. EPT has a disproportionate impact on small projects where investors are seeking a high IRR on their investment rather than a significant NPV, as illustrated in Table 2.1.

A commercial discovery bonus is common in the petroleum industry where it is perhaps more obvious when this event occurs (a single well can start producing oil, but a single drill hole into mineralisation does not convert this into a mineral project), but the only justification for applying this tax to mineral projects is where a company has benefitted from state-funded geological surveys.

The royalty rate is a tax applied directly to revenue, before the OpCosts are taken into consideration. It is therefore not possible to avoid and is essentially a resource rent that recognises that extraction of a natural resource permanently removes future value. A 1% variation has a much greater impact on NPV compared to a similar change in a tax rate applied after allowances.

11.4.2 *Gearing optimisation*

Once you decide to proceed to the FTFS stage (see Section 8.5.2), then you need to consider funding options. This requires building a financial model which incorporates both debt and equity, and then discounting the cash flows using WACC (see Section 2.5.2). The starting point is that you need to make sure you select the correct net cash flow row in the financial model spreadsheet. That is NPV ATBI (after normal tax that includes relief on OpCosts but before tax relief on interest). DCFs for PAIBT and PAIT inflate the NPV.

The more general point is that when funding includes a component of debt, DCFs need to be integrated into the financial accounts otherwise you end up with an incorrect NPV. As WACC will be a function of the cost of equity derived from the CAPM and the variable cost of debt, further optimisation of NPV can be achieved through gearing.

In reality, corporate cost of capital is what is imposed on subsidiaries of the major mining companies much to the frustration of project teams on an operating mine seeking to justify capital expenditure. They are obliged to use a high cost of capital that in many cases artificially depresses the NPV and detracts from expansion plans. The disinvestment of a major from a former subsidiary may well permit the new owners to go directly to the investment banks and raise debt independently. This can have a significant positive impact on the viability of the project.

The investment bank can also assist with an equity rights issue for an independent operation as well as being able to set up matching hedges to ensure the promoters can cover repayment of interest, balance of loan and OpCosts. The proportion of metal that needs to be hedged is a constraint on the level of gearing as equity investors want the project to benefit from increases in prices.

11.5 Base Metals: A Short Case Study

The critical issues in the project financing of nickel sulphide projects can now be assessed by modelling a hypothetical case scenario set in Western Australia (see Table 11.1). Though not based on any existing operations, the case example is a realistic representation of current nickel mining practice in Western Australia, and the figures used are reasonable reflections of those that might be encountered.

The project sponsors are seeking up to 70% debt funding of the total Capex and have been offered an interest rate of 8.5% on the loan capital. The assumed cost of equity is 15%. NPV will be calculated using the WACC, reverting to the cost of equity once debt has been paid off. A tax rate of 30% is assumed.

Table 11.1. Base case for an open-pit nickel mine.

Mine reserves	150.4 million tonnes
Commodity grade/plant recovery	Nickel 0.6% (65% recovery) Copper 0.1% (90% recovery)
Ore SG	3.2
Mining capacity	30,952 tonnes ore per day
Stripping ratio	3.2:1
Mining recovery	85%
Dilution	5%
Working days per year	360
Commodity sale prices	Nickel \$14,000/t Copper \$3,000/t
Capex mine/mill	\$165 million
Capex processing plant	\$275 million
Capex overheads	10%
Permitting years	1
Construction years	2 (60% Capex yr 1, 40% yr 2)
OpCosts	\$2.5/t mining ore \$0.75/t mining waste \$3.5/t processing \$10 million per year fixed costs
Working capital	25% of annual OpCosts

The banks require straight loan annual repayments over 5 years and are willing to grant a 2-year grace period on repayments. An upfront fee of 1% of the total debt is assumed with a 1% commitment fee. Fixed financing charges will amount to US\$0.5 million and there is a contingency of 10% to act as a cushion against unexpected cost rises. The cash flows for the first 5 years are given in Table 11.2.

The annual cover ratios as outlined in Section 8.6 are of particular interest to the lender as they provide an indication of the project's ability to function economically while servicing debt. Generally lenders will require that the interest cover, principal cover and debt service cover ratios in any given production year are considerably greater than one in order to satisfy concerns over the project defaulting on the debt repayment schedule.

Gearing optimisation based on different levels of debt are summarised in Table 11.3. This demonstrates that optimisation of NPV is achieved at a traditional debt:equity ratio of 60:40.

Table 11.2. Sample of DCF model worksheet — nickel sulphide project example.

WA_Ni_Sulphide	1	2	3	4	5	6	7	8	9	10
Cash flow										
Inflation	100.00%	100.00%	100.00%	100.00%	100.00%	100.00%	100.00%	100.00%	100.00%	100.00%
Reserves at start year (M/y)	127.84	127.84	127.84	127.84	121.47	112.98	102.37	91.76	81.15	70.53
Ore tonnage mined (M/y)	0.00	0.00	0.00	6.37	8.49	10.61	10.61	10.61	10.61	10.61
Rem reserves at end year (M/y)	134.23	127.84	127.84	121.47	112.98	102.37	91.76	81.15	70.53	59.92
Gross Rev (M$)	0.00	0.00	0.00	364.85	486.47	608.08	608.08	608.08	608.08	608.08
Royalties (M$)	0.00	0.00	0.00	0.00	−10.95	−14.59	−18.24	−18.24	−18.24	−18.24
Annual OpCosts (M$)	0.00	0.00	0.00	−00.16	−84.88	−103.60	−103.60	−103.60	−103.60	−103.60
Op margin (M$)	*0.00*	*0.00*	*0.00*	*298.69*	*390.64*	*489.89*	*486.24*	*486.24*	*486.24*	*486.24*
Capex (M$)	*0.00*	−290.40	−193.60	0.00	0.00	0.00	0.00	0.00	0.00	0.00
Wcapt (M$)	0.00	0.00	0.00	−16.54	−21.22	−25.90	−25.90	−25.90	25.90	25.90
Change in working capital (M$)	0.00	0.00	0.00	−16.54	−4.68	−4.68	0.00	0.00	0.00	0.00
Environmental & closure costs (M$)	0.00	0.00	0.00	−1.50	−1.50	−1.50	−1.50	−1.50	−1.50	−1.50
Cash flow (before interest and tax) (M$)	**0.00**	**−290.40**	**−193.60**	**280.65**	**384.46**	**483.71**	**484.74**	**484.74**	**484.74**	**484.74**
Ann disc. CF (before interest and tax) (M$)	*0.00*	*−240.00*	*−145.45*	*191.69*	*238.72*	*273.04*	*248.75*	*226.13*	*205.58*	*186.89*
Ann cash flow (before interest and tax) (M$)	*0.00*	*−290.40*	*−484.00*	*−203.35*	*181.11*	*664.82*	*1,149.56*	*1,634.29*	*2,119.03*	*2,603.77*
Tax paid before funding (M$)	0.00	0.00	0.00	−77.68	−105.26	−135.03	−133.94	−133.94	−133.94	−133.94

(*Continued*)

Table 11.2. (*Continued*)

WA_Ni_Sulphide	1	2	3	4	5	6	7	8	9	10
Cash flow (net of tax) (M$)	**0.00**	**290.40**	**193.60**	**202.97**	**279.20**	**348.67**	**350.80**	**350.80**	**350.80**	**350.80**
Ann Dis. CF (Net of tax) (M$)	*0.00*	*−245.93*	*−150.88*	*145.57*	*184.27*	*206.68*	*183.25*	*156.33*	*125.28*	*86.71*
Accumulated cash balance (M$)	*0.00*	*−290.40*	*−484.00*	*−281.03*	*−1.83*	*346.85*	*697.64*	*1,048.44*	*1,399.24*	*1,750.04*
Total costs associated with financing (M$)	−8.84	−1.74	0.00	0.00	0.00	0.00	0.00	0.00	0.00	0.00
Interest (M$)	−0.56	−20.92	−35.71	−35.71	−35.71	−32.14	−25.00	−17.86	−10.71	−3.57
Tax paid after funding (M$)	0.00	0.00	0.00	−66.96	−94.55	−125.39	−126.44	−128.58	−130.73	−132.87
Debt funding (M$)	6.61	239.47	174.07	0.00	0.00	−84.03	−84.03	−84.03	−84.03	−84.03
Equity funding (M$)	2.83	102.63	74.60	0.00	0.00	0.00	0.00	0.00	0.00	0.00
Cash flow (after funding and debt service) (M$)	**0.05**	**29.04**	**19.36**	**177.97**	**254.20**	**242.14**	**249.27**	**254.27**	**259.27**	**264.27**
Cumulative cash flow (after funding and debt service) (M$)	*0.05*	*29.09*	*48.45*	*226.42*	*480.62*	*722.77*	*972.04*	*1,226.30*	*1,485.57*	*1,749.84*
Pay back period (ATBI) (Years)	5.01									
Max cash exposure (ATBI) (M$)	−484.00									
NPV (ATBI)(M$)	1,008.36									
IRR (ATBI)	46.19%									

Table 11.3. Scenario analysis of nickel sulphide project example. IRR for all levels of gearing remains at 46%.

Debt: equity	Loan interest rate (%)	CAPM (%)	WACC (%)	NPV ($ million)
0:100		12		1,081
60:40	8.0	12	8.160	1,212
70:30	8.5	15	8.665	1,008
80:20	9.6	18	8.920	870

Any detailed review of the model also needs to take into account metal price assumptions and hedging. At a 60:40 debt:equity ratio, some 30% of nickel will need to be hedged to cover OpCosts and debt service repayments. While this can detract somewhat from the potential for the project to benefit from an increase in nickel price that equity investors would look for, they do have the comfort that in order to secure this level of debt the bankers would have undertaken a rigorous technical review of the project.

The grace period is normally 2 years and if the ramp-up period is longer than this then it is unlikely a bank would insist on a straight loan — a production loan is more likely as payment would then be proportional to revenue. The loan period is unlikely to extend much beyond 8 years as there is too great a drain on the cash flow as interest burden will be high. A geared model should be generated based on the variable WACC or the cash flows are discounted by the initial amount across the fixed term of the loan regardless of the fact that the tax shield is being sequentially lost over that period before reverting to being discounted by the cost of equity.

Capex and OpCosts assumptions will be derived from the FTFS and the uncertainty in Capex estimates (normally ±10%) should not be confused with provision for contingency that is to cover the unexpected. It would be prudent to set up Capex funding requirements at the base case plus 10%. Contingency of 5% would be prudent, 10% would be expensive.

Reserve tail assumptions are based on the premise that once the debt has been repaid, at least 30% of the original reserve should

Figure 11.7. Palabora Open Pit showing side wall failure. Reproduced with permission from Palabora Mining Company.

remain as the lender's final recourse. While this may seem generous, technical risk needs to be considered, as indicated in Fig. 11.7.

Fines from the waste rock are starting to report at the draw points in the underground block caving operation resulting in dilution and drop-off in head grades. This is discussed in Section 8.8.3. This type of scenario can reduce the reserve tail and is a good example of the convergence of technical and financial risk.

Sensitivity analysis demonstrates that the project can tolerate Capex and OpCosts of up to 20% above those used in the base case without compromising commercial viability. To be complete, the financial model should also incorporate functionality that generates an NPV for the different stakeholders that could include a partner with a free-carry, the promoters of the project and fund managers that might expect a higher return on equity than the 12% that is used in the optimised debt:equity scenario of 60:40.

11.6 Longwall Coal: A Short Case Study and the Role of Infrastructure

The longwall mining scenario considered in Section 6.4 takes into account the relationship between fixed mining costs of \$15/tonne, plant performance and differential prices for the different product streams. Running the model using IC-CoalEval demonstrates that the return on an investment of \$31 million in a longwall mining system is highly dependent on the utilisation of the equipment. The base case assumes that coal will be cut at a rate of 2.4 million tonnes per annum. The cost form is given in Fig. 11.8. This scenario generates an NPV of \$35 million and an IRR of 33%.

If production is 20% less than the target 2.4 Mt and only 1.92 Mt is produced then, according to the cost estimation empirical formula given in Section 8.3.2, OpCosts would increase from \$15/tonne to \$17.15/tonne. The NPV would then drop to \$6.71 million and the IRR to 18%.

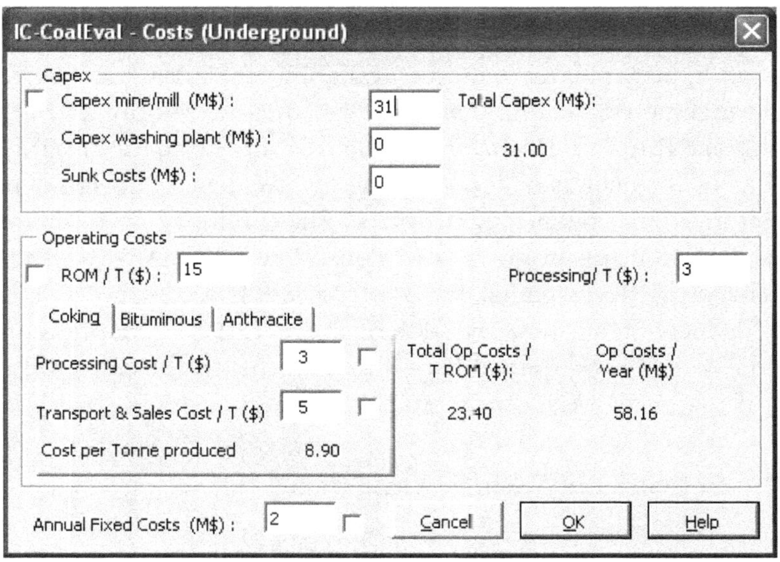

Figure 11.8. Cost menu taken from IC-CoalEval.

The fundamental problem with any coal project is that the product is a low-value commodity. The only way an investment can generate adequate returns is to aim for a high level of production well beyond that of the base case used. Not only does this amplify the margin between revenue and OpCosts, economies of scale mean that the cost of producing a tonne of coal decreases with an increase in production.

To put this into an international context, in 2012 Sasol invested \$250 million in their Thubelisha underground mine in South Africa that is designed to extract coal using room and pillar mining methods. It has the capacity to produce 10 million tonnes of coal per annum. While it could be argued that Sasol's product is used in their oil-from-coal operation justifying the high rate of production, Anglo-American produces coal for the international markets. Their Zibulo Colliery in South Africa produces six million tonnes of coal per annum from underground mining using room and pillar methods. A single section using one continuous miner and two shuttle cars produces 750,000 tonnes of run-of-mine coal per annum.

A further key factor in the commercial viability of a coal project is transport costs. For a project to derive premium prices associated with an export market requires availability of infrastructure. This would include rail-loading facilities, a dedicated railway and a port such as the Richards Bay facility in South Africa (see Fig. 11.9). This level of investment usually needs the involvement of government or the international finance institutions. The similarity with the development of iron ore projects is obvious. The alternative to a major infrastructure development for coal projects is a contract to supply coal for local steam-powered electrical generation. A captive power station would have a quite different relationship to the coal producers than if the latter were captive to the former.

11.7 Petroleum: A Short Case Study

An oil company has received technical data relating to a potential project and now needs to evaluate its viability.

http://www.transportworldafrica.co.za/

Figure 11.9. Coal infrastructure in South Africa. Top left: Loading facility. From author's collection. Bottom left and right: From Transport World Africa website and reproduced with their permission.

The project relates to a hydrocarbon reservoir containing oil only — no associated gas or condensate occurs. The company's technical experts have undertaken subsurface and engineering studies which suggest it could potentially produce oil for 13 years from the start of production. According to the scenario in the development plan, the production would ramp up from zero at the beginning of year four, to a plateau production rate of 12,000 bpd at the beginning of year five (i.e. a 2-year ramp-up period).

The plateau production would last for 3 years, after which the production rate would decline. The decline can be modelled as a simple 40% decline rate, where the average production rate in any year is 60% of the value in the previous year. The profile will appear as follows in Fig 11.10.

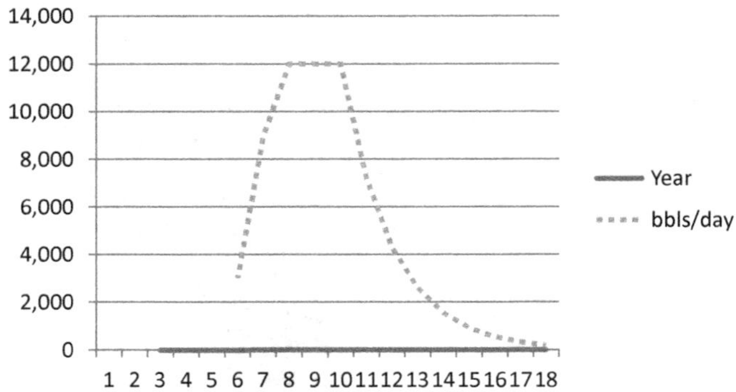

Figure 11.10. Petroleum production profile.

The oil company is the sole "contractor" and is responsible for all OpCosts and Capex. Details of the field development and OpCosts are given below. The government does not invest in the project.

The fiscal regime is a simple tax and royalty concession. There is an oil royalty of 5% of gross revenue. The contractor is also liable for corporate tax at a rate of 20%. The oil royalty is deductible against taxable income. Capex is depreciated using a 5-year straight line method for tax purposes. Tax losses can be carried forward indefinitely and both the royalty and tax liabilities are paid in the year in which they are incurred. Additional information available includes the following:

- Assume the inflation forecast is zero (i.e. do not model inflation).
- Assume a constant oil price of $100 per barrel.
- While the field is producing, it will incur fixed OpCosts of $40 million per year.
- The capital development costs are $50 million in year one, and $500 million in year three.
- There are no decommissioning costs.
- The company uses an "annual end-of-year" discounting method (i.e. assume cash flow in any 1 year all occurs at the end of each year).
- The company's nominal WACC is 6%.

A simple cash flow model for the total project will determine the contractor's and government's cash flows and allows the following metrics to be calculated:

- The field technical oil resource is 23.98 millions of barrels.
- The year of the field economic limit (the final year of economically viable production) is year 12.
- The field economic reserve is 23.24 millions of barrels.
- The total undiscounted project cash flow is $1,413.85 million.
- The NPV of the contractor's net cash flow is $592 million.
- The NPV of the government's cash flow (using the contractor's discount rate) is $241 million.

The results of sensitivity analysis on the base case are given in Table 11.4. This demonstrates that while the contractor may benefit more than the government at the higher base case oil price, the opposite happens at the lower price. This may not be an optimal arrangement as government would want a fiscal model that continues to provide incentives to the contractor to continue production during periods of low oil prices.

When we consider petroleum fiscal models, the level of complexity in both tax and royalty regimes as well as production-sharing contracts (which are essentially complex tax models) unintended consequences can occur. Agreements then have to be renegotiated. Furthermore, the relatively simple interrelationships between tax given in the financial model for a metal project and the linked economic model breaks down in a petroleum fiscal model. Petroleum fiscal models are therefore normally discounted using a flat corporate cost of capital.

Table 11.4. Sensitivity analysis of the petroleum model.

Oil price $/bbl	Contractor NPV $ million	Government NPV $ million
100	592	241
75	300	150
50	7	61

Figure 11.11. Cartoon by Roger Beale first published in the FT's Business Education section on Monday 20 Feb 2012 and reproduced with permission.

11.8 Final Thoughts

Do not introduce complexity in a financial model for its own sake as this can result in a bias that generates an outcome that you want. This is illustrated in Fig. 11.11 which is apposite given that as an undergraduate the first author did own a Triumph 650 Bonneville motorbike. The key characteristic of a financial model must be utility aimed at supporting robust investment decision-making.

Appendices

Appendix A

Extended Case Study 1

A Technical and Financial Appraisal of a Gold Project in Canada's Low Arctic

In Collaboration with Jean-Baptiste Krautter and Christopher Worcester

A.1 Introduction

Gold prices have swung between two extremes over the last decade. From around US$430 per ounce in August 2005, it reached a maximum of about US$1,900 per ounce in July 2011 and the prices as of January 2018 were around US$1,250 per ounce. This is one of the principal concerns in the gold mining industry as it can dramatically affect the viability of future projects.

The probability density function (PDF) used for the gold price is the log normal distribution with high gold price volatility (around 34% over the period 2005–2015 based on a mean of $1,114, a standard deviation of $375) as illustrated in Fig. A.1. It is the price used for the base case financial model for this case study.

The aim of the case study is to evaluate the future potential of a hypothetical gold project located in the Nunavut Territory (Canada's low Arctic) that is marginal at current gold prices. It is assumed that the project has probable reserve plus an indicated resource of more than 10 million ounces of gold of which 3.3 million belongs to reserves.

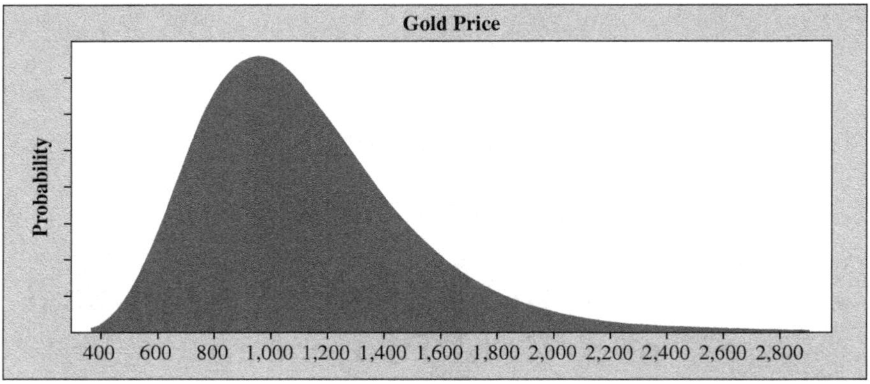

Figure A.1. Probability density function for gold price over the period 2005–2015.

A.2 Valuation Methodology

This study considers the project's base case and then applies quantitative financial modelling in order to consider alternative strategies and funding options. The base case assumes that the vein systems can be exploited using a combination of surface and underground mining. The valuation of the project derived from a deterministic discounted cash flow analysis, a stochastic discounted cash flow analysis, and finally a real option valuation (ROV). Sensitivities are undertaken on variables that do not affect the life of the mine, in order to assess the parameters having the biggest influence on the net present value (NPV). ROV is based on the Black–Scholes (BS) theory as outlined in Chapter 11 and aims at determining if a deferral option would demonstrate that additional value can be generated by deferring development.

A.3 Technical Assumptions

The project aims to exploit a series of sub-parallel shear-hosted gold deposits comprising quartz vein systems which vary in thickness from a few centimetres to several metres. These pinch and swell and are notoriously difficult to evaluate and require an extensive programme of drilling to delineate. Visible gold is present in some samples so any grade estimation will be associated with a high nugget effect.

The base case scenario assumes a resource of 9 million tonnes of ore at an average gold head grade of 9 grams per tonne and around one million tonnes of marginal ore, with an average gold grade of 3 grams per tonne. This marginal ore will come from the mine development. It will be stockpiled before being processed at the end of the mine life (Year 9). The underground operations are designed to produce around 3,000 tonnes per day using long-hole mining methods. The stope height is set at 25 m. The underground infrastructure consists of 23 levels, from 100 m to 650 m below surface (25 m intervals). Access will be provided via three ramps. The ore recovery will be maximised by backfilling the stopes using a mixture made of cement, sand and tailings or dry rock from the open-pit operations.

The economic parameters used to define the ore and the marginal cut-offs are a gold grade of 4.80 grams per tonne and a gold price of US$1,150 per ounce. All the material with a grade between 1.8 and 4.80 grams per tonne is considered as marginal and will be stockpiled. The model assumes a 95% mining recovery to all stope tonnages. The dilution is variable for each lode.

Pyrite is the predominant sulphide and the mineralisation can be described as non-refractory. This means it can be recovered using standard cyanide treatment. The base case assumes that the initial circuit will have a 3,000 tonnes-per-day capacity scalable up to 5,000 tpd.

A.4 Methodology for the Project Evaluation and the Quantitative Modelling

A.4.1 *Deterministic discounted cash flow*

The weighted average cost of capital (WACC) is a discount rate directly linked to the company's business and the financial risks. This is derived from the following formula:

$$WACC = K_e \times \frac{F}{V} + K_d \times \frac{D}{V} \times (1 - T),$$

where

- K_e is the cost of equity
- K_d is the cost of debt
- E is the market value of equity
- D is the market value of debt
- T is the corporate tax rate
- V is the market value of the equity plus the debt.

The Capital Asset Pricing Model (CAPM) is used to derive the cost of equity (K_e) from the following formula:

$$K_e = R_f + \beta_e * EMRP,$$

where

- K_e is the cost of equity
- R_f is the risk-free rate
- βe is the equity beta of the investment
- $EMRP$ is the equity market risk premium.

The risk associated with a particular equity is represented by the beta (unsystematic risk) from the following formula:

$$\beta_e = \frac{Cov(R_i, R_m)}{\sigma^2(R_m)},$$

where

- R_i is the return of the company's stock
- R_m is the return of the Toronto Stock Exchange (TSX)
- $\sigma^2(R_m)$ is the variance of the TSX.

These relationships are used to generate the curves given in Fig. A.2 which indicate an optimum WACC of Debt to Equity of 31:69.

The variables are summarised in Table A.1.

The cash flows will not, however, sustain this level of gearing and a debt:equity of 18:82 is needed. The result of the deterministic DCF is given in Fig. A.3 indicating a negative NPV of −C$73M.

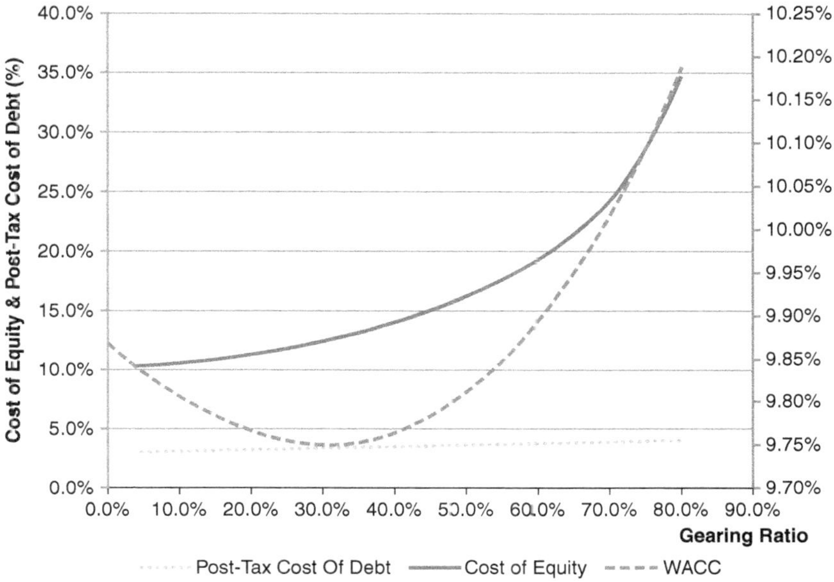

Figure A.2. Determination of optimum WACC.

Table A.1. Determination of WACC.

Theoretical computations		
Beta equity (the company)	βe	1.02
Beta asset (the company)	βa	0.85
Effective tax rate	Tr	27.00%
Risk-free rate	Rf	1.42%
Equity market return premium	EMRP	9.94%
Equity risk premium	β(Rm-Rf)	10.1%
Equity rate of the company	Re	11.56%
Debt	%	31.00%
Equity	%	69.00%
D/(D+E)	%	31.00%
D/E	%	44.93%
Pre-tax cost of debt (the project)	%	4.56%
Post-tax cost of debt	%	3.33%
Beta equity (project, re-levered)	βe	1.13
Cost of equity of the project	%	12.64%
Post-tax WACC of the project	%	9.75%

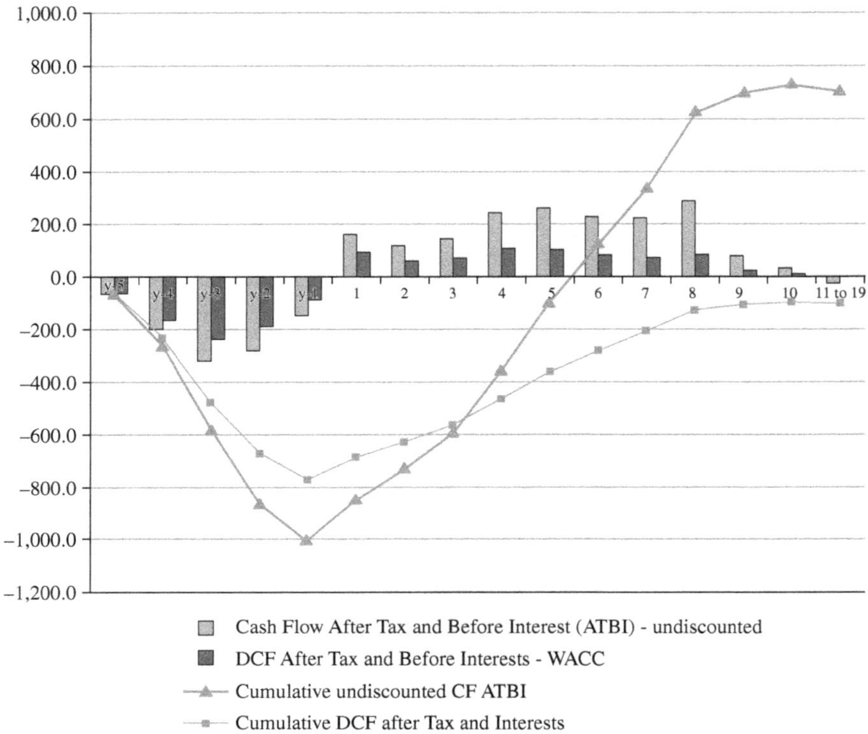

Figure A.3. Results of a deterministic DCF based on a debt:equity ratio of 18:82 and a WACC of 9.8%. This generates an IRR of 8.1% and an NPV of −C$73M.

A.4.2 *Probabilistic discounted cash flow*

Flexing gold price in a DCF model has exactly the same impact as grade and plant recovery because revenue is derived directly from the product of each of these three variables. The revenue row in a spreadsheet is of course the most important series in the whole model. No technically helpful insights are generated by flexing gold price or running a Monte Carlo (MC) simulation on all three of these variables. Running an MC on grade, plant recovery, Capex and Opcost to generate a distribution of NPV will, however, be useful as it gives an indication of risk at the fixed gold price selected.

Of course, gold price is the key variable in this case study and while the future price is not known, the rear view mirror can be used. It is not the trend that is relevant but the volatility of the gold price over the period selected. This is the driver for the ROV in which the MC simulation generates a distribution for the present values of the free cash flows, the volatility of which is used in the Black–Scholes (BS) model. The only input used in the simulation is the historical gold price volatility which is known.

Real option analysis involves the application of the BS model which can be used to examine any "contract" whose worth depends on the uncertain future value of an asset. A call option gives the right but not the obligation to buy the underlying asset by a certain date at a certain price (see Chapter 10). To apply the technique involves defining the stochastic variable which will be the gold price. The discounted cash flow model is then built using the WACC to determine the present values of the development costs, and of the free cash flows for the project (FCFF) during the production phase. An MC simulation is then run based on the volatility of the gold price to derive the volatility of the present value of the FCFF during the operational period. The results are then applied to the BS model.

The BS formula is given as follows:

$$\mathrm{V} = \mathrm{A}_0 N(d_1) - \mathrm{X}e^{-\mathrm{rT}} N(d2),$$

where

Selection of the inputs for the Black–Scholes–Merton model		Project
V	Value of the deferral option	
A_0	Present value of the FCFF* during operational period (at $t = 0$)	C\$702M
X	Present value of the development costs (i.e. the initial Capex)	C\$775M
r	Risk-free rate of return (per annum)	0.8%
T	**Time of deferral**	**6 years**
σ	Volatility of the present value of the FCFF during the operational period	64%

Notes: $N(d_1)$ and $N(d_2)$ are the cumulative probability distribution of a standardised normal distribution. *FCFF: Free cash flows for the firm.

The classic valuation methods based on a deterministic approach demonstrate that the project is marginal.

- *Deterministic DCF*: NPV of – C$73M
- *Probabilistic DCF*: NPV (mean) of – C$125M, 35% chance of having a positive NPV.

Nonetheless, consider:

- The project as a European call option
- Volatility of the underlying commodity (34% from 2010 to 2015)
- Volatility of the free cash flows for the firm (64%)
- Managerial options.

Then the time value of the 6-year deferral option is $C390M.

In general, the deferral time for an ROV should be linked to a tangible constraint such as the duration of a mineral licence. This would be the time to expiration in the BS model. An exploration licence is typically awarded for a 5-to-7-year period during which a programme of exploration and evaluation drilling will have been completed. If this was achieved within, say, 3 years, it may have exceeded the overall expenditure requirements to retain the exploration licence for the full 5 or 7 years. If at that point the project is marginal but you do not want to relinquish the licence, there is a role for applying the technique of ROV. If this generates a deferred value, you would have the justification for putting the company into care-and-maintenance. If the gold price recovers at the end of the period, an application to renew the exploration licence or convert it into a mining licence can be made. An esoteric quantitative finance technique provided the basis for a pragmatic business decision to proceed or abandon the project. These are still subjective considerations though and the application of ROV is no substitute for commercial acumen. The case study represents a boundary condition when purely technical and financial considerations are transitioning to business leadership factors. Of course, price forecasts and forward curves are fundamentally different concepts. All the forward curve tells you is the price that gold produced today can be sold or bought at, at a fixed time in the future.

Appendix B

Extended Case Study 2

Andean Polymetallic Skarn Silver, Lead and Zinc Project*

B.1 Introduction

The objective of this case study is to evaluate different alternatives that a mining company operating in the Peruvian Andes may have following the discovery of an undeveloped deposit close to its operating mine. This grants them the options such as the opportunity to extend mine life, increase annual production and to introduce a drastic change in the mineral processing method. The scenario proposes a change in the recovery method from flotation and cyanidation to a purely lixiviation process in order to produce silver bullion only and benefit from the sale of high purity silver ingots at the spot price instead of selling silver in lead and zinc concentrates at a discount due to net smelter return terms. This scenario was considered for deposits characterised by a considerably higher silver grade in contrast to relatively low grades of lead and zinc.

B.2 Geological Setting

An analogue for this case study would be the Uchucchacua deposit which is one of several skarn-rich mineral districts in central Peru. It lies close to the continental divide in the Western Cordillera,

*The corresponding IC-MinEval-generated Excel financial model is available for downloading at the following url: https://www.edumine.com/courses/.

approximately 170 km north–northeast of Lima. The mine plant is at an altitude of 4,500 m with peaks in the district reaching above 5,100 m. Mining levels range from 4,360 to 4,730 m. A variety of silver-, manganese-, lead-, and zinc-bearing minerals is associated with veins and skarn located around minor intrusions of dacite. Host rocks are Cretaceous limestone that have been folded, thrust, and displaced by steep normal and strike-slip faults. Ore occurs in veins and massive ore bodies which formed in faults and wall rocks by a combination of fissure infill and replacement (Bussell *et al.*, 1990).

B.3 Scenario

Exploration has identified a secondary deposit nearby, and it is proposed to expand the current mining and processing operations. The project is strengthened by significant amounts of silver that are found associated with the lead and zinc ores.

The proposed mine will produce 7,000 t/d (using 340 operating days per year) using cut-and-fill methods accessible by a main decline, from a mining reserve of 21.61 Mt of *in situ* ore. The deposit averages 1.5% lead, 1.5% zinc and 500 g/t silver. Mining recovery is likely to be 90%, with 20% mining dilution. A change in the recovery method is also proposed to switch to the production of silver bullion rather than selling silver contained in lead and zinc concentrates. This has the benefit of allowing the silver to be sold at the spot price, rather than at a discount if contained in a sulphide concentrate. The project will operate at 75% capacity in the first year of production, 90% in the second year, and reach full capacity by year three.

Run-of-mine (ROM) ore is taken to the mill where it will first report to comminution to liberate the mineral particles. In the previous process, a number of flotation stages followed, with regrinding in some instances, in order to produce the Ag–Pb and Ag–Zn sulphide concentrates. This is now being changed to a purely lixiviation process. Metallurgical recoveries for lead, zinc and silver are 90%, 50% and 82% respectively.

Capital expenditure for procurement of mining equipment and the construction of the mine and mill is estimated at US$147 million. The cost to build the processing plant is estimated at US$82 million. Capex overheads are allocated at 5% of the Capex. A 3-year pre-production period is envisaged in order to construct the plant and mine. 20% of the total Capex will be incurred in the first pre-production year, 30% incurred in the second pre-production year, and 50% incurred in the third pre-production year. There is no delay for permitting. Mining costs are estimated to be US$75/tonne ore. Processing costs are estimated at US$18/tonne ore. US$8 million fixed costs are estimated each year and working capital is calculated to be 25% of annual operating costs.

Silver doré is produced on site, therefore transport costs are considered to be negligible. The assumed prices are US$2,200/t Pb, US$2,560/t Zn and US$17/oz Ag.

Amendments to metal price forecasts are carried out through an allowance for concentrate toll treatment or purchase. In addition, credit and penalty adjustments arising from the concentrate's chemical and physical properties as well as the smelter's specific requirements are also taken into consideration.

Assume a tax rate of 29.5% of taxable income. Capital allowances can be claimed as straight-line depreciation over the mine production life. A royalty of 4% of gross metal sales value is payable. Environmental costs amount to US$5 million per annum during mining, rising to US$10 million per annum for 2 years after mining.

B.4 Capital Structure

From the CAPM formula, the return of the market (rM) and the riskfree (rf) are known and fixed, the beta of the equity is computed for each level of gearing ($\beta k = \beta e$), then a different cost of equity (Ce) for each equity beta. As a result, Table B.1 and the corresponding chart in Table B.2 were generated.

A pre-funding scenario based on a discount rate of 12% and no debt derived from Table B.2 generates a NPV of $598M with an IRR of 50%. This can be compared to a scenario based on 60% debt

Table B.1. Cost of equity using the CAPM of comparable companies.

Comparable portfolio	Beta	D/E
Buenaventura	1.0151	0.2559
Hochschild	1.8100	0.4682
Pan American	2.2779	0.0321
Fresnillo	1.8310	0.2808
Fortuna Silver	3.0871	0.0790
New Gold	1.4250	0.3813
Coeur Mining	0.5147	0.3663
Tahoe Resources	2.4707	0.0175
Hecla Mining	0.4348	0.3426
First Majestic Silver	2.8227	0.0717
Nogagold	2.5244	0.3053
Ludin	2.6407	0.2935
	1.9045	**0.2412**
Relevered beta		
βa unlevered	1.5344	
Targeted D/E	0.2500	
Targeted debt	0.20	
Targeted equity	0.80	
βa relevered	**1.8049**	

Table B.2. Change in the cost of equity as a function of the change in the gearing of the project.

Market premium	3%										
Risk-free rate	7%										
Corporate tax	30%										
Gearing (D/D+E)	0%	10%	20%	30%	40%	50%	60%	70%	80%	90%	99%
D/E ratio	0%	11%	25%	43%	67%	100%	150%	233%	400%	900%	9900%
Equity beta (βe)	1.5344	1.6546	1.8049	1.9980	2.2556	2.6162	3.1571	4.0586	5.8615	11.2704	108.6299
Cost of equity	11.9%	12.3%	12.9%	13.5%	14.4%	15.6%	17.5%	20.6%	26.8%	45.3%	379.3%

funding of the total Capex and an interest rate of 8.3% on the loan capital with the corresponding assumed cost of equity equal to 17.5%.

The banks require straight loan annual repayments over 5 years and are willing to grant a 2-year grace period on repayments. An up-front fee of 1% of the total debt is assumed with a 1% commitment fee. Fixed financing charges will amount to US$5 million and there is a contingency of 5% to act as a cushion against unexpected cost rises. The NPV will be calculated using WACC, reverting to the cost of equity once debt has been paid off. The modelling generates a NPV of $483M. The IRR remains the same as it is that discount that generates a NPV of zero.

The project finance parameters all indicate a higher level of gearing is possible, but by re-running the model based on 40% debt and a return on equity of 14.4% an improved NPV of $547M is generated. This demonstrates that while minimum WACC determined from Table B.2 (WACC Computations and Optimal Funding) suggest optimisation is based on 60% gearing this does not take into account free cash flow generated by the model.

A prefunding scenario based on a discount rate of 15% generates an NPV of $460M indicating that 40% debt generates an NPV that exceeds the pre-funding NPV. Using debt also means that the full Capex of $460M does not have to be met from the cash flows of the parent company from existing operations which can better be distributed as dividends. This in turn enhances share price and allows the equity portion of the capital requirements to be raised through a rights issue by maintaining credibility with fund managers when seeking to raise fresh equity. This must also have been a significant driver behind the fantastic enhancement of Antofagasta's market capitalisation since the 2008 financial crisis. Equity investors also have the comfort that, in order to secure this level of debt, the bankers would have undertaken a rigorous technical review of the project. This case study also recognises that the best investments are often located at existing mining operations where extensions to mineralisation have been delineated by geologists. The role of independent engineers appointed by the investment banks providing project finance also ensures technical robustness with design, realistic capital cost estimates, and adherence to construction schedules.

The results are summarised in Table B.3.

The insensitivity of the WACC to gearing is due to the relatively low rate of tax at around 30% and the very high cost of equity at 14%, even at the lower 40% rate of gearing. The investment bank would expect to hedge a proportion of the metals equivalent to the payments of interest and principal as outlined in the term sheet plus operating costs. This is to allow the mine to remain in production should metal prices fall below those used in the financial model used to justify the investment. If the hedge is based on silver alone, then this would require 56% of the metal produced to be hedged. That in turn would act as a disincentive to a fund manager being asked to provide the equity component, as the upside would be capped. The investment bank, recognising this, would normally therefore cap the proportion of metal hedged at around 40%. Unless lead and zinc production were also to be hedged, then the gearing would have to be adjusted downwards to around 30%. The reserve tail of 32% indicates that an adequate amount of mineralisation is left in the ground after the loan has been repaid based on the grace period and the term of the repayments. While this constrains the choice of a five-year repayment schedule, a longer period means greater capitalisation of interest that will reduce NPV, but there may be advantages in modelling a seven-year repayment schedule for a longer project life.

Table B.3. NPV for different discount rates. IRR for all scenarios = 50%.

Gearing	Discount rate	NPV
0	12%	\$598 M
0	15%	\$460 M
60%	10.51 (WACC)	\$483 M
40%	10.61 (WACC)	\$547 M

For large corporations, it is inappropriate to evaluate a project based on the way it is financed as this leads to the varying of NPV for otherwise identical projects for no clear economic reason. This means that although project debt reduces with time, company debt stays constant as money is borrowed for other projects. However, in this case study, financing is considered from a "ring-fenced" project perspective in which the applicable WACC varies throughout the project life according to the debt–equity ratio.

Appendix C

Extended Case Study 3

PGE Deposit, Platreef of the Bushveld Complex, South Africa

C.1 Introduction

For the PGE mines in the Rustenburg area, the challenge is the narrow Merensky and UG-2 reefs that are just over a metre wide; if the stopes are going to be wide enough to handle even low profile mining equipment dilution will increase and head grades will drop. Reduction in operating costs/tonne need to offset loss of head grade if the strategy is to succeed. If mechanisation is implemented, this will have social implications as unskilled labour makes way for skilled operators. These operational changes will inevitably draw attention to the potential of the Platreef with high grade zones which are at least 10 m wide and amenable to both open pit and mechanised low cost underground mining operations.

The first author mapped the Platreef from Townlands up to Overysel in the early 1980s. Based on theoretical and experimental work on sulphur solubility systems undertaken as part of a PhD and postdoctoral year at Imperial College as described in Section 5.5, DB was responsible for developing the system of zoning for the Platreef (Buchanan *et al.*, 1981). DB then undertook, with Isobel Clark, the first geostatistical resource estimations of Tweefontein up through to Overysel. More recent drilling is illustrated in Fig. 7.10.

C.2 Scenario

It is proposed to exploit a Platinum Group Elements (PGE) deposit on the Platreef in the Bushveld Igneous Complex in the North West province of South Africa. The property will be developed as an underground mine some 800–1000 m below the surface. This will have a capacity of 11,000 tonnes of ore per day (in calculations use 360 working days per year).

The mining reserves are 80 million tonnes of *in situ* ore with an estimated grade of 1.76 g/t Pt, 1.87 g/t Pd, 0.13 g/t Rh, 0.10 g/t Ir, 0.7 g/t Ru, 0.01 g/t Os and 0.26 g/t Au. There is also 0.15% Cu and 0.32% Ni in this ore. It is estimated that mining dilution will be 8.5% and the mining recovery will be 95%. The operation's major product will be a high quality nickel/copper sulphide concentrate, containing the PGE, for sale to a nearby smelting and refining facility.

The project will operate at 30% capacity in the first year of production, 82% in year two and will reach full production capacity by year three. The mine will be worked via four vertical shafts. Shaft No. 2 will be the main shaft which is already in place having been sunk as part of a trial mining exercise, while Shaft Nos. 1, 3 and 4 will be ventilation shafts established using raise boring techniques.

Underground stoping (recovery of ore) with backfilling from tailings will be performed using highly productive mechanised long hole open stoping methods. ROM ore will be trammed from the active mining areas to the bottom of Shaft No. 2; after being crushed, it will be hoisted to the surface, taken to the mill where it will undergo comminution and go from there to a sulphide froth flotation treatment plant. The plant is capable of recovering 88% of each of the PGEs and copper and 70% of the nickel all contained in a nickel/copper sulphide concentrate.

The unit costs of mining have been estimated at US$30.0 per tonne for ore but in this type of underground mine there is negligible waste mined. Processing costs are estimated to be US$12.0 per tonne of feed ore. There are annual fixed costs of US$14 million and working capital is calculated at 25% of annual operating costs.

The metals are to be sold on contract to a nearby smelting and refining facility and the cost of transporting the sulphide concentrate is so small as to be considered negligible. The assumed platinum price is 1,400 $/oz, palladium 700 $/oz, rhodium 1,200 $/oz with no revenue for iridium, ruthenium and osmium.

The nickel price is US$15,000 per tonne and for copper US$7,000 per tonne of metal-in-concentrate. Revenues assume a net smelter return or off-take agreement. Amendments to metal price forecasts are carried out through an allowance for concentrate toll treatment or purchase. In addition, credit and penalty adjustments arising from the concentrate's chemical and physical properties as well as the smelter's specific requirements are also taken into consideration.

Raise boring, purchase of mining equipment and construction of the mill will cost approximately US$733 million. The capital investment required to construct the processing plant is estimated at US$273 million. There will be Capex overheads of 10%. Since the mine is in an area where there is already extensive mining it is considered there will be no delay for securing permitting requirements. There will be a 4 year pre-production period to construct the plant and mine infrastructure, 11% of the capital cost will be incurred in the first pre-production year, 16% in the second, 27% in the third and 46% in the final year.

Assume a tax rate of 28% of taxable income. Capital allowances can be claimed as straight line depreciation over the mine production life. A royalty of 5% of gross metal sales value is payable.

A bullet payment of US$18 million is planned at the end of the mine life for environmental work. There will also be annual environmental costs of US$1.2 million and additionally annual rehabilitation costs of US$3.9 million. There will be a period of 2 years post closure for environmental clean-up.

The project sponsors are seeking 50% debt funding of the total Capex and have been offered an interest rate of 8% on the loan capital. The assumed cost of equity is 12%. NPV will be calculated using WACC, reverting to the cost of equity once debt has been paid off.

For large corporations, it is inappropriate to evaluate a project based on the way it is financed as this leads to the varying of NPV for otherwise identical projects for no clear economic reason. This means that although project debt reduces with time, company debt stays constant as money is borrowed for other projects. The same assumptions used in the second case study apply where financing is considered from a "ring-fenced" project perspective in which the applicable WACC varies throughout the project life according to the debt:equity ratio.

The banks agree a straight loan annual repayments over eight years and are willing to grant a two-year grace period on repayments. An up-front fee of 0.5% of the total debt is assumed with a 0.5% commitment fee. Fixed financing charges will amount to US$7 million and there is a contingency of 10% to act as a cushion against unexpected cost rises.

C.3 Analysis of Results

Output is given in Tables C.1 and C.2.

The project is viable and the Loan Life and Project Life ratios, Cash Cover, and Reserve Tail ratio all permit the level of debt used in the model. A five-year repayment schedule results in LLRs that fall well below the limit of 1.5, hence the need for the eight-year period

Table C.1. Financial performance indicators for the Platreef project.

Year	5	6	7	8	9	10	11	12	13
Load Life ratio >1.5	1.62	1.71	1.60	1.70	1.78	1.87	1.97	2.07	2.18
Project Life ratio >2.0	3.13	3.35	3.36	3.87	4.53	5.43	6.77	8.98	13.37
Cash Cover >1.5	1.49	4.15	2.21	2.40	2.52	2.65	2.80	2.96	3.15
Reserve Tail >30%	99%	95%	90%	85%	80%	75%	70%	66%	61%

Table C.2. Economic Performance indicators for the Platreef project.

Pay back period (ATBI) (years)	8.9
Maximum cash exposure (ATBI) (M$)	1,107
NPV (ATBI) (M$)	537
IRR (ATBI) %	18

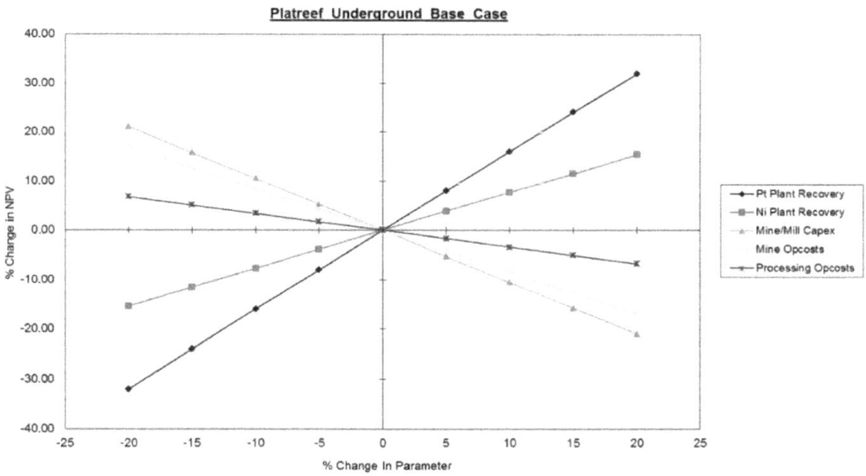

Figure C.1. Sensitivity analysis on key technical variables.

selected; however, this results in greater capitalisation of interest. The eight-year period is possible as, at 21 years, this is a relatively long-life mine with nearly two-thirds of the reserve unmined even after the loan has been repaid.

Sensitivity analysis is given in Fig. C.1.

As can be seen, the key technical variables relate to Pt and Ni recovery in the plant. This provides a clear indication of the importance of mineral processing in assessing technical risk. Any financial modelling of investment decisions in a PGE with base metal by-products must also take into account the boundary conditions between a processing plant and the thermodynamic constraints of smelting complex ores with revenue assumptions based on a model of a net smelter return. This is indicative of the level of detail that is needed when making investment decisions for all mineral resource projects.

An MC simulation undertaken on plant recovery, Capex and mine Opcosts is given in Fig. C.2.

This stochastic approach further illustrates the risk associated with developing complex polymetallic projects but the zero probability of a negative NPV demonstrates that the Platreef does provide sound investment opportunities.

There is never a definitive and final scenario – a model is subject to endless modification aimed at converging on the most likely predicted outcome. It is only when a business decision is made to proceed that the mining company will embark on the task of raising the capital through a combination of debt and equity.

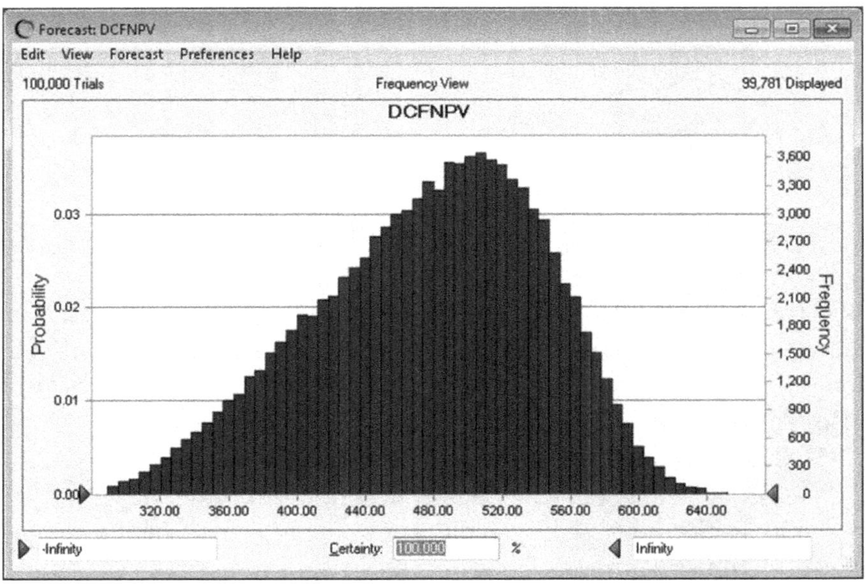

Figure C.2. Results of a Monte Carlo simulation derived from plant recovery, Capex and mine opcosts distribution assumptions.
Note: This figure was generated by an academic version of Crystal Ball licensed to Imperial College London.

There is of course no uncertainty associated with the documentation related to the actual capital raising. The bank will have a term sheet that states precisely the amount to be lent, the drawdown schedule derived from the Full Technical Feasibility Study, and when the payments are due and their precise amounts.

The equity portion of the capital raised is likely to be through a rights issue, with the price of the new shares set to ensure that the value of the overall holding for each shareholder is maintained. This obviously requires that the increase in the traded share price offset the cost of acquiring the new shares. This is illustrated in Extended Case Study 5 (Appendix E). If the project is being promoted by an existing company where they have used cash generated by existing operations to enhance dividends, this will have maintained credibility with markets when seeking to raise fresh equity.

Setting the price of the rights issue is clearly a task that requires considerable skill and, like the bank term sheet, incorporates a precise number with a harsh exposure if the (well-paid) adviser gets it wrong either way. If the price of the share drops after the raising, then investors could have acquired them for a lower cost. Conversely, if the price increases significantly on trading, then a higher proportion of the capital could have been derived from equity, reducing the level of debt (and gearing) needed.

While the performance indicators (annual cover ratios, etc., as shown in Table C.1) support the level of gearing selected, there is the related narrative of the level of hedging that would need to be implemented. Any decision to hedge a significant portion of palladium in order to generate the level of revenue needed to cover bank repayments (principal plus interest) and operating costs would be a disincentive for fund managers when evaluating the merits of an equity rights issue. The upside of this key metal would be capped. A better strategy would be to spread the hedge over platinum, palladium, and nickel.

An alternative strategy is to sell concentrate into the market under an off-take agreement rather than enter into a hedging programme normally required when securing project finance. An off-take agreement would have a price participation clause, so equity stakeholders would then benefit from price volatility, which would otherwise be capped under a straight hedging agreement. Traders no doubt would promote this type of benefit to an operating mine.

Of course, you may also need to reduce the level of debt below the 50% that was proposed in this model. While an investment bank would not normally want the period of the loan to extend beyond eight years, this included the grace period. A repayment period of eight years excluding the grace period results in a significant level of interest being re-capitalised, adding a significant burden on the cash flow. Reducing the repayment period to six years also reduces the level of metal that you need to hedge. At this level of gearing, a cost of equity set at 12% looks about right. If the CAPM is generating a higher cost of equity, then you might need to reduce the gearing to obtain greater benefit from discounting the cash flows using WACC.

Finally, given that this is a polymetallic deposit, there may be merit in entering a streaming arrangement. Based on the conservative gold price of $1,200/oz, the model generates a revenue of $670 million. This could be used to reduce the capital needed to build the mine.

Appendix D

Extended Case Study 4

Share Performance Metrics and Valuation of a Single Operation Copper Mining Company

In undertaking a valuation of a listed mining company derived from its share performance metrics and a discounted cash flow model, a base case would ideally require 100% ownership of a dedicated mining operation exploiting a discrete deposit. In the case study, the holding company operates a single mature open-pit copper mine in Spain that produces concentrate.

A MinEval-generated discounted cash flow model was produced for the operation based on an *in situ* resource of 189 million tonnes of copper ore grading 0.5% with a stripping (SR) ratio of ore:waste of 1:1.8, mining recovery of 90%, dilution of 10%, and plant recovery of 90%. Production of ore was 15.43 million tonnes/annum, giving an 11-year project life. Costs included sustaining capital of $20 million per annum over the first five years, with an overall operating cost of $374 million per annum. At a copper price of $8,500/tonne and a tax rate of 12.5%, an NPV of $844.08 million was generated using a discount rate of 10%. Earnings before interest, taxes, depreciation, and amortisation (EBITDA) were $154.13 million per annum.

The company is listed on an international stock exchange and has a share price of $4.24, earnings per share of 24 cents, and a market capitalisation of $595.63 million (implying 140.48 million fully diluted shares outstanding). Net debt stands at $77 million. US Dollar to UK Pound = 0.79.

The valuation of public companies is derived from a range of share performance metrics, as outlined in Section 2.3.1. The compilation of these together with the DCF model of the operation is given in Table D.1, together with an analysis of the results generated.

The NPV is derived from an estimate of the future cash flows that are expected to arise from the continuing use of the existing mining infrastructure, and no provision is made for the sunk capital historically invested in the operation. See Section 2.3.2 on the treatment of sunk capital. The NPV is based on an investment of sustaining capital needed for items such as pre-production development, with mine life based on the reserve (as defined in accounting terms). Cash flows never go negative, so an infinite IRR is generated, which means that this performance indicator has no utility in undertaking a valuation. A valuation by a seller (vendor) of the operation may seek to add sunk capital to the NAV, probably based on the original nominal cost, and this might allow an IRR to be generated.

In a DCF model, costs can be expensed against profit or capitalised to increase the amount assigned to fixed assets. For a processing plant, shafts, and pre-production underground development, this would normally be treated as a capital investment. The future benefit could be over 20–40 years of the life of the mine, with the tax relief based on, say, straight-line depreciation. This would have less advantage in determining NPV compared to loss-carried-forward if the tax code permitted it. For an active operation, it would be better to expense some activities, such as an open-pit push-back against profit rather than assigning this to capitalisation, again if the tax code permitted this. See Section. 11.4.1 on tax and company structure.

The NPV model in the case study was based on a deterministic approach assuming dependent and independent variables that do not change over the project life (for example, Capex and Opcost and plant recovery and grade, respectively). This is justified given that the valuation is based on an operating mine where accurate data are available, albeit subject to inflation and changing operating circumstances.

Table D.1. Share performance metrics.

	Description	Variable	GBP	Euro	USD	Indicator
Trading comparables	Share price		£3.34	€3.87	$4.24	
	Earnings/share (2022)			€0.22	$0.24	
	Market capitalisation (millions)		£469.00	€544.04	$595.63	
	Fully diluted share outstanding (millions)	140.42				
	Price/earnings. 20–25 is good, the lower the better. A low price compared to earnings suggests doubt about viability.					17.61
Capitalisation	Market capitalisation				$595.63	
	Debt			€70.00	$77.00	
	Enterprise value (millions). Market capitalisation + debt – cash – investments. The minimum amount needed if the company was an acquisition target.					$672.63
	Copper price $/tonne	$8,500				
	NPV (DR 10%) (millions)				$844.08	
	Debt (millions)			€70.00	$77.00	
	Net asset value (Millions). NPV – debt + cash + investments. Intrinsic worth of the company. A benchmark if the company was an acquisition target.					$774.08
	NAV/share ($/share)				$5.51	
Valuation	P/NAV (share price/NAV). A ratio below 1 is a good multiple since it suggests that that the shares are undervalued.					0.77

(*Continued*)

Table D.1. (*Continued*)

Description	Variable	GBP	Euro	USD	Indicator
EV/NPV. A ratio of one means that the discounted cash flows confirm the minimum amount needed for a bid if the company was an acquisition target. Less than one means there is good upside potential.					0.80
EBITDA (Millions) per annum. After taxation used to provide a dividend stream and can be used for share buyback.				\$154.13	
EV/EBITDA. A ratio of 10 means that undiscounted earnings would generate an income approaching the market capitalisation. A higher value could be indicative of a long life quality project.					4.36

A variable such as grade should ideally be modelled using a probabilistic approach based on geostatistical resource estimation principles. Deterministic estimates will be associated with uncertainty which is amenable to stochastic valuation methodologies, such as Monte Carlo simulation. Given the variable mineralogy, this is bound to impact plant recovery, which would also be amenable to stochastic treatment.

The discipline of quantitative finance can be applied to share price, with volatility treated using a stochastic approach through the CAPM and beta being derived from market performance. If the unlevered one-year beta for the holding mining company is given as 1.26, assuming a risk-free rate of return of 5% and an expected market return of 10%, then the cost of equity would be 11.3%. With a gearing of less than 20%, there is obvious scope to borrow, and assuming a 6% cost of debt at the tax rate of 12%, then 60% debt would generate a WACC of 7.7%. Gearing optimisation would need to consider the amount of cash being generated, which would place a limit on the amount of debt that can be carried.

While capacity was 15.43 million tonnes/annum, a stripping ratio of 1.80 was used. This assumes an average over the mine life. Pit optimisation based on the application of techniques such as the Lerchs–Grossmans process assumes that this is based on a DR of 10%. See the case study on mine scheduling. The application of the concept of WACC permits cash flows to be discounted by the corporate cost of capital of, say, 8%, which would result in a lower SR and therefore a higher NPV.

While the intrinsic value of a mineral project is still a key consideration, understanding the interrelationship between technical and financial risks to truly understand the long-term value of an asset helps companies make better investment (or divestment) decisions. Companies that can secure debt finance for both the development and acquisition of advanced projects have greater strategic flexibility. Understanding how debt impacts the valuation of projects allows for an objective approach to determining the levels of gearing; this is relevant to both the investment banking and mining communities.

The valuation is based on 100% ownership of a dedicated mining operation exploiting a discrete deposit. For a holding company with multiple separate operations based on different deposits that are geographically diversified, the task of generating a valuation becomes more complex.

Appendix E

Extended Case Study 5

Rights Issue with Accretion for a Nickel Laterite Project at the Development Stage

You are advising on securing equity and debt funding for a company planning to develop its first mining operation located in Brazil. This comprises a planned open-pit nickel laterite mining operation that mines a 27.5 million tonne (Mt) mineral reserve of a 119 Mt mineral resource to produce 52,000 tonnes of ferronickel (FeNi) (containing 14,500 tonnes of nickel) a year, for an initial 28-year LOM. The metallurgical process comprises a single-line rotary kiln electric furnace to extract FeNi from the laterite ore. The capital cost will be \$440 million. A discounted cash flow model generated an NPV of \$1.38 billion at a DR of 8% and a Ni price of \$20,000/tonne.

The company raised an additional £70.5 million by placing 78 million shares with new and existing investors. This represented 41% of the ordinary share capital issued prior to the fundraised amount of 190 million shares. The enlarged number of shares in issue immediately following the fundraise was therefore 268 million. The placing price was 0.90p (£70.5 million/78 million). This reconciled with the share price at the time, which gave a total market capitalisation of £171 million (190 million $\times$ 0.90).

After the raising, the total equity attribution would have been £171 million + £70 million = £241 million. Share price went up to £1.40, so the market capitalisation was £375 million (£1.40 × 268 million) and an accretion of £375 million – £241 million = +£134 million. Presumably, the comment that "the Board decided to upsize the Placing" was recognition that at 90p the placing price was attractive. The metrics and share price movements are given in Tables E.1 and E.2

A shareholder who held 110,000 shares on 31 December 2022 compared to 100,000 the same time the previous year will have paid £9,000. Post-raising, the initial value would have increased from £90,000 to £154,000. This is a net gain of £55,000. The rights issue was therefore accretive for shareholders. See Extended Case Study 6, Appendix F.

There is the related narrative of the company taking on debt, thereby securing a tax advantage on interest payments. The most recent statement indicates a debt facility of $135 million compared to a market capitalisation of £375 million and cash in the treasury of $154 million, with the project in construction. So, this is adequate to meet the cost if it is 40% completed, but linking this to gearing is probably a non-trivial task and may not even be relevant at

Table E.1. Rights issue: Statement of equity.

Description	Variable	GBP	USD
Number of new shares (millions)	77.9		
Number of shares pre capital raising (millions)	112.1		
Exchange rate ($/£)	0.79		
Cost of new shares (£)		£0.90	
Cost of new shares ($)			$1.14
Total proceeds ($ millions)		£70.50	$89.24
Share outstanding (millions) pre-raising in October 2022	190.0		
Percentage of issued ordinary share capital after raising	41%		
The enlarged fully diluted number of shares in issue immediately following the fundraise	267.9		
Total proceeds ($ millions)		£70.15	$88.80

Table E.2. Share performance metrics.

Description	GBP	USD
Share price on 5 October 2022	£0.90	
Share price post-raising	£1.40	
Market capitalisation pre-raising (millions)	£171.00	$216.46
Total equity attribution post-raising	£241.50	$305.70
Market capitalisation post-raising (millions)	£375.12	$474.84
Accretion	£133.62	$169.14
Development cost		$440.00
Debt facility		$135.00
Cash		$154.00
Total to invest		$289.00

the development stage of a mining company. Intuitively though, the project looks robust.

What of course remains is the analysis of the technical risks associated with developing a nickel laterite project. Murrin Murrin remains a reminder of the pitfalls associated with HPAL-based metallurgical processing. Anglo American made a further foray into this deposit type through their Barro Alto project, which is similar to this project in terms of primary ultramafic precursor petrology and secondary weathered lateritic mineralogy. The interface with the metallurgical process selected then becomes critical, as Mg/Si ratios, the types of clays present, and beneficiation potential become important.

An announcement that the plant is commissioned and production is meeting performance as outlined in the full technical feasibility study should represent an inflection point in the share price with market capitalisation converging on NPV. The corollary that the project is not developed as expected which is a not unusual occurrence in the mining industry. The market capitalisation would be impacted by the dual negative effects of an increase in predicted capital cost and a delay in the start of production. This would have a dramatic impact on share price. Not only would additional investment need to be raised for the project to be completed, but any delay also has a disproportionate effect on NPV given the way in which DCF models work, with present value factors having the most impact at the start of the project life. Although the project cannot now achieve the performance indicators on which the original decision to develop it was made, there are clear incentives for existing stakeholders and shareholders to provide the necessary additional funding needed to bring the operation into production.

Appendix F

Extended Case Study 6

Rescue Capital Raising for a PGE Operation Based on Lonmin plc

In Collaboration with Val Brophy

Lonmin plc was a well-established integrated mining company that produced the whole suite of platinum group metals. In 2018, it was taken over by Sibanye-Stillwater as a distressed asset. By 2018, the total cash invested by shareholders since 2011 was $1,202 million.

In 2012, the share price started off in April at around about £10 or £11 a share and dropped substantially over the next few months as it became more obvious the seriousness of the company's problems. See Fig. F.1.

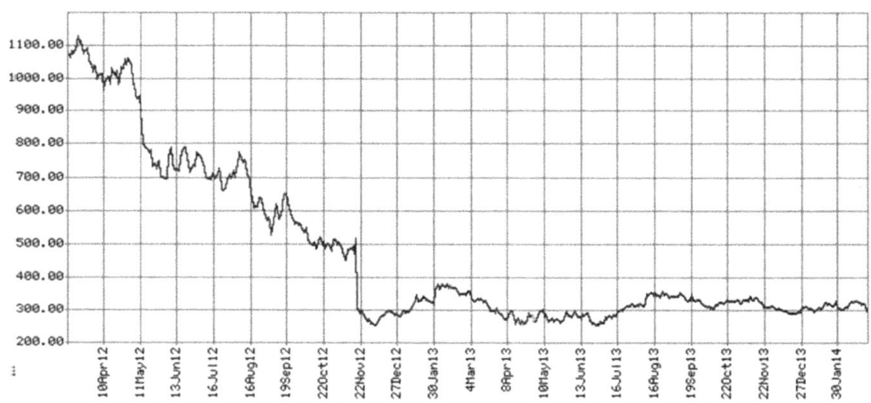

Figure F.1. Lonmin plc share price in pence for the period from April 2012 to January 2014.

The board of Lonmin Plc was considering an offer of a rights issue to shareholders in late November 2012, as the company was under pressure to reduce its bank debt. Existing profit covenants might have been breached, and bank loans would be repayable on demand. The rights issue permits changes replacing profit vs. debt with equity vs. debt. The proceeds from the proposed issue were intended to eliminate the company's long-term debt of $613 million and improve its liquid cash position.

The final proposal that was being considered was to offer nine new nominal 1$ shares for purchase at a price of £1.40 each for every five shares held: cost: 9×£1.40 = £12.60. Value of existing holding: 5× £4.53 = £22.65. Total =£35.25. Value =£2.51/share. If you are the only shareholder who doesn't take up the rights issue, then you do lose out as an individual. If, however, nobody is prepared to pay the extra money, then the company is gone. Furthermore, without participation, there would be a dilution of existing stakeholding that would further reduce the value of the holding. Shareholders are therefore obliged to take up the offer.

The figures anticipated are given in Table F.1.

Table F.1. Statement of equity as of 1 October 2012. Rights issue announced on 9 November 2012.

Description	Variable	GBP	USD
Number of 1$ shares offered (millions)	203.1		
Rights issue offer per share (nine extra for five original)	1.8		
Theoretical max uptake of new 1$ shares (millions)	366		
Exchange rate ($/£)	0.63		
Cost of new shares (£)		£1.40	
Cost of new shares ($)			$2.22
Total proceeds ($ millions)			$812.40
Underwriting and other associated costs (%)	0.50%		$4.06
Less associated issue costs ($)	4.10%		$33.31
Share premium increase ($ millions). Reflects the excess of what is being paid into the company by the shareholders over that for nominal share price of £1.00			$413.51

Table F.2. Share performance metrics.

	Variable	GBP	USD
Share price on November 9, 2012		£4.53	$7.19
Fully diluted share outstanding (millions) on November 9, 2012	366		
Market capitalisation (millions) as of November 9, 2012			$2,629
Share price on November 30, 2012		£3.00	$4.76
Fully diluted share outstanding (millions) on November 30, 2012	569		
Market capitalisation (millions) as of November 30, 2012			$2,708
Prior market price per share (November 8, 2012)		£4.53	
Following price range of share in November–December 2012		£2–£3	

As can be seen in Table F.1, the market capitalisation after the rights issue remains essentially the same, so the share premium increase of $413 million is not treated as adding value by the market. The value of the rights issue is preserved but not accretive (Table F.2). See the Extended Case Study 5 (Appendix E), which was accretive for shareholders.

While shareholders are forced to take up the rights issue and buy the extra shares in order to avoid being diluted, they do actually have shares in a rather more valuable company from an equity point of view. After the rights issue, the shareholder has now half the value of the shares in terms of the balance sheet, but they've got more than 50% of those shares now held for $69 million instead of $203 million. So, that's a way of looking at some of the benefits, real or imagined, of the value of the rights issues to the shareholders. After the rights issue, shareholders expect a bright future, looking for an annual return in the form of dividends as well as hopefully capital appreciation for them in the market. Realised the following year up to 30 September 2013, Lonmin made a profit of £198 million, but over the next two years, the situation had deteriorated.

This is illustrated in Table F.3.

Table F.3. Statement of equity.

At 1st October	2012 variable	2012 USD	2013 variable	2013 USD	2018 variable	2018 USD
Ordinary shares	203	$203	569	$569	586	$569
Share premium (millions from Ppt #23)		$997		$1,411		$1,816
Capital redemption reserve (millions from Ppt #23)		$80		$88		$88
Retained earnings (millions from Ppt #23)		$1,208		$1,341		(1,733)
Total equity attributable to Lonmin shareholders		$2,488		$3,408		$757
Equity ($) per nominal 1$ share (at balance sheet date)		$12.25		$5.99		$1.29
Sibanye offer at end of September 2018						$370
Equity ($) per nominal 1$ share of Sibanye offer						$0.63

At the time of the Sibanye offer in 2018, Lonmin was reported to be valued at £285 million (exchange rate 0.77). The annual Report for 2017 published late in January 2018 reported a loss of £1,152 million.

Exploration and evaluation costs (development costs) are capitalised if future economic benefits are reasonably assured. This requires "Probable Reserves" to have been defined and confirmed by a competent person. Construction of physical facilities, both above and below ground level, will also be considerable. These were the residual assets that Sibanye acquired with the takeover.

Appendix G

Extended Case Study 7

Mine Scheduling Open-Pit Optimisation Exercise

In Collaboration with Wenzhuo Cao and Sevket Durucan

Consider the ore grade block model in a 2D vertical section for an open-pit mine as follows:

(1,1) 0.05	(2,1) 0.15	(3,1) 0.40	(4,1) 0.30	(5,1) 0.50	(6,1) 0.03
(1,2) 0.17	(2,2) 0.14	(3,2) 0.45	(4,2) 0.60	(5,2) 0.15	(6,2) 0.12
(1,3) 0.15	(2,3) 0.40	(3,3) 0.12	(4,3) 0.10	(5,3) 0.50	(6,3) 0.18

(1,1)	→ Block number
0.10	→ Ore grade (%)

(a) Ore blocks are worth \$10/block per 1.0% ore grade, and the mining cost is \$2/block. Blocks with ore grades below the cut-off grade are treated as waste. Convert the grade block model to an economic block model.

(b) Identify blocks within pit limits using the floating cone technique.

(c) Two constraints related to the ultimate pit are: (1) the pit slope angle is 45°; and (2) each mining level can be entered through only one entry. Assume a production rate of 1 block per unit time period and a discount rate of 8%. Use the block sequencing method to determine the order in which the blocks are mined to yield the maximum NPV.

(d) Assume a discount rate of 30%, and keeping other factors unchanged, determine the order in which the blocks are mined to yield the maximum NPV.

Answers:

(a) The relationship between ore grade $x\%$ and the net value y (\$/block) is $y = \begin{cases} 10x - 2, \ x \geq 0.20 \\ -2, \ x < 0.20 \end{cases}$. The economic block model converted is:

(1,1) -2.0	(2,1) -2.0	(3,1) 2.0	(4,1) 1.0	(5,1) 3.0	(6,1) -2.0
(1,2) -2.0	(2,2) -2.0	(3,2) 2.5	(4,2) 4.0	(5,2) -2.0	(6,2) -2.0
(1,3) -2.0	(2,3) 2.0	(3,3) -2.0	(4,3) -2.0	(5,3) 3.0	(6,3) -2.0

(1,1) → Block number
-2.0 → Block value

(b) The first incremental cone includes blocks (3,1), (4,1), and (5,1). The second incremental cone includes blocks (2,1), (3,2), and (4,2).

The ultimate pit identified is:

(2,1) -2.0	(3,1) 2.0	(4,1) 1.0	(5,1) 3.0
	(3,2) 2.5	(4,2) 4.0	

(c) Based on the ultimate pit identified in (a), first identify the last block in the optimum sequence with a positive value, which is block (3,2) with a value of 2.5. Then, examine the remaining sequence of blocks and identify the latest negative block scheduled for mining, which is block (2,1) with a value of −2.0. Determine the present worth for the sequence extending from the identified negative block to the end. The NPV for this sub-sequence (blocks $(2,1) - (3,2)$) discounted to the beginning of time period 5 (the end of time period 4) is $NPV = \frac{-2.0}{1.08^1} + \frac{2.5}{1.08^2} = 0.3 > 0$. Therefore, this sub-sequence is retained in the optimum sequence.

As all the other 4 blocks have positive values, it is easy to identify the optimum sub-sequence subjected to constraints: blocks $(5,1)$ – $(4,1)$ – $(3,1)$ – $(4,2)$. The overall optimum sequence is $(5,1)$ – $(4,1)$ – $(3,1)$ – $(4,2)$ – $(2,1)$ – $(3,2)$, with a total $NPV = \frac{3.0}{1.08^1} + \frac{1.0}{1.08^2} + \frac{2.0}{1.08^3} + \frac{4.0}{1.08^4} + \frac{0.3}{1.08^4} = 8.4$.

(d) The NPV for the sub-sequence (blocks $(2,1) - (3,2)$) discounted to the beginning of time period 5 (the end of time period 4) is $NPV = \frac{-2.0}{1.3^1} + \frac{2.5}{1.3^2} = -0.1 < 0$. Therefore, this sub-sequence is dropped from the optimum sequence.

As all the other 4 blocks have positive values, it is easy to identify the overall optimum sequence subjected to constraints: blocks $(5,1) - (4,1) - (3,1) - (4,2)$, with a total $NPV = \frac{3.0}{1.3^1} + \frac{1.0}{1.3^2} + \frac{2.0}{1.3^3} + \frac{4.0}{1.3^4} = 5.2$.

Bibliography

Ala, M. (2017). *The Imperial College Lectures in Petroleum Engineering — Volume 1: An Introduction to Petroleum Geoscience*, World Scientific.

Baxter, M. and Rennie, A. (1996). *Financial Calculus*, Cambridge University Press.

Bingham, N. H. and Kiesel, R. (2004). *Risk-Neutral Valuation*, 2nd ed., Springer.

Björk, T. (2009). *Arbitrage Theory in Continuous Time*, 3rd ed., Oxford University Press.

Blunt, M. J. (2017). *The Imperial College Lectures in Petroleum Engineering — Volume 2: Reservoir Engineering*, World Scientific.

Buchanan, D. L. (1988). *Platinum-Group Element Exploration*, Elsevier, Oxford.

Buchanan, D. L., Nolan, J., Suddaby, P., Rouse, J. E., Viljoen, M. J., and Davenport, J. W. J. (1981). The genesis of sulfide mineralization in a portion of the Potgietersrus Limb of the Bushveld Complex. *Economic Geology*, **76**(3): 568–579.

Bussell, M. A., Alpers, C. N., Petersen, U., Shepherd, T. J., Bermudez, C., and. Baxter, A. N. (1990). The Ag–Mn–Pb–Zn vein, replacement, and skarn deposits of Uchucchacua, Peru; studies of structure, mineralogy, metal zoning, Sr isotopes, and fluid inclusions. *Economic Geology*, **85**(7): 1348–1383.

Cairns, A. (2004). *Interest Rate Models*, Princeton University Press.

Duffie, D. and Singleton, K. (2003). *Credit Risk: Pricing, Measurement and Management*, Princeton University Press.

Filipović, D. (2009). *Term Structure Models*, Springer.

Halsall, C. (1989). *Intrusive Magmatism, Volcanism and Massive Sulphide Mineralisation at Rio Tinto, Spain*. PhD dissertation, University of London.

Hayes, C. (2014). *Modern Valuation Techniques Applied to a Development Stage Uranium Junior*. MSc (Metals and Energy Finance) dissertation, Imperial College, London.

Houlding, S. (2000). *Practical Geostatistics, Modeling and Spatial Analysis.* EduMine Online Course.

Hull, J. (2017). *Options, Futures and Other Derivatives*, 10th ed., Pearson.

Lane, K. F. (1988). *The Economic Definition of Ore*, Mining Journal Books.

O'Hara, T. A. (1980). Quick guides to evaluation of orebodies, *CIM Bulletin* **73814**(2): 78–99.

Robb, L. (2004). *Introduction to Ore-Forming Processes*, Wiley-Blackwell, Hoboken, NJ.

Underhill, J. R. and Stoneley, R. (1998). Introduction to the Development, Evolution and Petroleum Geology of the Wessex Basin, in Underhill, J. R. (ed.), *The Development, Evolution and Petroleum Geology of the Wessex Basin*, Geol. Soc. London, Special Publications, 133, pp. 1–18.

Wells, J. (1998). *Bre-X: The Inside Story of the World's Biggest Mining Scam*, Orion, London.

Index

D

G

H

I

www.ingramcontent.com/pod-product-compliance
Lightning Source LLC
Jackson TN
JSHW011558200225
79206JS00002B/4
* 9 7 8 1 8 0 0 6 1 6 6 2 2 *